WORLDLY
THEOLOGY

WORLDLY THEOLOGY

The Hermeneutical Focus
of an Historical Faith

CARL MICHALSON

CHARLES SCRIBNER'S SONS
New York

To my students
and colleagues

ACKNOWLEDGMENTS

Grateful acknowledgment is made to the following publishers for permission to
reprint material from the books or periodicals indicated:

ABINGDON PRESS

for Chapter XI which appeared first as "The Finality of Christ from an
Eschatological Perspective" in *The Finality of Christ*, edited by Dow Kirkpatrick.
Copyright © 1966 Abingdon Press.

(The following page is an extension of the copyright page)

FOREWORD

by John D. Godsey

Readers of this book will begin to sense the reason for the profound feeling of loss that spread through academic and church circles as news of Carl Michalson's untimely death moved around the world. An evangelist endowed with remarkable gifts of discernment and expression was gone—gone overnight, gone with the wind.

It was no ordinary human being whose life was snuffed out when the jetliner plowed into the hillside near Cincinnati on the evening of November 8, 1965. At the age of 50 Carl Michalson enjoyed an international recognition and esteem as a Christian writer, lecturer, and teacher. Although firmly anchored as a teacher of systematic theology in Drew University since 1943, his interest and experience were world-wide. Since receiving degrees at John Fletcher College, Drew University, and Yale University, he had studied at the Universities of Tübingen, Basel, and Strasbourg in Europe, and had lectured at Japan's Tokyo Union Theological Seminary and Aoyoma Gakuin University. An ardent advocate of Christian unity, he had participated in the Faith and Order Conference at Lund, Sweden, the International Missionary Conference at Willingen, Germany, and the World Student Christian Federation Conference at Strasbourg, France.

Probably no American theologian was more effective in interpreting the meaning of Christian faith to the growing masses of searching and bewildered college students than Carl Michalson. Constantly in demand throughout the United States and Canada, he fulfilled a ministry to students that was almost unique, and his influence was steadily expanding through the media of radio and television, not to mention the growing indirect influence exercised through his teaching of a generation of seminary students who are now pastors or teachers of religion. Few who heard his polished, scintillating lectures, delivered without manuscript or notes, realized the amount of study and anguish that went into their preparation.

In large measure a theologian is remembered for his books. Carl Michalson's writings are outstanding, not only for their erudition and relevance, but for a literary style that is at once vibrant and tasteful. Besides editing *Christianity and the Existentialists* (Scribners, 1956) and a "Reflection Book" called *The Witness of Kierkegaard*, he wrote *Faith for Personal Crises* (Scribners, 1958), *The Hinge of History* (Scribners, 1959), *Japanese Contributions to Christian Theology* (Westminster, 1960), and *The Rationality of Faith* (Scribners, 1963). It is my conviction that with *The Rationality of Faith* Carl Michalson had reached, after a long and arduous pilgrimage, a mature theological position—or, at least, frame of reference—which he felt was true to evangelical Christianity and worthy of articulation in the twentieth century. This position, which might be characterized as doing theology within the realm of history alone, is lucidly and persuasively advanced and expanded in this new volume, *Worldly Theology: The Hermeneutical Focus of an Historical Faith*. Here is the crown of his life's work, and it is an impressive legacy indeed. The manuscript, which incorporates several articles that have appeared elsewhere in recent years, had been completed before death struck. It needed only to be typed, and this was done with loving care by one whom Dr. Michalson had called a poet, Mrs. Marilyn Plowman Haney.

Carl Michalson died "with his boots on," so to speak. He was a Methodist circuit-rider of the modern age, substituting the jet for horseback but carrying with the same sense of urgency the message of the gospel to a needy world. He was to speak the next morning on the subject: "Life and Its Setting: The Meaning and Experience of Existence." That address is lost forever. But the witness of Carl Michalson perdures. Gradually, ever so gradually, the terrible sense of loss experienced by those who knew him is being transmuted into a deep feeling of gratitude for his legacy of victorious faith and an ineluctable summons to be concerned with his concern: the liberating news of God's redemption of the world in and through Jesus of Nazareth.

Gone with the wind? No, Michalson's thought is blowing on the wind!

Drew University
Epiphany, 1966

CONTENTS

ONE

History and the Question of Faith
—Fifty Years of Theology in Retrospect

The major clue to what has been occurring in theology during the last fifty years may be found in the movement known as historicism. A list of major influences upon the intellectual development of the Christian faith in this epoch would surely include three distinct phenomena: first, the widespread sense of dearth experienced in world culture; second, the translation of the writings of Søren Kierkegaard into accessible language; and third, the discovery of "the strange new world within the Bible." These influences, however, have acted in concert. The key to their unitary impact is in "historicism" with its slow but pervasive penetration into the heart of all the major theological concerns.

By historicism I mean what Ernst Troeltsch called "its good sense." Historicism is the point of view which conceives of history as the only knowable reality and therefore of historical method as the way of knowing reality. Erudite men of the West had been writing history since the days of Herodotus and Thucydides. The difference between that history and the history of historicism, however, is as great as the difference between Ptolemy's universe and the universe of Copernicus. For historicism, history is the only reality man knows, so that the possibility of man's significance in the world is exclusively an attribute of what he finds in history. Man must strain out his livelihood in the stream of time as fish filter out their existence in rivers.

I

Fifty years ago Troeltsch proposed doing theology within the historicist framework. His importance to this period ought not be sought in his achievement or failure but in his conception of the project. He forecast a radical reorientation in theological method wherever historicism was taken seriously. The progress since discernible in theology is intimately related to the seriousness with which theologians have taken up Troeltsch's venture. The distinctive thing about contemporary theology is its attempt to overcome the problems of history entirely from within history and, what is the same, to claim nothing in theology which is not at the same time history.

That is why historicism can be said to be at the base of what might otherwise be regarded as the several major influences upon the last fifty years of theological work. For one thing, the cultural dearth of this period is accounted for in historicism. The reality called history, which historicism says is the only reality man knows, is as transitory and evanescent as time, of which it is made. It is a realm of complete relativism. Nothing that is made of time seems final. No standpoint from within time seems authorized to speak for all time. How, then, can theology proceed within such limitations? Historicism at least has this excellent advantage: it provides a point of view by which the cultural cataclysm of the world's last fifty years can be made intelligible. Nothing is ultimate in history. Therefore, utopian or demonic attempts to potentiate cultural life, illustrated in this period by bourgeois liberalism and totalitarianism, were fated to fail. History has an inherent tendency to exhaust itself. Historicism, frankly espousing that view, materializes as a modern version of prophetism, exposing the transitory character of life and condemning schemes which seek to evade such finitude.

To the extent of this critique of history, historicism is also the basic ingredient in existential thinking, which entered into theology during this period through Søren Kierkegaard. Kierkegaard won the title of modern father of existentialism by penetrating every claim to have overcome the limits of history from within history. Yet he himself uncovered one way in which this might be done legitimately. Working within the framework of history alone, he came upon one moment of time which exempted itself from the transience and relativity of time. That was the moment in which eternity announced its presence in time, the special moment of the presence of God in Jesus of Nazareth. If one adopted that exemption he ceased being "an existentialist" who, by definition, encounters only relativity and the absence of final meaning, and became a believing Christian. Christians who found ultimate claims in a single event he charged with perpetrating a "scandal of particularity." Kierkegaard's only warrant for proposing this scandal as the basis of one's existence was itself historical. That is, when one enters into the voluminous account of human history and assumes the interpretive burden implicit in historical existence, it is possible for him to come upon that one point at which transience declares itself to be overcome. Therefore, if by virtue of his Christianity Kierkegaard was not a thoroughgoing existentialist, he never broke with the spirit of historicism, if by historicism is meant the view in which history is the only reality one knows.

The method of historicism, with its existential seriousness, seems more than anything else to account for the rediscovery of the Bible in recent theology. The customary historical procedures of textual criticism and genetic explanation had truncated the Bible's full historicity. When historicism helped the theologian see history as the only reality man knows, the theologian ceased holding himself off from historical sources at an objective distance. He tested the sources hermeneutically. That is, he put a fundamentally historical question to the sources. He asked of the Bible whether there was anything in its story which would support life with significance. For historicism, such a question converts all history into contemporary history. That does not mean the end of the relation to the Bible as a book of the past. It simply translates the past into the present, where alone the past can be known. The Bible through this procedure could become in contemporary theology what the church originally composed and canonized it to be—"the story of our life." Karl Barth in the belfry of his parish church with his unsteadied hand falling against the bell rope is a symbol of how the word of God can sound when history throws itself upon the Bible. The uproar against Barth's exegesis of Romans which came from the established scholars was a sign that Biblical scholarship was not fully prepared to exchange its concept of history as erudition for historicism's incautious but thoroughgoing historical consciousness.

The only major test of contemporary theology's use of historicism occurred at the mid-point of this fifty year period. In 1934 at Barmen in Germany, Barthian theologians led the confessing church of Germany to repudiate all theological justification for National Socialism. Historicism had unwittingly contributed to the endorsement of political movements as acts of God, for it had implied a certain coalescence between man's activity and God's activity in the medium of history. Barth, however, had increasingly sensed the danger in historical thinking, regarding it as a new form of psychologism and anthropologism in theology. For him, the authentic source of the Christian faith was in the name of God as trinity. By that decision he meant to conserve the conviction that nothing is true in history which does not involve the reality of God himself.

When Barth commenced to construct his *Dogmatik* on this trinitarian foundation, cries of protest went up from his colleagues. Barth, they said, speaks about God in abstraction from history. Barth's God is a God *an sich*: a God who acts within the trinity but is detached from the process of history. A theology which discusses God's activity in abstraction from history secularizes history. To that extent the critics of Barth made a telling point. Barth's more recent emphasis on "the humanity of God" is sometimes taken as a belated concession to his critics.

However, the critics in making their case tended to lean too far in the opposite direction. Whereas Barth had said that nothing is true in history which does not involve the reality of God, Friedrich Gogarten, Karl Heim, and Emil Brunner all sponsored the conviction that nothing is true in history which does not involve the reality of man. In doing so, they spoke quite appropriately of God as a reality *pro nobis*, an historical reality who identified himself with the baby Jesus in the manger and with the carpenter on the cross. "Revelation is history," they said. The step toward affirming the consequent was a short one, and some of them soon found themselves asserting that "history is revelation." That was the trend against which Barth pronounced his loud *"Nein!"* Now the theologians of our time are known as the Post-*"Nein!"* fathers, for they have inherited a climate in which it is no longer considered appropriate to look for God in history except in the light of how God has disclosed himself there. History is revelation at one point only, and that is where God has announced himself to be present. Thereafter, only the witness to Jesus of Nazareth can be taken as the clue to what God is doing in history.

Once the Barthian repudiation of general revelation was politically vindicated, its prestige became distended. Significant elements in the historicist approach to theology were thereby overshadowed. Not until the end of the Second World War was the balance restored through the "demythologizing" project of Rudolf Bultmann. The significance of Bultmann's existential hermeneutic is that it reinstated a dimension of historical understanding which Barthians had obscured since Barmen. It is true, as Barthians insist, that God reveals *himself* in history and that revelation is what properly constitutes history. It is just as true that it is *in history* that God reveals himself. But history is the reality in which man has his life. Hence, if the revelation of God is historical it occurs in the medium in which man lives and it addresses itself to the fundamental perplexities which characterize man's life.

"Demythologizing" as a synonym for hermeneutical responsibility had been implicit in historicism from the outset. The past is fully historical only as it can be lived in the present. That in the past which cannot be lived is either chronicle, which is the corpse of history, or it is myth. Chronicle is a treatment of history which errs by its indifference to ongoing life. Myth is a treatment of history which errs by its excessively passionate, hence almost contrived concern. Myth is so preoccupied with fixing once-for-all the truth of God revealed to history that it states the truth in a medium in which the truth does not occur. Myth states historical truth in a non-historical medium, the medium of objective certainty. "Demythologizing" is a process of translating the myth back into the medium of lived reality, where God and man may meet. The revelation of God is identifiable with an event which facilitates interpretation without requiring capitulation, in which the interpretation remains indistinguishable from the event.

During the last few years an unacknowledged Barth-Bultmann axis has been developing in the theological world. It expresses itself as the overcoming of the old dichotomy between theology and anthropology which had Barthians against the world for so many years. Such an alliance was able to occur through the mediation of Rudolf Bultmann because he was the one theologian of major importance whom Barth had never attempted to annihilate. When Barth's little *Schrift* on Bultmann did eventually appear, the worst he could find to say of Bultmann was, *"Er ist ein Lutheraner!"* The strength of the admittedly tenuous Barth-Bultmann concordat among their disciples is the way in which it fulfills the original promise in historicism. Contemporary theologians are now in the very best position to know what it means to say that Christians are involved with a reality which is nothing but history. For the word "history" may now embrace a connotation inclusive of both divine and human reality. A properly historical event is an event in which *God* is present in a way which supplies *man's life* with the basis for its meaning. The occurrence of Jesus of Nazareth is just such an event. There theology and anthropology become one as history. That event can be repeated in the life of the world when the community which it forms is faithful in its reenactment of the event.

Where this historical understanding is operative in theology today, major conceptual revisions are occurring. A few of the more obvious bear noting. "Supernaturalism" tends to fall into disuse, for faith now refers to a reality which is neither natural nor supernatural but historical. "Rationalism," which locates the norm of theological authenticity somewhere within man's experience, gives way to hermeneutics, which finds the meaning of man's existence in an historical context engulfing man's whole life. "Dogmatism" becomes the symptom of a situation which has lost its spiritual power; for history, which expresses itself in meaningful assertions, carries its own power to convince. "Subjectivity" no longer connotes private feeling but refers to man's life in its tendency toward some concrete reality, some reality which man himself does not constitute. Therefore, the exclusion of the canons of "objectivity" from theology does not mean the abandonment from faith of all reference to an "objective reality." "Literalism" has become alien from historical thinking. Nothing in history is "literally" so, for history involves meaning, meaning involves interpretation, and interpretation involves hermeneutical risk. For the same reason, "authoritarianism" is no longer in good theological taste, for history knows no authorities. There are only frames of reference within which what was once meaningful for someone else becomes meaningful for you through your acts of interpretation. "Credalism" need not disappear as a result of this historical rubric so long as the propositions in which the faith is expressed are regarded as formative rather than normative. The propositions of faith, historically conceived, are not primarily objects of assent but access to meaningful existence. Faith is not realized in sentences which can be asserted to be true or false but in sentences which make men true. The propositions of faith are not meant so much to inform as to confer courage. Finally, "metaphysics" is not disallowed by historicism. It is more apt to be rendered superfluous, for historicism does not look for ultimate reality behind historical manifestations but within them.

II

To what extent, then, have some of the distinctive theologies of the past fifty years responded to this wave of historicism?

Probably the most conspicuous current illustration is the work of Paul Tillich. Tillich's method of question and answer is characteristically historicist, for where there is no putting of questions there is no history. But Tillich's historicism is not thoroughgoing. He chooses to frame his theological answers in formulations which antedate the rise of the historical consciousness. The historicist dimensions of existentialism structure his questions but the ontological dimensions of pre-historicist, classical philosophies structure his theological answers. One might say with Tillich, "I am only if Being itself supports me." That is an ontological judgment. Or, one might say with the historicist, "I am only if some fundamental meaning supports me." That is an historical judgment, and historicists do not feel that this judgment requires extension into ontology where "being" has more status than "meaning."

Process theology, inspired by Alfred North Whitehead's philosophy, is more suggestive theologically than the range of its influence would indicate. Its correlation with historicism, however, is very limited. Notwithstanding that it defines all reality as a continuum of events, history is not its primary medium. This philosophy is oriented primarily to the natural sciences, and therefore gives encouragement to causes which deplore the decline of cosmological categories in contemporary thought. According to the historicists, however, events of nature are knowable only to God, the Creator. They are deficient in meaning for man until they are interpreted. Yet when they are interpreted, they cease being nature and become history. Biblical theologians corroborate this development in historicism when they find the word "creation" functioning in the Bible as an historical and not as a cosmological concept.

The one American theologian most consistent in his delineation of the historical element in the Christian faith is Reinhold Niebuhr. Every major doctrine has become a hermeneutical tool in his hands. Creation, for instance, "means" that there is a purpose in history, however hidden. Eschatology "means" that the purpose of history is historically unrealizable. Jesus Christ "means" that perfection will always be crucified in history. Theologians trained in the ontological or naturalistic traditions tend to object that this treatment of Christian doctrines vitiates the solidity of the Christian standpoint. "Meaning" seems so insubstantial and so benign for coping with "the terror of history." According to the historicist tradition, however, nothing is more solid than where a man lives, and a man lives precisely where he holds his meanings. The realm of meaning, which is history, ought not be regarded as a shadowy, subjectivistic sphere, for it is the very reality which constitutes faith. Faith is meaning which shapes the future through the force of its present reenactment of the past.

Two quite recent intellectual movements are bringing considerable influence to bear upon theology in respect to its preoccupation with historical affairs. One is from the side of Biblical studies, the other from the side of philosophy.

The "new quest of the historical Jesus," pursued chiefly on the Continent by New Testament scholars of the Bultmann persuasion, has made it no longer admissible for theologians to take the eventfulness of Jesus with less than full historical seriousness. The old quest paradoxically subjectivized Jesus by seeking him as an object, the object of a scientific quest, hence finding only what was sought—a scientific object. Theologians who abandoned that quest seemed unwilling to proceed on the basis of an inner, spiritual witness to Jesus such as the early preaching of the church provided, without putting the question of his historical factuality. At this stage in the development of historicism, however, historical factuality inheres not in scientific objectivity but in a reality which transcends objectivity and subjectivity while embracing the intention of both. That reality is event as interpretation.

Does it matter to our faith that Jesus actually existed? In the recent past that question meant: if Jesus was not a fact, our faith is in vain. The question is just as important now, but it means something else. Bultmann's followers, Ernst Käsemann, Ernst Fuchs, Gunther Bornkamm, and Gerhard Ebeling, have criticized him for showing no adequate interest in the historical Jesus. James M. Robinson in America has perceptively organized and advanced their understandings. For Bultmann, the church lives from the preaching of Christ, the Christ of faith not the Jesus of history. The faith of the church is the faith of the apostles, not the faith of Jesus. Bultmann's major precursor in that line was Martin Kähler who distinguished between the historical (*historische*) Jesus and the historical (*geschichtliche*) Christ. Considering Bultmann and Kähler, the question about the historical Jesus now means: How can one say that the Christ of faith is the same reality as the Jesus of history? Is the church not led into docetism, worshipping a Christ who is only apparently historical, or even into mythology, understanding Jesus not from within the Nazarene's unique history but from the standpoint of the pagan and Jewish stories about the gods which were used by the apostolic church to describe him?

The new meaning of the question about the historical Jesus signals a theological shift which many today seem reluctant to make. The older concern about the historicity of Jesus was rooted in the quest for historical verification of revealed truth, a quest hostile to the very meaning of revelation as justification by faith alone. Scepticism about getting back to the historical Jesus made it possible in the past for theologians to reject the old quest and thus to prolong their dogmatic and confessional claims about Jesus. Now, however, the concern about Jesus is rooted in the quest for the historical meaning of revealed truth, revelation being a fully historical reality. New understandings of history and the study of history are dissolving the old historical scepticism and with it the ancient and current dogmas and philosophies which exploit the sceptical vacuum. The meanings of faith are historical meanings inaugurated in Jesus himself as the pioneer of faith and as the word made flesh. The post-resurrection faith is a pre-resurrection reality.

From the side of philosophy, the sleeping giant of logical positivism has lately awakened to an interest in theology through British analytical philosophy. Logical positivism had sponsored the physicalistic dogma that only those sentences are meaningful which can be perceptually verified. British analysts no longer work by that dogma. While they continue to identify philosophy with language analysis, they simply classify the various languages in use in common speech and referee their use for the sake of cutting down the confusion of tongues. Thus released from the positivist preoccupation with physical things, the British analysts, particularly at Oxford, have taken to examining theological language as one among the actual linguistic functions. The effect upon theology is strikingly similar to the effect of "demythologizing." What for Bultmann is mythology, for British analysis is a violation of the rules of the language game. Theologically, myth is using with reference to unverifiable reality a language which implies verifiability. The same mixing of language rules is called logical nonsense by the British analysts. However, a theological weakness is evident in the procedure of British analysis. Statements which are not perceptually verifiable are still persistently under suspicion. For that reason, the philosophical theology in this school tends to underrate unverifiable theological language, which usually includes the most kerygmatic elements in a Christian's credo. What is equally misleading is that it tends to underscore the theological statements which concern nature and human experience, statements which do lend themselves to verification, as if more validity resided there. This suggests a throw-back to an earlier day of theology as an empirical science. The most serious weakness of the method, however, is its deficiency in historiography. The role of human interpretation in history is underestimated. As did its progenitor, logical positivism, British analysis tends to view interpretations as expressions of how one feels, pointing to nothing objectively real; whereas for historicism interpretation is the very form which the reality of history takes. Documents and events in which historians find no interpretation either are not history or they have been handled non-historically.

A very muscular element in the historical thinking of contemporary theology and the one most likely to contribute to the development of a worldly faith is the view that modern secularism is a welcome product of Christianity rather than its archenemy. Traditionally the word "secular" has been the antonym of "religious." It has been taken to mean a way of life pursued without reference to religious realities. Where the functions of religious institutions are taken over by the state, secularization is said to have occurred, as in programs of education and social amelioration. Understandings of life without reference to the idea of God and His alleged intervention in the process of the world are called secular views.

The inception of secularism in western culture is usually dated at the Renaissance and ascribed to the inflation of human pride. Man at that epoch put himself at the center of reality and arrogated to himself authority over life and responsibility for it. Christendom since the Renaissance has been hard pressed to justify its theocentric universe and its traditional confessions to a God who is all powerful, to a man who is abased and weakened by finitude and sin, and to a system of things which is contingent upon the sustaining power of God as expressed in miraculous interventions in history and nature.

Friedrich Schleiermacher was the first theologian to attempt to express the Christian faith in terms of the new understandings of the modern world which the Renaissance introduced. Protestant theology following the First World War made Schleiermacher its primary target. The situation after the Second World War is quite different, even though the experiential grounds for man's despair over his secular adequacy have seemed even more obvious than after the First World War. Now it is being seen that secularism, far from being the enemy of the church, as theology in its medieval and Protestant Orthodox orientation has tended to hold, is the product of the Christian faith. The Protestant Reformation is held to be the only major attempt since the Apostolic Age to reintroduce the meaning of the Christian movement as the secularizing of the world.

In contemporary Christianity two theologians, mainly, have contended for this view. Dietrich Bonhoeffer, in fragmentary suggestions through his prison correspondence prior to his death, conceded that modern man had "come of age." That is to say, he is capable of handling his affairs without invoking a god. That is secularism. Bonhoeffer was probably unique in the conclusions he drew for his description of modern life, a description already patent in the Renaissance period. His conclusion for Christianity was that the church ought not force this modern, mature man to become weak in the world in order to convert him to faith. It might rather call him to discipleship at the point of his strength. For Bonhoeffer this was no simple compromise with modern man. It was the nub of the Christian revelation. The meaning of the faith is that God has allowed himself to be edged out of the world onto the cross. Because of the cross, therefore, man can know that the world is now left to him as his responsibility.

Friedrich Gogarten is the one who has given this theme its most systematic and comprehensive treatment. The major text for Gogarten's explication is Galatians 4: 1-7. The significance of Jesus of Nazareth is that in him God has called the world to obedience. The call to obedience is given in the context of God's gift of the world to man as his responsibility. In Jesus of Nazareth mankind is delivered from the time of its childhood and slavery where the world had become the vehicle by which man was required to justify his life before God. In the word of God in Jesus of Nazareth, it is God who justifies men. Men no longer need to justify themselves. That means that the world no longer needs to be exploited for religious purposes. To say it positively, that means God has given man the world as his responsibility, as a father gives his heritage to his son.

Nietzsche and Kierkegaard had both addressed themselves to the situation of secularism in the modern world. Both saw that secularism was a Christian outcome. Kierkegaard regarded the outcome as bad, and believed it was his responsibility to reintroduce a purer Christianity into the secularized Christendom. Nietzsche regarded it as good, but doubted that Christianity was an adequate basis for supporting the seculum it had inaugurated. Gogarten, on the other hand, believes Christianity is indispensable to the conservation of secularism. His reasoning is as follows: God has turned the world over to man as that for which man is responsible. If man does not continually receive the world from God as the one *to* whom he is responsible, he may make the world itself his new object of responsibility, as Judaism and Hellenism did before the time of Jesus, worshipping the creature rather than the creator and thus converting law and wisdom into demonic powers which thereby lost their status as instruments of responsibility. If man becomes responsible *to* the world, he will lose his capacity to be responsible *for* it. In the Christian proclamation through which man learns to receive the world from God, responsibility *to* God is kept alive, and with it, responsibility *for* the world, which is the condition we know in the modern world as secularism.

Finally, historical thinking has inaugurated a methodological revolution which in contemporary theology may have a very practical effect on the way we do our work. As scholars today must feel quite keenly, historicism puts in question the status of Biblical, historical, and systematic studies as independent disciplines. One can no longer easily distinguish Biblical and historical studies from systematic studies as if the former deal with history while the latter deal with interpretation. History may no longer be looked upon as a series of events simply open to interpretation. History is events which are interpretation. Therefore, it is as true to say that systematic studies are bound to history in respect of its occurrence, as to say that Biblical and historical studies are bound to history in respect of its interpretation. Moreover, one can no longer confidently assert that systematic studies deal with *contemporary* interpretation while Biblical and historical studies deal with interpretations of the *past*. The only data within the range of anyone's knowledge are historical data which, albeit past, have their mode of existence as past in the present of the interpretive act. If the intimations in this method are sound, when we pursue them with rigor, we may enter into an era of exhilaration in theology which will be characterized by interdisciplinary cooperation, dialogue, and possibly even unity.

III

What signs are there in the American scene today that this rich cultivation of theological possibilities during the last half century is coming to maturity among us?

Probably two factors in American life are mainly responsible for the perennial immaturity of its theology. One is that we have always depended upon Europe for our theological enrichment, a kind of theological Marshall Plan in reverse. American theologians still make jokes about how the way to become a creative theologian is to learn to read German. The other factor is that we have constantly had to contend with an expanding frontier. That means that as soon as we have received theological products from overseas, we have shipped them off to the front. The rapid transfer from import to export gave no adequate time for the theological fruit to ripen on our own vines.

The relationship to Europe remains strong. In fact, thanks to increased mobility in all areas of life today—in transportation, linguistics, ecumenicity and finance—the contacts with European thought are even more ample than ever before. In our efforts to break out of this exclusively European relationship and explore the contributions of other peoples, such as the Japanese, we have discovered that they, as we, are indebted to Europe.

The new factor, however, is that the relation is no longer one of dependence. The reasons for this are manifold. For one thing, the frontier, while it continues to be a psychological reality among us, is no longer a geographical fact. Some of our leading theological faculties now occupy the area only recently regarded as a frontier. For another thing, a new kind of resistance to the expansion of the church has forced upon us a form of theological reflection that did not seem so urgent in earlier times. The church itself is calling into question its customary image and is looking to its theology as well as to its sociology for insight into the nature of congregational life. The church is finding its expression, not in the edifice, and not in numerical expansion, but in the small group movements among laymen. European churches have seen it happen in their lay academies. The Japanese have developed it in the non-church movement. In America one finds these movements arising within established congregations. For these groups, the preaching service, around which the congregation typically rallies, tends to take second place to small assemblies of concerned laymen who probe their faith in depth through Biblical and theological studies. One might have called the group *ecclesiola in ecclesia*, except that these, judged by traditional standards, seem to be comprised of the faithless, those making a last desperate effort to remain in the church, but doing so under the auspices of the church.

A correlative shift of accent is occurring at the academic level. In America in the past, denominationally-supported theological schools, often isolated from a university setting, have been the main *loci* for theological reflection. Now non-church-related private universities are beginning to assume theological leadership through their faculties of religion. Even state universities have found a way of transcending the constitutional strictures against mixing religion and government and in many instances have gathered competent and influential theological faculties. European theologians have been known to express their pleasure at doing theology in state-supported rather than in church-supported institutions because they enjoy more intellectual freedom there. American church-related theological faculties, of course, manifest a wide variety of emphases on a spectrum ranging from control to freedom, depending on the denominational attitude toward theology. In communions where theology is somewhat cynically indulged, on the grounds that theology is no finally crucial factor in church life and in Christian piety, theologians experience a freedom bordering on indifference. The frontier mentality is residual to that permissiveness. The theology now being done under nonsectarian circumstances, however, is enjoying a freedom which goes beyond anything we have known in either Europe or America. One should add at the risk of confusing the case that many theologians deliberately choose to work within the church-related context, because they consider theology as a function of church existence. My point about the shift of theological studies to the universities is that theology is no longer for us simply a function of church existence. Questions of faith are more and more accepted in America as *bona fide* human questions, even to the extent of being granted a hearing in the humanities curricula.

One of the main evidences that this is true is the provocative theological note being discerned in America in literature and art. I do not refer so much to the standard Broadway fare, such as Mac-Leish's take-off on Job, Chayevsky's *Gideon,* or Osborne's *Luther.* Here the stage seems edifying and sometimes even permissive toward traditional prejudices. When religious groups on university campuses are unable to secure the services of an eminent theologian for their special conferences, instead of reaching for less prestigious theologians, they will often go for Edward Albee or James Baldwin. When they do settle for a theologian, they will require him to speak in a setting of modern art and will confront his contributions with performances of plays by Sartre, Ionesco, or Brecht. As a part of the orientation program at the theological school where I teach, almost one hundred entering students attended an off-Broadway theater in New York to witness Albee's *Zoo Story* and Beckett's *Krapp's Last Tape.* On the following day the theological classes began.

Drama of this *genre* produces a more ambiguous reaction than the usual Broadway offering. Therefore, because it cannot count on large public support as entertainment for the after-dinner crowd, it must be mounted in small and inexpensive theaters "off Broadway." The playwrights seem to have anticipated this necessity, even to the extent of limiting their casts to a single character (or two, if you count the tape recorder). The ambiguity of this kind of drama is that it is a direct onslaught upon the world of illusion, so that in the end it is difficult to know what is real and what is illusory. God, while rarely mentioned outside ejaculations of profanity, always seems to hover in the wings. Is he the reality who will finally overcome our last illusions, or is he the one large illusion which we will have to release before our life together can be real again? The laceration one undergoes in auditing this kind of art leaves one like a hand which has just grasped a nettle, astringently aware of one's own existence. The ambiguity remains, however. Is this awareness of one's human reality a springboard for the realization of God's existence, or is it a substitute for God and thus a rival to faith? Is it a dialectical stage on the way to God, or is it the legitimate mode God's presence can be expected to take today? That dilemma, I believe, describes the issue underlying present American theology. How are the theologians responding to it?

Before I outline the points of view developing in American theology which are attempting to cope with our situation, let me cite a number of features which all of them seem to share. Karl Barth and Rudolf Bultmann taught this generation of American theologians how to take their sources seriously. To be sure, Barth called history a *Hilfswissenschaft* to theology, but he found more there than most for whom history was a major science. Bultmann treated the Bible with an almost surgical penetration, yet he brought more to light of relevance for Christian existence than one was accustomed to associate with Biblical scholarship. It is also often reported of Reinhold Niebuhr that while his exegesis of the Bible was not always accurate, it was always interesting. In consequence, this epoch has witnessed the appearance of large bodies of first-class Biblical and historical studies which seem to have gathered their momentum under the inspiration of these great teachers.

Another feature of the times is the return to nineteenth-century theological sources. Within a span of twenty years Schleiermacher, F. D. Maurice, and Horace Bushnell have become transformed from aliens into allies. What they called experience and what was shunned in them for its anthropocentrism is now seen as the historicality of existence. What they described of the knowledge of God as a moral reality and was rejected in them as epistemological agnosticism is now being described as a faith-event with its own inherent structures of rationality. When they used theological language as if the theologian were better qualified to speak about man than about God, they were criticized for subjectivism, but now they are looked upon as the pioneers in the New Hermeneutic, where one does not speak about God but attends to the linguisticality of Being.

This juxtaposition of an American historical figure, Bushnell, alongside a German and an English figure is, in itself, a revealing phenomenon in America theology. We have long been aware that by contrast to other areas of the church, we Americans have scarcely any history. That rather self-conscious attitude has now been dissipated. Thanks to the impetus of such studies as *The Kingdom of God in America* by H. Richard Niebuhr and Perry Miller's investigations of the role of Puritanism in the formation of the American spirit, there has emerged a discipline in our theological faculties, "American Church History," which is considerably illuminating our theological picture. As my colleague in this field, Gordon Harland, is often quoted as saying, "An unexamined history tends to operate as a fate."

Openness toward philosophy is another feature of American theology. In the United States we have probably had only one indigenous philosophy, the pragmatism of William James and its successor in John Dewey's philosophy of education, called instrumentalism. James's position is sometimes thought to have had its roots in the common sense thinking of Benjamin Franklin, and Dewey's in the discussion method of the New England town meeting. Dewey's philosophy never received expression in *the* theological point of view, but it did inspire the religious education movement. James's pragmatism never found its way into theology. The sole philosophy developed distinctively in America to have been extended into a theological position is the process philosophy of Alfred North Whitehead and its current version in Charles Hartshorne. The philosophies which rival process philosophy in their bid for American theological attention are linguistic analysis, phenomenology, and existentialism. These I will take up in connection with the points of view among us today which draw inspiration from them. I only wish to say that far from being cautious of the role of philosophy in theology, present American theology tends to let philosophy be more than a handmaiden and more even than a midwife or dialogical partner. Some would regard this as sitting too lightly to the theological frame of reference, the Bible and the history of its interpretation. Nevertheless, I believe it can be taken as a sign of theological maturity for at least two reasons. For one thing, theology is no longer exploiting philosophy for theological purposes. For another thing, theology has a realistic appraisal of its limitations and how modest its own claims are, materially speaking.

The most startling outcome of all these affiliations is the determination to express the Christian faith without supernaturalism. It has long been understood by American theologians that we must not look for a God from the wings, a *deus ex machina*. How to express this conviction without seeming to betray the existence of God and without defaulting in one's ministry to existential needs becomes a major agenda for these theologians.

The point at which the non-supernaturalist theology is in the greatest agreement is that the life of faith must be a being-for-others. To illustrate how seriously this is meant, being-for-others expresses itself more explicitly in the form of social ethics, and social ethics tends to become almost the exclusive mode in which faith is being encouraged to formulate itself. The enormity and urgency of such problems as the development of the inner city and the momentum of the civil rights movement give credence to this direction. Therefore *The Christian Century* magazine can repeatedly criticize the American evangelist Billy Graham for his evasiveness on the integration issue, and the ministers of New York City can protest the election of Norman Vincent Peale to the presidency of the Protestant Council of that city on the grounds of his theological incompetence to deal with the subtle social issues there. Most striking of all is the noticeable waning of interest in the theology of pastoral care, so popular a decade ago. Americans are learning to live more easily with anxieties, finitude, and guilt than they can with social injustice.

In this matrix, then, what evidence is there that American theology is coming of age? What great dogmatic systems are emerg-

ing on our shelves under the auspices of our theologians? Barth
has posted his *Dogmatik* and Tillich his *Systematic Theology.*
Where are the American counterparts of these? Probably the major
claim to maturity in American theology is its realization that we are
living "between the times." That does not mean between the time
of Christ's appearance and the time of his coming again. That means
what Friedrich Gogarten meant when he first coined the phrase
now so famous in our century. We live between the time of the
theology which no longer makes sense to us and the time of a
theology which has not yet clearly dawned. Theology written in
this time between the times will not only be modest, it will be confused. It will not only decline to be systematic, it will be fragmentary, rash, and even chaotic. It will not nurse on its catechism in
secret, like an arcane discipline which is afraid of being misunder-
stood in the open forum. It will only utter short, sometimes ejaculatory sounds, sounds sometimes barely distinguishable from profanity because the words are more percussive and resonant than
their meanings seem to warrant, words like "God!", "Christ!",
"Love!", "Thou!", not fully knowing what they mean, but stabbing
from out of all our vast endowment of theological information for
the word or words which will illuminate our way into the time
beyond this time between.

IV

Four theological emphases in America seem most clearly rep-
resentative of our situation "between the times." These are enjoying an almost "honest to God" prominence in theological conversation today.

A. One is the "process theology" of Schubert Ogden and
John Cobb. This motif in American theology is relatively venerable,
but it had a major liability in its earliest form. It was an unabashed
naturalism. It expressed faith in completely this-worldly terms at
a time when nobody was concerned about getting rid of the "God
out there." The spokesman most likely to have received a hearing
at that time was Daniel Day Williams. He was the first theologian
to bring the process motifs into combination with other theological
traditions. Shortly after World War II, at a time when there was
wide dissatisfaction over both conservative and liberal trends in

theology, he showed how Christians were not limited to those alternatives. Process motifs could overcome the weaknesses in both while conserving their strengths. Mainly, liberalism was too optimistic and orthodoxy too pessimistic. Neither view had an adequate place for redemption, because the liberal did not need it and the orthodox delayed it eschatologically.

In Whitehead's view, God was transcendent in such a way as to be a part of the universe, not "out there" but entering into relation with the universe from within it. The tragic character of the universe was dramatized by the knowledge that not only is God in the universe, the universe is in God, filling up his being by its decisions. Nevertheless, through the appeal of God's aggressive love to man's freedom, the tragic universe is being moved in the direction of creativity and growth. Redemption can therefore be offered without indifference to the tragedy of existence.

Ogden and Cobb have now renewed process motifs by bringing them into relation to European theology, especially Bultmann's. Ogden contends that Bultmann, to be consistent, ought to get rid of the last myth, the myth of the uniqueness of Christ. Faith conceived along process lines knows no unique events, only decisive events. The *logos* is universal. Furthermore, faith must be able to stand the test of truth and not confine itself, as Bultmann seems to do, to kerygmatic proclamations. The claim to the reality of God is a metaphysical claim which should be able to stand independently of any particular faith expression. The responsibility of theology is to bring faith to understanding, to verify faith as truth. One way of fulfilling this responsibility is to find the formal intellectual system which can do it. Theology, then, is taken to be the search for the right philosophy. For similar reasons, John Cobb has shown how a natural theology can be done on the Whiteheadean model.

B. "Hermeneutical theology," mainly promoted by James M. Robinson, is the major American outlet for current European thinking but has also contributed creative elements of its own, as European works continue to acknowledge. While it is not formulated in opposition to process theology, its distinctive motifs clearly emerge in such a contrast. In theology as hermeneutics, faith is not the kind of reality which seeks understanding, because it is itself a mode of understanding. Truth is not something that can be tested, because truth is what is brought to light in events outside of which the truth is untrue. The revealed events of faith are not simply decisive, but unique. They are historical events, and in history all events are unique. The *logos*, therefore, which occurs in the Jesus of Nazareth event is not a universal. In history there are no universals. Nor is the *logos* the truth about God. In history one does not speak about God. One hears God's words in Jesus of Nazareth as the answer to the questions of the meaning of man's existence, and in that event of God's self-revelation, not God but the world is revealed.

This view is hermeneutical in the sense in which Martin Heidegger's "philosophy" has helped it to become so. In Schleiermacher and Dilthey hermeneutics had been an art of understanding, where the object of understanding was some fixed expression of human meaning, as in a text or work of art. In Heidegger, influenced as he is by phenomenological thinking, hermeneutics is a process of understanding in which the interpreter is himself both subject and object of interpretation. In a man's relation to a text it is he, the interpreter, who is understood.

The view of speech involved in this thinking is crucial. Words here do not point to things. Words, as in poems, bring a situation to light. "God"-words, then, do not require that the reality "God" be isolated as an object in order for their truth to be validated. "God"-words illuminate situations, and their truth inheres not in the correspondence of the word with the object, but in the luminousness of the event brought to light by their expression.

This combination of emphases on "event," "speech," and "interpretation" explains why "the new quest of the historical Jesus" is central to this position. Jesus' historicity is established by recent historiography and hermeneutics not in isolation from his influences but precisely in these influences. Therefore, the familiar dichotomy between Jesus and Paul is no longer entertained. In addition, Jesus' words, as in his parables, are inseparable from his deeds, because words have the historiographical function of illuminating events which might otherwise remain brute facts, with no capacity to interpret, and therefore with no real historicity. Thus one looks to Jesus' own words as interpretations of his cross and resurrection, not simply to the words of the post-resurrection Christ. The effect of this position is to locate the question of faith firmly within historical reality, to place theological conclusions in direct reliance upon the traditions stemming from the preaching of Jesus, and to confine the language about God to a mode of expression more reminiscent of poetry with its evocation of worlds, than of metaphysics with its denotation of beings.

C. "Secularizing theology" takes two quite different forms among us. One is in the work of Paul van Buren, who takes his cue from linguistic analysis, where statements to be "meaningful" must have some empirical reference. Van Buren believes that the man of today is a "secular" man. That is, he is oriented to human, historical, empirical type realities. His *milieu* is dominantly scientific and technological. "Non-objective" realities are meaningless to him and existential language strange. If the Gospel is to be made meaningful to the secular man, those aspects of the Gospel which lend themselves to empirical certification must be accentuated. So, for instance, Christology is more central than theology. Christ, especially in his humanity, is a more plausible object than God. In this preference, the contrast with process theology is explicit. The cross has the theological advantage of having been "two pieces of wood joined together."

Fortunately, van Buren does not seem to carry out the empirical promise in his project. In his delineation of faith he is more cognizant of the existential basis, except for one possibly ironical outcome. Van Buren believes there was no Christian faith prior to the resurrection of Jesus. That sets him against the "new quest" theology. On what empirical base does he place his theology, then? On the base of the history that comes into existence when the preaching of Christ is heard. That outcome has the irony of a double disadvantage for his case: the alleged empirical base is no more empirical than existential meanings are, and the historical significance of Christianity's historical origin in the pre-resurrection Jesus has been obscured for him.

The other form of secularizing theology is expressed in Harvey Cox's work *The Secular City*. While this is not primarily a theological work, it is a compendious and artistically conceived presentation of major trends in contemporary theology. "Secular" for Cox has the meaning it does in the work of Cornelis van Peursen and Gogarten. The secular man is not the scientific, technological man who never really bothers about the question of meaning. He is the man, as Bonhoeffer described him, who has learned to get along without

God, who has answered the questions of the meaning of existence without reference to the God hypothesis. The modern city is the best illustration. Many deplore that God has left the city. Cox finds that to be the theological charm of city life: it is mature enough not to "need" God. But that outcome is not, in this view of secularism, a merely cultural achievement. It is the situation of maturity for men which God himself initiated when, in Jesus of Nazareth, he turned the world over to men as their responsibility by making men his sons and heirs.

People who find no meaning in faith outside I-thou relations with God and neighbor will not appreciate this view. But Cox has proposed that God has permitted a kind of neighbor-relation which does not automatically become an it-relation when it is no longer a thou-relation. There is still the you-relation, so familiar to the anonymous life of the city. God may even have allowed himself to be so situated in the scheme of things as to be satisfied to be addressed as "you." Van Buren's secular theology seeks an empirical foundation and expresses itself as a revision of the meanings in the traditional doctrinal outline. Van Buren was a close follower of Barth before his new affair with linguistic analysis, and the Barthian positivism has found a new form through him in the lingering positivism of linguistic philosophy. Cox, on the other hand, speaks for a group of theologians who find the quest for empirical validation something required not by modern secular man, but by the immature and religious, who still seek a sign. Secular meaning in Cox's view is found in the socio-political responsibilities which faith inspires and illuminates.

D. Now one can see how in American theology God has been successively telescoped. His metaphysical independence as God has been telescoped into the historical reality of Jesus of Nazareth and from thence into the responsible relations of Jesus' followers to their society. What next step does that suggest? God could die out entirely. I would not want to claim that "the death of God theology" regards itself as the dialectical outcome of the views I have been reporting. But probably no current theological expression in America is more contrived to catch the secular ear than this one. "God is dead." Nietzsche's Zarathustra announced it. William Blake, Hegel, and Luther announced it before him. Today's world is just coming into that realization through the collapse of meaning in its God-words. William Hamilton and Thomas Altizer are the chief spokesmen for this view. They do not mean, as many have, that theistic positions regarding God have died. Nor do they mean that God has been momentarily eclipsed. Nor do they mean that men have learned to remain silent about a God they no longer quite understand. They mean that God has actually allowed himself to die. Therefore, they are not atheists. They believe in a God who was. Nor are they deicides. They have not eradicated God through their rapier-like theological wit. God in his wisdom and love sought to redeem the world by letting it be without him. God's death is the objective reality at the base of our life today, which is the major barrier to our any longer speaking meaningfully about God. The form which the Christian confession must now take is to affirm the reality of God's death. The holy history of the acts of God, when recapitulated by modern man, must now include the holy act of his death.

What the necrology of God precisely means in this view is necessarily vague. Possibly "death of God" states the case too strongly. Bonhoeffer's language about God "allowing himself to be edged out of the world" is probably more accurate, and sufficiently heady. These theologians do not seem to mean that God has really died, but that he is really absent. As Hamilton has said, "We are not talking about the absence of the experience of God, but about the experience of the absence of God." Therefore, God is not really present in the word of faith. He is dead for faith.

What is the theological structure of this view? Christology replaces theology and kenosis is redefined. God does not empty himself so as to become man. Rather, the man Jesus becomes the Christ by emptying himself and all the history which follows him of its godness. Christians who confess their faith in Christ at one and the same time confess the absence of God from history and the presence of man himself in his full humanity to the world in its complete worldliness. "My God, why hast thou forsaken me" is not a cry of dereliction but the essence of God's revelation in Jesus of Nazareth.

In conclusion, whatever one's judgment about the maturity of the four theological emphases outlined above, I believe that no theology can regard itself as mature which has not been engaged by them. My own conviction is that they are the most promising fruit of the last fifty years of theological work. Their promise does not reside in what they see so much as in how they focus our perspective. The major achievement of theology in our epoch will be in the way in which, through its concern for the reality of God as expressed in the history stemming from Jesus of Nazareth, faith will arise. Why that should be regarded as an achievement in our time will depend on whether one observes that faith emerges now as a wholly worldly reality. A theology which exists in the service of God and draws its insight from the historical reality of Jesus of Nazareth will express itself in the constitution of a meaningful world. The chapters which follow develop that thesis in two ways. The earlier chapters are experiments in the possibility of a worldly theology, made through the medium of some major movements in modern thought. The later chapters begin to focus more sharply upon the terms in which such a theology may find expression.

TWO

Existentialism and
the Humanity of Faith

Existentialism is one of the ranking philosophies in the world today. Its prestige is derived from its effectiveness in addressing the question of history, which is the question of the meaning of human existence. Since Christian theologians necessarily deal with the same questions, they are required to negotiate with existentialism. Such conversations between theologians and philosophers are not new to the history of faith. At every stage of its intellectual development Christianity was alternately bracing itself against or allowing itself to be seduced by the most commanding views of life developed outside the church. Inasmuch as faith occurs when the historical conditions of human existence are embraced by the historical message of the New Testament, and inasmuch as existentialism is as candid an examination of the conditions of human existence as occurs today, theology, which is vocationally responsible for the question of faith, cannot avoid the encounter with existentialism. It is a philosophy which illuminates faith, if only to the extent that it illuminates the structure of human existence. It is a philosophy which prepares the ground for the coming of faith, because its interrogation is so radical that no other answers satisfy its questions. What shape, then, is existentialism now conferring upon the Christian faith in its formulation?

I

To understand how existentialism affects Christian faith, one must first have some understanding of what existentialism is. The subject has been pretty thoroughly ploughed up in recent years. Therefore, I would like to structure my approach to it with the help of one of the lesser known existentialists, the Irish playwright and novelist Samuel Beckett. Three brief dialogues in his play *Endgame* seem to me to set up the main dialect in the existential position. No work of Beckett, of which *Waiting for Godot* is his most familiar, makes any sense as a whole. The strategy of fragmentation and open-endedness is calculated, for according to existentialism life does not make sense as a whole, either. However, brief episodes of illumination such as the three I have chosen jut through the more massive unreasonableness of the Beckett literature. The reader then becomes satisfied that the oracular utterances justify the incomprehensible remainder as sheer ad libbing until such time as the significant statement can be spoken.

A

Hamm: Last night I saw inside my breast. There was a big sore.
Clov: Pah! You saw your heart.
Hamm: No, it was living.
(*Pause. Anguished.*)[1]

St. Augustine once described existence in a similar way. It is a dying life and a living death. Man is a being who is irremediably mortal. What is meant by mortality is not the mere biological event of physical extinction. Some disease begins to eat away our hearts from the outset. Existentialism diagnoses the fatal disease as absurdity. Life is unreasonable. That is, there is no apparent reason for living. Therefore, Albert Camus, the Algerian-Parisian novelist, opened his early essay "The Myth of Sisyphus" with the line, "There is but one truly serious philosophical problem, and that is suicide." When the heart is dead the next step in the logic of life is suicide. The strange exhilaration of suicide seems to be that it is apparently the only sensible act in life. While no other existentialists take quite this position on suicide, their immediate analysis of existence is the same. Existence is absurd because it is an unresolvable conflict between the desire for eternity and the inevitability of death. Existence is the passion for meaning in a world that is taciturn and opaque. To some, it may seem strange that on the basis of such analyses Camus was awarded a Nobel prize for "illuminating the problems of the human conscience in our time." The noteworthy thing about the award is its discernment regarding "the problems of the human conscience." The ethical problem of existence today, according to existentialism, is not determining what is good and bad or what is true and false but finding a reason for living.

Man, as Martin Heidegger says, is a being who is thrown into the world. He is impacted here, as marble in mud, with nothing around him which adequately explains him. But he is restless and malcontent until he transcends the sheer stupefaction of being there. Man is as one who awakens from a dream holding tightly to the side of his bed. He is not satisfied until he can remember what he dreamed that makes him hold on so. The frustration and thirst and fatigue of reaching out for meanings for which one's world provides no clues is the anguish of the existing man. I believe it is possible to see this illustrated in Henri Rousseau's painting "The Sleeping Gypsy." A gypsy is lying on a vast stretch of sand with a moon above, and a lion and a lyre at her side. The picture is striking if one interprets it existentially rather than by the canons of Zen Buddhism, with its attention on the sharp eye of the lion or the oriental lilt in the lion's tail. The gypsy looks as if she is simply thrown onto the sand, as if from the outside: there are no footprints in the sand. When she awakens, she won't know where she has been. Therefore she will not know where to go. She will not even have a memory, and if one has no memory one will have no history. The gypsy will not even know her own name. She may have a process, like a crystal in a bottle. But she will have no history. Ibsen wrote *Hedda Gabler* after seeing an insect in a bottle which reminded him of someone he knew. Little wonder, then, that Beckett could write a novel about one person, have it take place entirely inside a bottle, and call it *The Unnamable*.

Existentialism as a philosophy depicts man as a wayfarer who comes to consciousness in a world which supplies him with no adequate clue to his identity. Therefore, existentialism is the philosophical cry of a man lost in his world. In one of his stories Camus has expressed this lostness with particular starkness. Like a scene from the apocalypse, the stage bristles with questions about the destiny of man. Then into the scene there hobbles an old man. He simply stands there, silent.

B

Hamm: What is he doing?
Clov: He's crying.
Hamm: Then he's living.[2]

One would be wrong to conclude from the foregoing discussion that existentialism is a philosophy of despair. It simply *begins* in despair, as Platonism began in wonder and Cartesianism in doubt. But despair is no final resting place any more than wonder or doubt were for philosophies in the past. The philosophical importance of existentialism is that in a world in which nothing seems certainly knowable one senses a panic in his inner life which at least communicates the awareness of one's own existence. That experience leads to an important epistemological point of departure. The hope for knowledge will be closely related to what I know about myself, in my concrete encounter with life as I come up against it. The existentialist, therefore, driven by the sting of an apparently meaningless life, consults the sting itself as a source of meaning.

The philosophical importance of this procedure is that the existentialist looks for truth where it appears, and not behind or beyond appearances. It is a philosophy which seeks answers to the questions about the meaning of existence from within the conditions of life where one is placed. The very resistances, the very silences, the very limits are consulted for whatever evidence they can yield. Karl Jaspers, the German existentialist who has taught in Basel for many years alongside Karl Barth, refers to these situations as boundary situations: suffering, death, guilt, the struggle for love and the struggle for power. Life may have no apparently ultimate meaning, but man is a being who is engaged in enterprises which constantly draw on the necessity for meaningful decision. Is there no clue to reality in this lively sense of one's own presence to himself which one experiences when the conditions of life are crucial?

Gabriel Marcel, the French Catholic existentialist, defines

man's life as essentially incarnational. By that he means one's existence is always incorporated, always inseparable from a body, always located in time and space. In the more idealistic philosophies of the past, incorporation was considered a limitation upon the appropriation of truth. Marcel turns the necessity into a virtue: one can use his immediate, corporeal contacts with life as clues to the shape of life. As Beckett says in *The Unnamable,* in lines almost directly transcribed from Heidegger's *Being and Time,* "I know my eyes are open because of the tears that pour from them unceasingly. I know I am seated, my hands on my knees, because of the pressure against my rump, against the soles of my feet."[3] But Beckett's original tutor was not Heidegger so much as Marcel Proust. Walking in despair of his own existence, Proust one day stubbed his toe on two flagstones. The shock dispelled his doubt. Beckett quotes Proust as saying, "Man is the creature that cannot come forth from himself, who knows others only in himself, and who, if he asserts the contrary, lies."[4] Truth is never apprehended *in abstracto,* outside one's own skin. That is why existentialism must not be written off as an irrationalism. Irrationalism is the effort to live by confused reasons. Existentialism is an effort to find lucid reasons, even if at the boundary of existence. Heidegger finds such lucidity in one fundamental question: "Why is there something and not nothing?" Camus finds it in the dynamics of the myth of Sisyphus. Sisyphus is condemned ceaselessly to roll a stone up a steep hill. He knows in advance that at each attempt the stone will roll back before he makes the grade. Yet Sisyphus continues to roll that stone. Why does he do it? That is a picture of man's absurd bargain with life. Beckett enumerates a few "hopes" which Sisyphus might enjoy notwithstanding his condemned existence. He can stop occasionally to scratch himself. He can take a different route each time. He can be the kind of person who is filled with satisfaction at "doing the same thing endlessly over and over again." But this kind of hope is at best a "hellish hope," unrelieved by the promise of something ultimately gratifying.[5]

C

Clov: Do you believe in the life to come?
Hamm: Mine was always that.
(*Exit Clov.*)[6]

The most authentic expressions of existentialism are the ones which hold the question of meaning open to the future, refusing to gratify their questions with artificial, sporadic answers. In one sense, these positions seem the most pathetic, like small boys who will not eat bread if they cannot have cake. In another sense, they seem to betray the initial motive of existentialism, which is revolt against a universe which does not reveal its own intent. Camus' later work seems to make a truce by settling for a form of mysticism with the world. It is a virtual abandonment of the quest for ultimate meaning for the sake of momentary meanings, as a man who cannot marry settles for the intermittent pleasures of promiscuity. Jaspers turns his negative answers regarding a meaningful life into positive clues: the dark clouds of existence could have a silver lining of meaning. That is possible. Marcel, of course, turns to Roman Catholicism, and it is often difficult to distinguish between his revealed theology and his philosophy.

The early Heidegger and Sartre, like Beckett, seem to play the game to the end. If there is meaning, as our inexplicable appetite for it suggests, then it must be in the future. The information existence yields up to Beckett, for instance, is not enough to tell him whether he is being born or whether he is dying or even who he really is. Therefore, we must wait, condemning all momentary claims to meaning which bid for our loyalty at insignificant levels. Sartre's philosophy, most rigorous of all in this regard, is a deliberate strategy of annihilating every block to man's openness to the future. Even death itself, which is the final testimony to a meaningless life, is repudiated by Sartre on the grounds that it compromises one's freedom for the future. That is why Sartre disagrees with Camus concerning suicide. An act of suicide for Sartre would be an effort to find meaning on a basis which is, absurdly, the termination of the hope for meaning. Thus what seductively appears as the one meaningful act is really the end of the possibility of meaning. If there is no real life in the present, man has only one hope left him, an eschatological hope. Thus the authentic existentialist is the one for whom the future is the primary historical category because it is the sole remaining possibility of salvaging existence. For existentialism as for J. D. Salinger's Seymour, of all the words in the Bible, the favorite is "Watch!"

II

The possibilities for this position in relation to ethics are most impressive. In his famous lecture on existentialism, Jean-Paul Sartre, the last existentialist to avow the title, tells of his refusal to advise a young man facing an ethical dilemma. In the subsequent discussion with the philosophers who heard the lecture, two criticized him. "You should have told him what to do," they said. One of these was a Christian, the other a Communist.

Existentialists make a virtue of not knowing what to do. They are not thereby as remote from Christian thought as some have judged. Basic concepts in Christian ethics are taken up into the viewpoint, especially in the attitude toward law and toward human freedom. Even the alleged acosmism, individualism, and atheism of existentialism have meanings which are closer to the Christian position than the casual observer generally concedes.

Living by laws, which is a way of knowing what to do, is regarded by existentialists as "bad faith" (Jean-Paul Sartre and Simone de Beauvoir). Any abridgement of human freedom is "bad faith." A legalistic ethic abridges freedom by taking decisions out of the hands of responsible selves. Søren Kierkegaard's treatise *Fear and Trembling* anticipated this view. Abraham was a knight of faith because he remained open to God's word. His willingness to murder his son out of obedience to God is higher than ethics because it does not force the future to conform to revelations of God given for the past.

In contemporary existentialism what Kierkegaard called "the teleological suspension of the ethical" is itself ethics. Openness to the future has primacy over conformity to the past. Not that one annihilates the past. To use Sartre's term, one simply "nihilates" it, which is to say, "suspends" it, in order to let the demands of the future emerge. The past tells a man what he ought to do. The future is a more reliable guide simply because it does not tell a man what to do, but appeals to him to "invest" or "create" in the light of the emerging situation.

Christian ethics has accomplished the same movement away from legalism. When the apostle Paul interpreted the preaching of Jesus as a reducing of the whole law to the one word "love," he rooted Christian behavior in "the trans-moral conscience" (Paul

Tillich), "an ethic without laws" (Paul Ramsey), an ethic of "creativity" (Nicholas Berdyaev) or "responsivity" (H. Richard Niebuhr). The transcendence of laws does not mean, however, the abrogation of norms. For existential ethics, freedom, by which one transcends laws in the direction of creative action, is itself the norm for freedom. Man is freedom. Freedom is the source of man's possibility to act ethically, because freedom is nothing—a lack to be filled, a power of resoluteness which lets situations reveal their needs. And what is the norm by which to discern in any situation what is needful? One must so act as to let others be free while oneself remaining free (Sartre).

In fulfilling this ethical program existentialists are known to be atheistic. What is less evident is that they are also acosmic. That is, they do not accept the world sponsored by cosmologists. If one could know why existentialism is acosmic, he would have important clues to why existential atheism is quite benign. The world of the cosmologist is an out-there world into which a man is invited to fit as a coin fits in a box. Existentialists, however, believe the world is not something one is *in*. Worlds are modes of *being-in*. There is the world of politics, of sports, of religion, of art. There is no "world" of ethics because ethics is the study of modes of being-in which result in revealing the possibilities for the worlds one creates through his modes of being-in.

The model from art comes the closest to exemplifying how an existential ethic works. The artist does not record a world that exists. He creates, through his aesthetic behavior, the possibility for a world one may not previously have known (Martin Heidegger and Maurice Merleau-Ponty). The Acropolis mobilized the earth, sea, and sky of Periclean Athens into a significant human world. Whether it still does so is questionable, so that artists continue to develop possibilities for today's world at the risk of reducing previous art works to the status of museum pieces. Ethics, like art, nihilates the world as cosmos (earth, sea, and sky) in order to create the world as a mode of being-in (the Acropolis). Now it can be seen why it is a mistake to call existentialism an individualism, implying that it has no social ethic. The primary term for existentialist ethics is neither "individual" nor "social" but "world," a reality in which the distinction between individual and social disappears, for "world" embraces *all* modes of being-in.

By analogy to acosmism, atheism does not mean the annihilation of God, but only his nihilation. God as a static reality is put in parentheses in order to let the world of man emerge as it is possible. Atheism has sometimes meant that men have killed God. In existentialism it means that men have used a static concept of God in order to endorse effete causes whose prolongation is murderous to men. Such a god is not simply dead; he is an executioner. Kierkegaard was a theist for the very same reason that existentialists today are atheists. Why is it that for Kierkegaard Abraham's willingness to slay Isaac was not a deficiency in his moral sense, so that he could be called a pioneer of faith? Because if there is a God, nothing else can be absolutized. All one's relations will be relative. Old worlds, like Isaac as the seed of Israel, must be allowed to die in order for new worlds to be born. In this case relativism does not mean the absence of standards, but the freedom (which entails responsibility) for creating in one's time, that is, being receptive to the relevant mode of being-in.

III

The eschatological suggestiveness of existentialism is the point at which it is most influential in Christian theology today. Camus once referred to the novels of Franz Kafka as "theology in action," because of the way they stripped all the artificial props away from life and left man exposed to some more final possibility. Existential philosophy is, in this sense, a secularized theology. Unlike almost every other philosophy, while it asks the question about ultimate meaning, it holds itself open to an answer which it does not itself provide.

The instance of the use of existentialism in theology today which is apt to occur to Americans first is Paul Tillich's method of correlation. Here the answers of the Christian faith are used by Tillich to fill the existential void. Now that there has been time to assimilate Tillich's position, it is being deceptively felt that his tactic is a very simple procedure which almost any Lutheran pastor would have used who desired to relate the faith apologetically. Therefore one should go beneath the apparently simple correlation of question and answer to a profounder level in Tillich's method. When one does, however, one senses another difficulty. His correlation is not a simple fitting of answers to questions but an ontology of question and answer in which the very asking of the question of ultimate meaning is already in some sense a participation in ultimately meaningful being. On that basis Tillich can regard the most violent, fragmented forms of contemporary art as the best expressions of the Protestant spirit and he can be more hospitable than most theologians are to the meanings in non-Christian faiths and in philosophies. Ontology for Tillich absorbs history and in doing so forecloses on the future. Avowedly, he is not a radical existentialist. No one has made it clearer than Tillich himself that when one becomes a Christian he ceases being an existentialist. What sometimes is not realized is that Tillich himself ceases being an existentialist *before* he becomes a Christian. Martin Heidegger led the way for this when he augmented his radical sense of the questionableness of life by the awareness of a revelation of meaning in the very asking of the question. Man gets his meaning as the one who asks the question of being. His very being becomes the locus for the appearance of the question of being. In this understanding, existentialism in Heidegger has been subordinated to a kind of ontological philosophy. In the light of developments in the thinking of the later Heidegger, it is now clear that Heidegger intended neither an ontology nor a philosophy but only a way of thinking and speaking more closely resembling poetry than anything else, where whatever "is" is allowed to come to appearance through speech. Tillich's systematic theology, however, has continued to build on the supposed non-existentialist ontology of the philosophy of the early Heidegger. In Tillich a philosophy of being becomes the common foundation beneath an otherwise radical existence and radical faith. Theologically, that means faith is never one's radical end: the revelation of meaning was already implicit in the fact of being. Philosophically, that means Tillich is among those associated with existentialism who do not play the game to the end.

The most influential existential view in theology today is the method of Biblical exegesis which Rudolf Bultmann sponsors. Irrespective of how his Biblical colleagues and former students react to him, the distinctive characteristic of his view philosophically and theologically is that he is one who does play the game to the end. He holds the same radically unanswerable existential questions which the existentialists and Tillich hear, but he knows of no possibility outside the Christ event for answering these questions. Of course, he is professionally unqualified, as any theologian is, to deny such possibilities. However, in his exegesis of the New Testament faith it becomes clear to him that the event of God in human history under the name of Jesus of Nazareth is "an eschatological event." That means that a Christian, who bases his existence on God's act in Christ, sees history as a reality to which God himself puts an end. The Christian, then, supplies the reason behind the existentialist's inability to find ultimate meaning in history. According to the Christian faith, history in general lacks the means of overcoming its own deficiencies because only God is Lord of history. At one point only is the predicament of history overcome; that is the holy event of Jesus in which God reveals his Lordship once and for all. All history is called to the decision about its ultimate hopefulness in that event.

Does not such a radical revelationalism remove Bultmann a great distance from all philosophy, and from existentialism in particular? Yes, and the two people who have seen this most clearly about Bultmann are Karl Jaspers and Karl Barth, although for somewhat different reasons. Jaspers rejects Bultmann because in making one historical event the absolute for all history he has shown himself to be too orthodox a Christian. Barth, on the other hand, defends Bultmann against the charge that he has made Christian faith synonymous with existential philosophy. "There are some philosophical fragments floating in the theological soup," Barth has said; and existentialism is no more definitive of Bultmann's theology than garnishing is to the soup.

A pivotal struggle going on in theological circles in America today is the struggle between Barthianism, which is just beginning to take hold, thanks to the English translations of his *Dogmatik*, and Bultmann's existential method of interpretation. Why should that be so when both have so much in common, as contrasted with Paul Tillich, in respect of their radical dependence upon the revealed character of the Christian faith? There are two central issues between them, and both depend upon an appreciation of how existentialism can be used in theology without compromising the radicalism of either existentialism or the Christian faith.

First is the issue as to how to interpret the Bible. According to Barth, it is the task of theology to criticize the preaching of the church in the light of the exegesis of the Scriptures. Bultmann's quarrel with Barth, however, is that Barth has no method of criticizing the Scriptures themselves. Now, both agree in rejecting the older tactics of Biblical criticism which approached the Bible simply as literature, with no sense of its normative value for Christian faith. How, then, does Bultmann's Biblical criticism differ from that of another day?

This is where his existentialism serves his interpretive task. The Bible is asking a certain type of question. These questions are strikingly similar to the questions existential philosophers are asking: "Why is there something and not nothing?", "What must I do to be saved?", "What is man?", "What wilt thou have me to do?", or as Beckett puts it, "that rumour rising at birth and even earlier, what shall I do? What shall I do?"[7] Existential philosophy is helpful in formulating theological questions, but is in no sense necessary to theology, for the Bible both asks and answers these questions. Only a man who comes to the Bible asking the questions the Bible is asking will understand it. One cannot read a book meaningfully unless he asks it the questions it is attempting to answer.

However, Bultmann detects that the Bible is also answering some questions which it is not asking and which the seriously existing man does not ask, either. They are answers rooted in curiosity and the instinct for evidential certainty and speculative explanation which do not speak in a primary way to the final concerns of life. Such answers participate in a myth-making tendency manifest in all religions, which is the tendency to express the truth of the eternal as if it were as verifiable as the facts of the world. It is one of the responsibilities of the Biblical interpreter to criticize these elements in the Biblical literature for the sake of allowing the truth of the faith to emerge. The Bible can in this way be criticized without jeopardy to its status as rule of faith inasmuch as the standard for judging it is itself a Biblical standard. That is, when the Bible is found to be answering questions which the Bible is not itself asking, there is a standard from within the Bible itself for judging the Bible.

The second issue between Barth and Bultmann has to do with what is meant by the historical character of Christian truth. Both affirm that Christian truth has to do with an event in history. Barth has persistently defined the event primarily from the standpoint of the doctrine of the trinity, that is, from the standpoint of God's participation in the event. The tendency of Bultmann and his followers has been to define the event more broadly than Barth from the standpoint of man's participation in it. The difference is at the point of inflection, and the inflections show up the relative esteem for existential matters. For Barth, revelation is not true unless it is *theologically* meaningful, that is, unless it involves God himself. For Bultmann, revelation is not true unless it is theologically *meaningful*, that is, unless it involves man himself. For Barth, Christian faith has to do with God *and* his relevance for the here and now, not with God *in* his relevance for the here and now. That is the characteristic Barth decision in theology today which separates him from those for whom the reality of God is in some sense at stake in history, in acts of interpretation, and for whom God's reality is not event simply, but historical event, or, event inseparable from man.

The outcome of Bultmann's method is a theology of existential interpretation in which the revealed events to which the faith witnesses are translated into the basis for a meaningful existence. The position is more familiar to Americans than often suspected, thanks to the pioneering which the Niebuhr brothers have done in our midst in the same vein. A highly sophisticated manifestation of the method can be found in the works of the Göttingen theologian Friedrich Gogarten, who has been at the center of the continental theological dialogue since the early twenties. Interesting and somewhat creative new departures are occurring in Europe in the generation of Bultmann's and Gogarten's disciples, particularly Gerhard Ebeling and Ernst Fuchs.

In a theology of existential interpretations, theological propositions are not intended as statements of truth, but as access to the illumination of existence. For instance, statements about God as creator are not so much literal truths about God as they are invitations to man to assume his role as creature. Statements about creation are not meant to compete with or much less to corroborate the findings of natural science but to give man the confidence that there is a purpose in history, however hidden. Statements about eschatology do not point to something in a chronological timeline of world history but support man's history with the realization that the hopes of history are not historically realizable and that he receives his life from beyond himself. The statement that children should honor their parents is a true statement only when uttered by a child. The importance of this trend for an understanding of Christian truth is enormous. When a man comes up against a hot stove he may conclude "The stove is hot," or even "Hot stoves burn." But he does not have the truth about the stove until his existence is qualified by caution in the presence of hot stoves.

This method of thinking is being undermined today from two sides. One is the old, familiar Barthian complaint that existential interpretation reduces theology to anthropology. But Barth himself has softened that complaint in his later works, where a new appreciation of the pietist tradition and the "humanity of God" has become quite evident. The more serious erosion is from the side of the friends of the method who carry it too far and thus appear to substantiate the Barthian objection. Fritz Buri of Basel is the chief illustration of this direction. Buri finds that the meaningful statements of the Christian faith are symbols which are not necessary derivatives of the historical events in which the faith first arises. They may as well be symbols of existence alone, and they may function valuably even though independently of any special event in history. Wilhelm Kamlah, a German theologian turned philosopher, contends somewhat more bluntly that existential philosophy has everything the Christian faith offers, so why be a Christian theologian. Other followers of the line of existential hermeneutic, sensing this erosion of the Christian foundation of their faith at the hands of existentialism, have leaned more to the right to become Roman Catholics. I refer principally to Heinrich Schlier, New Testament professor at the University of Bonn in Germany, and Gerhard Krüger, professor of philosophy at the University of Frankfort.

The irony of this latter movement is in the way in which Roman Catholics themselves are increasingly receptive to the existential trend. These are the new modernists, such as Jean Daniélou, Yves Congar, and Henri deLubac in France and Karl Rahner in Austria, who were the object of papal rebuke in the 1950 encyclical, *Humani generis*. The rebuke, however, was so gently and appreciatively made that in some circles it was interpreted as encouragement, and it is true that these same theologians, disciplined by the Vatican in 1950, were employed as *periti* or theological specialists for Vatican Council II from 1963 to 1965. The force of the existential concern in Roman Catholicism is twofold. It is giving the Catholic faith a point of contact with modern times which no longer seems available in the categories of scholasticism, and it is reopening Catholic interest in the Bible which the creeds and the developing tradition of the church had been allowed to overshadow. Existentialism could do this for Roman Catholicism because it made the Christian aware of a kind of redemptive concern within the Bible which was not adequately represented in the more speculative and theologically defensive formulations of the ancient ecumenical councils.

At least one question remains poised over the discussion of the role of existentialism in theology today. The thoroughgoing existentialists are those who play the game to the end. They are witnesses to the absence of final meaning in history and to the unreasonableness of that condition. The theologies cited here claim some kinship if not indebtedness to existentialism. Yet, in proposing Jesus of Nazareth as the presence of ultimacy in history, have they not also failed to play the game to the end? That, of course, will depend upon what Christianity means by its alleged maturity, finality, and eschatology. That is to say, it will depend upon how faith, which Jesus of Nazareth inaugurates, clears up the ambiguity of our world by bringing it to some viable focus. Or, as Beckett himself implies, it will depend upon what is meant by "Christ's parthian shaft, 'It is finished.' "[8]

THREE

Linguistic Analysis and the Context of Faith

Contemporary analytic philosophers have defined their task in such a way as to put every intellectual discipline, including theology, in debt to philosophy. The debt is joyfully acknowledged, for this philosophy does not attempt to bind other disciplines to itself as the one which sees the deepest truth. This philosophy is no overlord but a handmaiden. It performs a modest service, yet without subjugating itself. Let me state it with perilous simplicity. Every discipline uses a language. Its language is peculiar to its own subject-matter. The task of philosophy in the analytical definition is to patrol the border between the various functioning languages. One ought not say "Obst!" when ordering fruit in France, unless the mechanisms of translation are known to be in operation. Analytic philosophy is a philosophy which limits itself to language about the use of language. Its purpose is to help users of language avoid the confusion of crossing language boundaries unawares.

Why are philosophers needed for that? Why not simply *ad hoc* committees from language departments? Philosophers are needed because linguists deal with the syntax of language, but philosophers deal with its logic.[1] Inter-disciplinary vigilance committees of language departments could patrol the boundaries between, let us say, history, biology, and sociology and never challenge sentences in which "father of" was used, so long as their syntax was correct. Hence unsuspecting students could hear in one hour that "Washington is *father of* his country," in another that "the fruit fly is *father of* prodigious eye-color mutations," in still another that "the American male is *father of* a social unit now subject to novel forms of deterioration." Unaided by philosophy, grammarians would have no way of explaining the giddy sensation of inexactitude which this use of language can produce on campus. For languages can have radically different *logical* characteristics notwithstanding their impeccable *syntactical* symmetry. What if one were not alert to these logical discrepancies hiding behind smooth syntax? He would contribute to a chaos comparable to playing basketball by the rules of football. Analytical philosophy emerges as referee of the various university language games. The price it pays for this modest role is to play no game itself. In this definition philosophy is not a varsity language. It is a meta-language,[2] a language about language, a spectator language.

The therapy which philosophical analysis effects in the realm of meaning is nevertheless impressive. Picture a Kafkalike situation in which a judgmental voice comes from nowhere with the indictment, "That was an illegal pass!" What moral confusion can overcome you if you cannot identify the logic of the language. Is it athletics, is it traffic control, or is it social life! When the philosophical analyst asks the question, "How are these terms functioning here?", he has not simply resuscitated the grammarian. He has introduced an aseptic element into modern speech. What is involved is not mere stylistic finesse but the prevention of systematic—that is, logical—ambiguity which results from what Gilbert Ryle calls "category-mixing," or shifting terminological meanings in the middle of conversational streams.

Consider some instances. In using the word "time" it is important to throw up a warning flag at the moment its meaning shifts from designation of "a space" to designation of "a flow." When one refers to "action" it is important to know if the reference ever slips from the "causal" to the "motivational" gear. "History" is a term frequently used to specify more than one class of events, so that to say "This is all that happened during that time" can be highly misleading. Even the simplest combinations of words require vigilance, such as "This is his." Is it a descriptive statement, merely naming a thing? Is it an ascriptive statement, designating what belongs to whom? Or is it a "performatory" statement (J. L. Austin), actually effecting a transaction? Take the innocent little word "same." Does it operate unambiguously under all circumstances? Does "same" in "the same situation" have the connotation it does in "the same man" (Stuart Hampshire)? "Laughing" and "sneezing" are both participles. Does it make any difference in their logical form that one is less voluntary than the other? Do the "data" of the oculist have the same logical form as the "data" of the surgeon, if the oculist *knows* what the letters are but the surgeon *does not know* how the pain feels (Gilbert Ryle)? "Evidence" is a status word in academic vocabularies. Consider a situation, then, in which a painting is discovered which is purported to be a Goya (A. J. Ayer's illustration). The experts, after making every appeal to the evidence, still disagree. They do not despair, however, for they are confident the solution resides in the evidence. Then a philosophical amateur among the experts speaks up. After all, a picture, he says, is "a set of ideas in the perceiver's mind." What happens to the examiners' contented focus on the "evidence"?

Philosophical analysis is having an especially salutary effect upon the discipline of theology. This has only lately occurred in any direct way, thanks to the efficient circulation of the news that contemporary analytic philosophy has relinquished its former verificationist criterion. In the logical positivist epoch, language analysis meant testing assertions for their verifiability. The only canon of verifiability was that executed by the physical sciences. Sentences which did not lend themselves to verification were judged to be "nonsense," which really only meant that those certain sentences were not "sensibly," that is, perceptually, either verifiable or falsifiable. At present language analysis means that there is a great variety of language in operation, and that the task of philosophy is not to judge which languages are meaningful in terms of their verifiability, but to adjudicate the lines between the various functioning languages, in order to prevent confusion. The most crucial area of confusion, of course, is still between languages which do lend themselves to verification and languages which do not. Those that do not are not ruled out. They are simply contained. They must make no statement which implies verifiability if, in fact, the statement deals with what is not verifiable.

This demand for linguistic rigor is not new to theology. The effectiveness of some of the major theologians of the church has been in direct proportion to their analytical clarity. Probably the most conspicuous instance is Thomas Aquinas. Even John Wesley materializes as a primitive Oxford analyst after one has noticed the recurrent insistence in his sermons on overcoming ambiguity by the scrupulous use of words. Today Rudolf Bultmann's "demythologizing" project is based on the very desire for terminological clarity which comes with freedom from "category-mixing." Myth is a form of assertion which refers to the unverifiable in a language which suggests verifiability. When "son of God" is taken as a genea*logic*al judgment, faith is mythologized. When "end of the age" is taken as a meteoro*logic*al judgment or "people of God" as a socio*logic*al judgment, categories are mixed and mythology has set in. Demythologizing does not call for the abandonment of myth from sacred literature, but simply for its translation into the language appropriate to the *logic* of its claims.

Notwithstanding these and other grounds for gratitude to philosophical analysis, I as a theologian am sad about the current prominence of this point of view as philosophy. I call attention to my position "as a theologian" in order to warn the general reader not to trust my competence in philosophical matters, and also to advise the philosopher that I do not wish to tamper with his affairs. I only say that something is happening to analytical philosophy which is bound to impoverish theology, whatever else it may do to philosophy. The real apprehension of the theologian is not with the direct effect of logical analysis upon the statement of the Christian faith but with its indirect effect. Most of its direct observations refer to popular belief or to what these certain analysts remember of their childhood religious training. Theologians are as critical of immature expressions of faith as these analysts are. What the theologian fears is not what this philosophy is doing directly to the faith but what it is doing to philosophy, and hence indirectly to a faith which relies so heavily upon hearty dialogue with philosophy. The story of theology's life with philosophy records a relation in which philosophy has helped theology formulate its questions and conceptualize its faith. A maieutic force is always being exerted by philosophy upon the body of Christian faith which helps deliver the faith into intellectual comprehension. If analytical philosophy were to become what it aspires to become, namely, philosophy itself, I for one would fly my flag at half-mast. It would be a sign that theology had lost its closest dialogical partner. Then I would be forced to go in search of some other discipline, perhaps history or literature, to do what philosophy traditionally had done but would now no longer be qualified to do. The grounds of this disqualification, as I see it, support Boyce Gibson's complaint that "the fashionable mature accommodation between an empirical philosophy and a declaratory religion . . . is not even a marriage of convenience; it is a frostily amicable bilateral quarantine."

My recurrent reservation upon entering into dialogue with philosophical analysis is the sense of the ghost of logical positivism lingering in its procedures. When "leprechauns-in-watches" become analogues of selves-in-bodies or of God-in-the-world, suspicion is aroused that a value judgment is being smuggled in. When the name "Pickwick" is said to function differently from the name "Napoleon" because the former is fiction and the latter historical fact, one surmises that the constitutive power of Dickens' literary imagination has been culpably downgraded.

Philosophical analysis is an empirical philosophy, but we are repeatedly advised that it is not so in the same sense in which logical positivism was empirical. For logical positivism, empiricism meant the perceptual verifiability of a language. For contemporary analytical philosophy, empiricism means simply the examination of *the use* of a language. If one did not realize how radically the connotation of the word "empiricism" has changed in the later phases of analytical philosophy, he would be quite puzzled to know what the Oxford analyst Ian Ramsey means when he says that without "empirical anchorage all our theological thinking is in vain." By empirical he is referring to the location of theological assertions in the logic of "worship, wonder, and awe." He does not mean that theological statements find some kind of sensory verification in liturgical acts. He simply means that when the sense of these statements is sought in detachment from their liturgical use, confusion is at hand.

What can be meant, however, when the analyst deplores the incursion of the language of drama upon philosophy, if not that it inspires the evasion of verification, an "evasion of that abiding and ultimate question—*on what grounds* ought I assume an attitude of obedience before the New Testament and not before, say, the Koran" (Ronald Hepburn)? Why should virgin birth and resurrection be held more "conceivable" than the Trinity just because they are "historical" while the Trinity presumably is not" (J. J. C. Smart)? Why is religious language said to have "an insecure status" which makes it "controversial in a way in which scientific language is not" (Anthony Flew)? What makes the "at least this, at least that" of scientific predication more acceptable to analysts than the "not this, not that" of mystical *via negativa* (John Wilson)? I judge it is the ghost of logical positivism which, though renounced, still lurks in their analytical machinery.

The ghost of positivism haunts the work of the very most well-intentioned philosophical theologians among the analysts, in the guise of what has been called "eschatological verification" (John Hick).[3] According to this view, the verification of certain propositions, especially religious assertions, may be possible only after death or at the end of history. Take the claim that "human personalities survive bodily death," or that "the love of God and human suffering are not incompatible." As long as the obvious facts of life which tend to falsify these statements are liable to revision by information that may still emerge beyond death or at the end of history, these claims enjoy the logical status of assertions. The device is reminiscent of John Wisdom, who has said, "to know that something is so, is with a proper basis to believe that it is so and be right." Everything hinges on the leap between "a proper basis" and "be right." Eschatological verification means that the end of the game vindicates as knowledge the move one took in mid-game by faith. Or, to say it wryly, as Wisdom does on another occasion, winning a race is one of the most "settlable" disputes in language. Theologians could say of their religious concepts what F. Waisman of Oxford has said of empirical statements in general: there is a "porousness" about them, an "open texture" such that "we can never fill up all the possible gaps through which a doubt may seep in." But they would themselves be tricked into coddling the ghost of logical positivism if they anticipated even a final moment, however remote, when the last gap would be filled. The verification which positivism required has nothing in common with theological reasoning. Specific facts, which are surely no sufficient cause of religious belief, are no necessary cause either. To say so underestimates the radical effect which personal belief with its intentionality of consciousness has upon the logic of the reality with which faith is involved.

That suggests another occasion for theological restlessness in the presence of analytical philosophy. Christian faith is primarily an historical reality, but analytical philosophy is notably deficient in historiography. What kind of dialogical partner, then, is a philosophy which yawns at the very moment in the conversation when theology begins to show an interest?

Analytical philosophy appears to have a sensitive approach to history. This is evidenced in its refusal to accept the concept "history" as embracing a simple reality. History exists in "levels," and languages which use the word as if it meant the same thing in every operation contribute to confusion. For instance, there are two pasts: the irrecoverable past which no one will ever again know, and the past which is knowable as a dimension of one's present. That distinction is fairly patent. But there are also two futures: the future which has not yet occurred and the future which never comes. Historical sceptics have a field day if they can confine history to the temporal modes of past and future, and then purvey the understanding that everything past is simply irrecoverable and everything future will simply never come. The analytical approach to historical language is a refreshing exposé of such reductionistic sleight-of-hand.

History can also be classified in respect of its grades of generality. There is what is called "the ideal limit" or the "book of the recording angel" view of history where every slightest detail of history is embraced. I detect that this view of history corresponds to the "God knows" convention, where "God" is the formal equivalent to "an infinite number of infinitely efficient observers and computers" (J. O. Urmson). At the opposite extreme there is the lowest level of historical generality, probably biography, where the historian is limited to anecdotes accidentally available in his sources of information.

One ought not be shocked by now to hear the analyst observe that these two extremes are "equally good history." "We do not get a better or a worse view of a field according as we take a bird's eye, or a man's eye, or a worm's eye view of it, though we get a different view" (A. M. MacIver). Philosophical analysis does not evaluate; it simply classifies according to the logic inherent in the language. Hence, to call these levels "equally good history" is really redundant. A man's history is the only history a man has, therefore the terms "better" or "worse" are inapplicable.

Here, however, the ghost of logical positivism stubbornly persists. The analyst does not see how possible it is for a *man, himself,* to have more than one kind of history, and how one kind may be more suitable to his humanity than another. This distinction may not require the exercise of value judgments, but it does require more finesse than is manifest in most philosophical analysis (with the possible exception of the recent work by Stuart Hampshire, whose residual positivism is dissolved partially by a trend toward phenomenology).

Philosophical analysis is deficient in historiography because it does not sufficiently distinguish what phenomenologists call "the natural standpoint" or *prima facie* evidence from the "phenomenologically reduced" standpoint. Efforts of historians imaginatively to reconstruct and participate in the events of the past are dismissed as subjectivistic caprice. Lest one fail to recognize where to draw the line between sensitive personal involvement, which is the stuff of history, and sheer inventiveness, philosophical analysis approves as history a single view not fully human. There is some plausibility in the observation, therefore, that linguistic analysis flourishes as philosophy chiefly in a land noted for its "national taste for landscape painting."

"The Skylark" is prominent in the analytic landscape. Logical analysts simply do not want historians avowing Shelley's bird that "never wert." The mistake the analyst makes is assuming the reality of only one kind of bird. Of several possible birds, which does the historian deal with? The natural standpoint dictates that the historian deal with the orbitho*logic*al bird. In fear of snaring the bird of aesthetic daydreams instead (i.e. "bird thou never wert"), the analyst seems to choose the orbitho*logic*al bird. It has been said of the man's, worm's, and bird's eye views of history, "They are all views of the same field" (A. M. MacIver). That is the simplistic mistake of the natural attitude, for there is also the historian's bird.

Now, the temptation is to say that, while the ornithologist's bird is not the sufficient cause of the historian's bird, it is the necessary cause. To yield to that temptation is to be seduced by the natural standpoint, which is the ghost of logical positivism. History must not be thought to be a common field of objective events simply subject to a diversity of subjective interpretations. History is a realm of events which are interpretations. Interpretation is the objective reality of these events. Such events will not be historically recovered, therefore, except by acts of interpretation. To back away from interpretative responsibility in the effort to get to some object itself is to create a new object from which the interpretation is squeezed out, and hence an object which is deficient in historical reality. The necessary and sufficient cause of the historian's bird is the historical bird. The ornithologist's bird never makes history, for it is the bird in the bush, the *prima facie* bird. The historian's bird is the bird in the hand, the bird constituted by the fact of its existence in man's world. Philosophical analysis dehumanizes history by an implicit value judgment that a bird in the bush is worth two in the hand.

This leads to my main anxiety over the prestige of language analysis as philosophy today. Clear justice is not done to the effect of the personal dimension upon the logic of reality. The cardinal illustration is John Wisdom's parable of the two travellers who stumble upon a garden. One traveller concludes that a gardener must exist; the other concludes that no gardener exists. The purpose of the parable is to mark the transition in contemporary British philosophy from logical positivism to linguistic analysis. When two travellers can derive opposite results from the same field of evidence, what shall the philosopher conclude? He may now accept both conclusions as equally valid, with no responsibility to verify either. The situation is parallel to two viewers in the presence of a work of art. One says, "It's beautiful!" The other says, "I don't see it!" Both have the same picture before them, but draw opposite conclusions. That is taken to mean their tastes are different, and analytical philosophy does not adjudicate tastes. It only helps to indicate which way the languages function. The validity of their conclusions is a matter of indifference.

The repeated assumption of the analyst that the nature of the human question has no bearing upon the kind of reality one encounters is rather too bland. As I have said, it is philosophy's own show if it wishes to delimit its act in this way; but it is a calamity to theology that its dialogical partner has so depersonalized the philosophical medium that cries of wretchedness over the inability of the universe to answer critical questions about reality are put off with counterquestions about the use of the words which phrase the cry. That the passion is left unsatisfied is not the fault, but that the passion has no chance to enter into the emergence of the appropriate reality.

"Time" is sketched with terminological precision, but no sense is left that time is running out. The "future" is categorized with verbal clarity, but no burden of choice before its imminence remains. The existence of "other minds" dominates the dialogue, but there is no tension of struggle for love and power in the conflict with these other selves. The problem of "pain" for logical analysis is the question of how to overcome solipsism. This philosophy is so enamoured of liberation from the epistemological privacy of the pain experience that it forgets to cry out in anger, "Why the pain!" "God" is a formal concept which stands for omniscience, but there is no sense of the holy such as an ultimate personal presence or even absence would inspire. "Who am I?" is always asked in the sanitary Cartesian sense where the continuity of the self is treated as a technical problem. The astringent query of Pascal, "Am I?", or of the medieval mystics, "Why am I something and not nothing?" drops out of range. Philosophy begins in "doubt," as Descartes knew, and doubts in philosophical analysis are "requests for decision" (John Wisdom), but only the decision concerning the proper form of the language to be used. What of the question of the proper form of human existence to adopt? What of the question of "ultimate meaning?" That is the question which, for some philosophy today and in the past, has made suicide the number one philosophical problem. "Meaning" for analysts, however, no longer connotes "importance" but "the implications words carry." "Ultimate" refers no longer to "what makes life worth living" but to the circumstance that "a fact has in some sense only one set of terms" (John Wisdom). Why should philosophy as a discipline be permitted to arrive at the place where its metamorphosis from deep human questions to language-and-logic questions is experienced as a chill?

A. J. Ayer recently deplored certain philosophers who "see tragedy in what could not conceivably be otherwise." By that he meant they cannot seem to live with equanimity in the presence of the inability to know anything for certain. Logical analysis quiets all sense of tragedy in philosophy by moving the concern of philosophy beyond what produces tragic awareness. Such philosophical ways of evading what is so integral to being human may become acceptable to philosophy, but they make philosophy unacceptable to enterprises which insist upon transparency to the basic human questions. Christian theologians, in looking for a dialogical partner, do not seek philosophies which are already Christian. They only seek for methods which admit the human questions where they are most profoundly raised. By design, philosophical analysis abrogates this responsibility. Insofar as it does so, it ceases to hold the interest of the theologian.

FOUR

Apologetics and
the Communication of Faith
—Karl Heim's Theology

One of the best illustrations of sensitivity to the theological significance of worldly enterprises is the thought of Karl Heim, late professor of systematic theology at the University of Tübingen in southern Germany. His work has exhibited with an astonishing range and versatility the historical scope of the task of theology today. Over a period of more than fifty years he wrote on the history of religions, philosophy, and natural science with the same vigor and skill that characterized his theology and ethics. He also produced Biblical expositions and historical studies, including a treatise on Alexander of Hales and another on the problem of certainty in Christian doctrine to the time of Schleiermacher. Scores of his sermons were published, several volumes of which are in English. They reveal a fascinating combination of tender piety and disciplined penetration into personal and cultural needs. No crisis in the life of the German people seemed to escape his theological scrutiny. A fat volume, *Faith and Life* (*Glaube und Leben*, 1926), which someone has called "a thesaurus," embraces these essays from a period of twenty-five years.

Heim saw the care of the soul portrayed in the ministry of Jesus. Contrary to the image most have of the German theologian, he made pastoral concern central to his own vocation. Ecumenical involvement begun in his youth as secretary of the German Student Christian Movement persisted throughout his most mature work. To the very end of his life he deliberately resisted what he felt to be the theologian's cardinal ambition—the writing of a *Dogmatik*. During an Oxford Group meeting in England that ambition was revealed to him as a sin of pride and he surrendered it. In 1931 he began his closest approximation to a *Dogmatik*, a six-volume work entitled *The Evangelical Faith and the Thought of the Present* (*Der evangelische Glaube und das Denken der Gegenwart*). The first volume, *Faith and Thought* (*Glaube und Denken*) is his most significant work. In his preface he announced that he was definitely not writing "in the form of a *Dogmatik*. . . . We have enough textbooks on dogmatics." At least one theologian in Europe found it impossible to take that announcement lightly, for Karl Barth just four years earlier had launched his own leviathan.

Probably best known to the English speaking world of the pre-World War II period was Heim's Protestant manifesto, *Spirit and Truth* (*Das Wesen des Evangelischen Christentums*, 1925). This was written in open dialogue with his famous Catholic colleague at Tübingen, Karl Adam. Since World War II Heim has been known across the world for his writings on natural science. This is a calamity, for it by-passes his most distinctive contribution, which is the methodological structure underlying his entire literature and which, more than the concerns of piety, dictated the direction of his theological writing. Heim aimed his communication of the Christian faith at levels of the human spirit which are often left untouched by the theological traditions stemming from seventeenth-century Protestant orthodoxy and from nineteenth-century liberalism. It is not mysterious, therefore, that many pastors in Germany today continue to regard him as their principal teacher.

Here the mystery begins, however. The continental theologians who remember him have appended him to their courses in the history of doctrine. His phenomenal life-span has made that a possibility. He was beyond eighty years of age when he died. But what of the contemporary pertinence of his work? I believe there are mainly two reasons for the relative neglect of Heim's thought among his colleagues today. The more immediate reason seems to be that the Barth and Bultmann circles have almost completely absorbed current theological attention. The less evident but more instructive reason is that the theologians have been too disconcerted by Heim's method to sustain their interest. My account of Heim's contribution will attempt to provide the key to both circumstances. It can be found in what Heim conceives to be the responsibility of Christian apologetics.

I

The theologians who have noticed Heim have exhausted themselves attempting to locate his position within some standard camp. One group has labelled him "a rationalist." Did he not develop a philosophical basis for the Christian view of life? Was he not concerned with the intellectual possibility of the certainty of faith? Did he not restlessly seek for "a category" by which to express the Christian faith in terms comprehensible to contemporary culture? Is not that device reminiscent of the Schleiermacher-Troeltsch-Otto succession, with its tactic of religious *a priori?*

The testimony of this group is very confident. "Anyone who accepts Heim's world view is not yet a religious man," says one interpreter. "Heim's whole effort is a blunder which can be traced to his preoccupation with artful abstraction," says another. "Insoluble logic is more important to him than personal relations. His God is an 'it' and not a 'Thou'." "He employs the experience of despair as a device for securing the certainty of faith." "In his desire for a science of the ultimate he wishes to stand where only God can stand." "He does not speak from a place within the Church." He "fails to follow the proper task of theology, reflection on the testimony and message of the Bible."[1]

These charges would be serious were it not for the almost comical fact that another block of interpreters arrives at a completely opposite conclusion about him. His tendencies, they say, are those of "an irrationalist." Does he not elevate God beyond the reach of human reason? Does he not exemplify a simple trust in the Biblical revelation with its miracles and unique revelation? One rejects him because he denies that man is able to have communion with God outside of Jesus Christ. Another says, "He imports a *deus ex machina* into a sceptical philosophy." Another, "He is a reactionary irrationalist." Still another, "He neglects the rational in order to found religion on an irrational source."[2]

By these contradictory testimonies the critics fall against each other and the Heim mystery deepens. The more patient and discerning critics see both rationalist and irrationalist tendencies in Heim's work but they fail to see how he has resolved these tendencies. He presents the puzzling appearance of one who attempts contradictory aims. Therefore, these analysts ask, "How can one combine in a single viewpoint an emphasis both on what is beyond the reason and what is a necessity within the reason" as Heim seems to do? "How can an intellectual impossibility become the basis for the intellectual possibility of Christianity?" "How can one express Tertullian's fideism in the patterns of pure mathematics?" Has not Heim "vacillated indefinitely between an austere metaphysical theology and a theology of individual experience"? [3]

That more cautious and well-balanced critique is as misguided as all the others, however. All seem to miss a central key which unlocks the mystery of Heim's theological significance. One may state it briefly. Heim's theological method is instructed by a sensitivity to the polarity, the tension in human existence which is ineradicable from within existence. How does he know about this tension? In two ways and not just one. He both lives as a man and is the beneficiary of the revelation which names the truth "Jesus Christ." These two standpoints are nowhere held in separation in his position. The human situation is seen to be riddled with the agonies one associates with doubt, social hostility, suffering, guilt, and death. These agonies are the more acute for the fact that there appears to be no satisfactory relief from them within the human situation. How does Heim know that? Has he personally played all the registers of life? That is not required of a man who has heard from within his life as a man the message of justification by faith alone. It is precisely the priority of faith in his method which makes it possible for him to participate profoundly in the life of the world.

For instance, he wrote as a *phenomenologist*. Indeed, his first book in 1902 was an analysis of Husserl's phenomenological method. That means, he dealt with the problems of life *as it appears*, and not simply as a deduction from the Christian revelation. Yet it was his position from within the faith that gave him his warrant for proceeding as a phenomenologist does, in honest pursuit of the problem of life as it appears, for that process of fundamental questioning would surely culminate in the thirst for a meaning which does not necessarily appear. He also wrote as an *existentialist*. Heim was one of the first theologians in Europe to introduce Kierke- gaardian insights, as well as being one of the first to take up the crucial work of Heidegger into theological reasoning. Yet, it was as a steward of the faith that he had the confidence that the pursuit of meaning involves *all* one's faculties and commits one to decisive action upon the results of his search. He wrote as an *ontologist*. That means he was not simply a *metaphysician* seeking for the origin or causes of things, for first principles. In that regard he was instructed by Ritschlianism. To say he was an ontologist means he examined and illuminated the fundamental structure of being in such a way as to relate the whole of one's life to the ultimate mean- ing in the whole of life. Along with Tillich and others in the days between the wars, he defended the role of ontology in theology. However, it was clearer to him than to some others that theology precedes ontology and makes it possible, as even Plato and Aristotle seem to have believed. He wrote with a *hermeneutical* accent. By that is meant that the fundamental realities with which a theologian has to deal are meanings. This accent ought not be confused with a variety of Gnosticism for which sheer theological information was held to be redemptive. The intellectual propositions of a hermeneutical theology are different from those which specify that life means this or that. The meanings which resolve the manifest and hidden agonies of life will be breathed with intimacy through such confessional language as, "You mean everything to me!", and by that communication change the structure of life.

II

The primacy of faith in Heim's system ought to safeguard his otherwise secular methods from being dismissed, as Barthian influ- enced theologians tend to dismiss them. Karl Barth has said "Nein!" to almost every major theologian of this century, and he has done it, as he himself says, like a roaring lion. His main prey have been theologians with an *Anknüpfungspunkt* mentality, which is a species of natural theology, deriving theological insight from sources other than God's special revelation in Christ. Therefore, to join forces with Heim would seem like an invitation to annihila- tion at Barth's hands, considering Heim's apparent deafness to the

Barthian warning. The following typical citations from Heim's works are impressive evidence of his apparent methodological flirtation with natural theology.

"All reality speaks a common language." "Morality and religion are one and the same movement of life under two different viewpoints." "Every fleeting wish is indeed already a religion in miniature." "The demand of human relations is for another who himself needs no other." "There are only two possible reactions for the man in battle—stupefaction or prayer." "There is no experience of despair that does not give light to the horizon." "The despair which the conscience experiences is the foothold in the visible for the leap into the invisible." "Every forcible suppression of doubt is a direct blow at conscience. It destroys our reverences for truth, the highest faculty within us, which must be kept alive if we wish to know God." "An atheistic ontology is only possible on the grounds of an abstraction which neglects the why and wherefore of the existence of the real man." "We must find an answer to the question about how we may find a way from creation to the creator." "The leading of God can come to one in an entirely reasonable and commonplace form in which, after a laborious rational process through which I examine a given situation according to my best knowledge and conscience and enumerate all the reasons *pro* and *con*, I become stamped with the seal of certainty: 'this way must in the name of God be taken'."[4]

Barth's own critique of Heim was relatively benign until he read Heim's statement disavowing works on dogmatics as acts of pride. It can truthfully be said of Barth that he never fought an offensive war. In the case of Heim, the casual sentence in his preface provoked Barth's counterattack. In an open letter to Heim appearing in the periodical *Between the Times*,[5] Barth asked Heim to explain what he meant by that statement. But he said more. The students who moved back and forth between the two universities where Heim and Barth were teaching had told Barth some of the things Heim was saying about him in his lectures. Heim was alleged to have said that Barth's *Dogmatik* was "the summit of the unpleasant pride of modern secularism." To that Barth replied that Heim's theology was "the most recent form of equally unpleasant humility of modern pietism." While Heim's personal history is laden with pietism, as his recent autobiography quite explicitly reveals, Barth's charge was theological in intention. Heim's approach to the Christian faith, he said, was a form of "psychologism," the very kind of anthropological exaggeration which makes bedfellows of nineteenth century liberalism, pietism, and scholasticism. Each is a trend toward "point of contact" thinking or natural theology.[6]

Barth's criticism of Heim is wrong. Heim's theology has never been anthropological, except in the sense that his Lutheran Christology is anthropological. To begin with God's word in Christ, however, does not prohibit taking one's humanity with theological seriousness. Since the Enlightenment, of course, any alliance between the revelation and human discernment has been looked upon with suspicion by both theologians and philosophers, for at that time philosophy declared its independence from theology and theology felt obliged to return the compliment. Therefore, in modern life philosophies have tended to absorb the functions of faiths. Barthianism alone of all the theologies today has attempted, like medieval scholasticism, to absorb the functions of philosophy.[7]

Heim's understanding of the relation of theology to non-theological disciplines antedates this curtaining off of the human and the divine disciplines. It is probably best exemplified in the philosophical theology of Augustine. Karl Heim can really be understood only in this setting. For that reason, judgments aimed at him from within the philosophy-blind post-Enlightenment theology are apt to miss the mark. If theology is separable from other spheres it is insulated against their judgment. At the same time, however, in such a relation the judgment of theology upon other spheres is blocked by its own defences. If theology is in any way dependent upon other spheres, its autonomy is threatened, being subject to the judgment of these other spheres. One of the rewards of that risk, however, is that the methodological lines by which theological perspective is communicated to other spheres are at least kept open.

It would be better to find a new name for what theologians used to do than to allow the theological task to be pinched by restrictions forced upon it by either secular or sacred sciences. Heim believed this so firmly that he entertained the notion of a completely different name for theology, namely, the "Science of the Ultimate." Such a science is interested in but one question: "What are the ultimate presuppositions which support our life and how is the certainty of this foundation established?"[8] Heim would not concede that there is a distinction between theological responsibility and the type of search for a basis in life which goes on outside theology, such as in the novel and the drama, or even in newspapers and in politics. All are concerned explicitly or implicitly with the ultimate in existence, be they inside or outside the Church.[9]

As a result of his method, Heim believed he was able to achieve at least the outlines of a Christian ontology. There does seem to be a convincing overlap between the human situation as lived through by the concerned man and the divine revelation as witnessed within the Christian Church. One would expect, therefore, that the effect of Heim's method would be to break down the wall, if not to construct a bridge, between the Church and the world, between theology and philosophy, between faith and culture. It should be carefully noted that Heim proposed no theological bridge "between God and man." That task is out of the theologian's hands and where attempted is nothing but a *Schneebrücke*, a bridge of snow.

Two major data dominate Heim's ontology. One is the thoroughgoing relativism of human existence. The other is what he calls God's "dimensional" transcendence. These data are complementary. If there is a God of the sort confessed by the Hebrew-Christian faith, then man has a permanent basis for his life. The basis, however, would be not in man's life but in God's. Therefore, Heim could press man relentlessly with the question of ultimate meaning, because he knew from the outset that a life unrelated to God is relatively meaningless. "A man must have something permanent," Heim believed.[10] Human experience needs it, not because it feels the need, but because the need is revealed to be inherent in the very structure of life.

By relativism Heim meant that in existence, as one can know it by himself, there is no absolute point of reference. The ontology underlying this assertion is constructed out of a view of time. Man is completely embedded in time, or better, time is completely embedded in man. The very structure of existence is time, and, like time, existence is running out. Within existence there is no security for existence. Man's life is a continuous trek across a never-ending watershed. Behind him is the irrevocable and certain past, powerless to help him in the present. Ahead of him is the uncertain future. Without the help of any final knowledge, man must act decisively toward the future. In the nature of time, moving forward as it does irreversibly, suspension of decision would be itself a decision to let time decide. The mistake of man is either to accept something in time as if it were final, or to fail to despair of its lack of finality. Either state would be a condition of "radical Godlessness," which Heim describes as the lack of an archimedean point for the orientation of one's life.

How does the human reason function within this time reference? Reason leads man restlessly from island to island but never finds a continent on which to build firmly. Within the ever-receding infinity called existence, the reason comes upon nothing which is not staggered by the question, "Why?" But the conscientious reason, the moral reason, the reason which is concerned with the total destiny of the person on behalf of whom it functions, is not content with this situation and tantalizes itself in an endless and exhausting search for a clue to transcendence beyond the situation. Life under these conditions can only result in either the crushing spiritual poverty one has learned to call despair, or a leap into some sort of saving faith. No faith could be regarded as a saving faith which does not transcend the limitations of the "time-form" from which it professes to bring deliverance. In his autobiography, *Ich gedenke der vorigen Zeiten* ("I remember the days of old"), Heim recapitulates the sheer geographical and political relativity he experienced in a trip around the world just after the First World War. Add to this experience his knowledge of Einstein's theory and you have what he called "the fundamental negative idea at the base of my whole theological work."[11]

The Christian belief in the transcendence of God both explains the relativity of the time-form and brings deliverance from it. Where there is only one God, all else is related to him, that is, all else is relative. Where there is only one Absolute, all else presupposes this Absolute. The very effort to know the Absolute depends upon the prior existence of the Absolute. Is God so transcendent, then, that He is out of touch with human experience? On the contrary. God is transcendent because he is so near, not because He is so remote. He sustains man's whole life, and one cannot see the place on which one stands. Is man therefore destined to live in ignorance of the one reality the knowledge of which can bring authenticity to his life? Not at all. The experience of thoroughgoing relativism is the presupposition for the raising of the question about the ultimate. The question simply waits upon the answer which only the ultimate can give, and give in its own way. The Christ-revelation is taken to be the answer of God to the question implicit in the structure of man's life. As such, it is an answer which arises not from the relative situation but transcendent of the situation.

Yet, throughout Heim's work he makes the claim for the rational certainty of the Christian faith. What could that mean within this ontological scheme of human relativism and divine transcendence? The allusion to certainty is a residuum in Heim for another day. The meaning, however, does not hinge upon the language. Heim is convinced that it is rational to affirm what is needed to make experience possible. The Christian revelation, then, notwithstanding man's inability to come upon it by himself, is a "rational event," as Barth himself once called it.[12] For Heim it is not the revelation but only the need of revelation which is given in human experience. When Barth complains that one cannot end with faith-certainty unless one has begun with it, he requires exactly what Heim has proposed. His theology begins from within the human situation at the point where the Christ revelation brings the ultimacy of the transcendent God to the contingency of existence.

III

The general lines of Heim's ontology were present in his theology from his earliest work. Pertinent elements in the new physics and biology, in existential philosophy, and in the political fortunes of the world have been blended with Luther's doctrine of justification by faith. The result has been no flatulent philosophy in waiting for some doctoral candidate to place it in the history of thought. Heim's work has been a spur at the flank of continental life for over half a century.

The mobility of Heim's intellectual forces during this time is most impressive. In each succeeding decade he has shifted his key concept, always improving without essentially changing his fundamental structure. To shift the figure, he has felt it important to erect a readily traversible bridge between the Christian message and the world. It must be remembered that the bridge connects the Church and the world, not God and man. To use an Augustinian figure, the bridge is traversible when illuminated, and one who believes in the Christian doctrine of justification by faith, or what is the same, the doctrine of the Holy Spirit, knows that this is a *lumen aeternae* for the coming of which one can only wait. This primacy of God's action, however, in no way obviates for Heim the importance of building bridges.

In *Psychologismus oder Antipsychologismus* (1902) Heim set the pattern for his entire theological literature. In this very difficult little study of Edmund Husserl's pioneering work in logic, he attempted to show how it is possible to do theology without either metaphysics, on the one side, or the logic of the natural sciences on the other. An epistemology is required which will allow that at the base of thought processes there are presuppositions which are themselves unknowable. In his recent memoirs he notes how Martin Heidegger's *Sein und Zeit*, which virtually attempted the same kind of analysis, has now made that early work of his superfluous. I cite this comment simply to observe that he makes no such statement with reference to his other works.

Das Weltbild der Zukunft (1904) established Heim as an author at a time when he would rather have become a professor. The book was a study of reality documented from the modern sciences and from philosophy. His thesis was that in reality as it appears one has to do only with relationships, never with ultimate data. This very relativity of phenomena forces men to make decisions, even though a secure basis for such decisions is not given in the phenomena. It does not seem unreasonable, therefore, that there would appear to man what man himself needs but cannot voluntarily conjure up—the revelation of an absolute basis for decision in God's own decision.

Heim does not hide his disappointment at not being called to a chair of systematic theology as a result of this work. Actually, it was not the kind of work expected of dogmaticians in Germany at that time. Just to show that he could do it, he subsequently turned to more traditional historical studies, one on Alexander of Hales and the other on the problem of certainty. Karl Barth is said to have confessed a similar motive behind his own *Anselm* study. Not until 1914 was Heim finally called to a professorship at Münster. Because of the war, he could not take up this call until 1918. Two years later, he won the post at Tübingen which he held until retirement. I say "won" because a contest actually ensued with Rudolf Otto for that position. In his early student movement days Heim felt shunned by circles in Germany which associated with him an American brand of practical Christianity and a Methodist brand of evangelical piety. On one occasion when he sought the advice of Reinhold Seeberg concerning his vocational possibilities as a professor of theology, he was shocked when this famous teacher told him he should seek a chair of practical theology.

In 1916 his original insights concerning the decisional character of reality were sharpened in the direction of more fundamental theological concerns in the volume called *Glaubensgewissheit* (*The Certainty of Faith*). In the second edition of this work, appearing in 1920, the first significant shift in his position occurred. The "decision" category was replaced by a "destiny" category. Man's windowless decisions do not simply presuppose some transcendent light. They suffer a light burning in upon them. This category, suggested by Oswald Spengler, offered Heim the occasion to introduce into his method the more aggressive connotations of the revelation, theologically expressed in the doctrines of predestination, grace, and the witness of the Spirit.

Within three years, a third edition of *Glaubensgewissheit* appeared which further clarified the structure in the relation which God's destinating decision sustains to man's relative decisions. God is "the non-objective perspective," drawing all visible experience up into the unity of His being, but Himself remaining invisible. This perspectival unity is at the ground of all experience as the very possibility of experience. One cannot know the non-objective perspective point of all objective perspectives, but one cannot know anything else without it. The dependence here upon motifs from Kant is avowed.[13]

This development of categories prepared the way for the emergence of the category on which Heim based his *opus magnum, The Evangelical Faith and the Thought of the Present.* I refer to his most famous category of "the dimension." Heim believed that one who understands the meaning of the "dimensions" has come upon the primary and most important basis for understanding the mystery of existence. The illustrations are patent. The two-dimensionally-minded primitive man was unable to make sense of his universe until someone announced the existence of the third dimension. The third dimension was nothing he could see, for one's perception presupposes it. Width and height stretch out before us, but depth is a straight line. If we observe it, we see only the end of it, a pinpoint on the two-dimensional width-height surface. If we observe on the basis of it, however, the surface becomes deep with perspective. To say it more technically, on the basis of two-dimensional experience, it is contradictory to assume that more than two straight lines meet at right angles. Analogically, the God-relation is the depth dimension which, when one hears of it, comprehends all other dimensions and clarifies existence, without itself being perceptible.

The God-dimension is hidden, and it is the presupposition of a meaningful existence. But it is not a silent relation. It is characterized by "the word," an encounter similar to the relation between persons. Hence the analogy from dimensions serves an additional function. Heim has used it to express in somewhat logical language the poetical insights of Martin Buber's *I and Thou*. There are two kinds of spaces: I-spaces and it-spaces. It-spaces are filled with contents which are exclusive of all other spaces, like the spaces on a checkerboard. The conflict in personal relations is a result of attempting to make it-spaces out of I-spaces. Either we draw circles around ourselves in such a way as to exclude others, or we introject the others into the circle of our own existence in such a way as to rob these others of their independence. I-spaces, however, are not content-spaces. They are dimensional-spaces. Therefore there may be an infinite number of these spaces without their excluding one another. An infinite number of lines may converge perpendicularly at the same point if there is a third dimension beyond height and width. At the same time, these dimensional spaces can meet without losing their distinctive identity. Two infinite planes may intersect without jeopardizing either their infinity or their distinctness. It-spaces meet by contact. I-spaces meet by encounter. The God-relation is of the nature of I-spaces.

The analogy from space has not overlooked the time analogy in which Heim's ontological structure was conceived. It-spaces are past time and I-spaces are present time. God Himself is an I-space with the unique character of eternal presentness. God is the "dimension of dimensions" which comprehends all other dimensions. That dimension actively confers meaning on all reality when the word of God, which is the point at which the world of experience is related to God, is present.

With the rise of National Socialism in Germany, Heim's categorical bridge-building suffered a moment of uncertainty. Since 1902 his method had assumed the ontological impossibility of relativizing the absolute, and absolutizing the relative. Obviously it was always considered *morally* possible to invert the structure of life, to exchange the truth about God for a lie and worship the creature rather than the Creator. National Socialism, however, seemed to illustrate the possibility of embracing relativities as absolute without undergoing existential despair. Hence in the third edition of *Glaube und Denken,* which was the first volume of his six-volume work, Heim stressed what had nonetheless always been implicit. This volume is translated into English as *God Transcendent.* In it, Heim indicated that analogies from the world are too weak to turn man from preoccupation with the world to faith in God. Man cannot by any observation of his own attain to the Christian knowledge of God. "We are thrown back on God's own revelation."[14] As Heim had said in his *Glaubensgewissheit,* "The hammer with which the smith strikes the anvil cannot forge itself. . . . Nor can thought prove its own presuppositions."[15]

IV

The best clue for understanding Heim's theology is what he believes to be the responsibility of a Christian apologetic. At this point he is most clearly different from the two dominating figures in continental theology, Barth and Bultmann. The questions that emerge from a comparison of these three theologians are now helping to form the theology of the future.

In Heim's method an apologetic has three obligations. The first is to unmask the idols which the world destructively reveres. This is the offensive phase of apologetic. As such, it is simply a propaedeutic to Christian preaching. The second obligation is to preach the positive Christian message. The third is to provide a Christian view of life, a Christian ontology, a science of the ultimate that would relate the Christianized world meaningfully to its total environment. This is the phase of consolidation, organic to apologetics in general.[16]

The old variety of defensive apologetic in which the theologian felt called upon to justify the Christian message before the so-called "bar of reason" is utterly foreign to Heim's method. As he said, "We need an attitude which we do not need to defend . . . indeed, which can change the strategy from defense to attack."[17] Equally foreign is the still older method of rational attack upon non-Christian systems, characterized by Franz Overbeck as the intellectual equivalent of the medieval crusades. Heim is rather in the tradition of Pascal and Kierkegaard, applying a relentless critique to the roots of man's existence, and always upon the presupposition that the God revealed in Christ can alone re-establish the uprooted man on the soil of His truth. Apologetic attack is analogous to the way a physician attacks an illness. He is not so intent on defending his professional reputation as he is in effecting a cure.

Apologetic can lead only to the threshold of a Christian solution. Even then, the threshold is no closer to heaven than to hell. The method is informed by Socratic midwifery, the maieutic method which Kierkegaard introduced into theology through his concept of irony. But where Socrates used the process of fundamental questioning to deliver the mind of its own innate wisdom, the great Christian apologists have simply disabused the mind of its barriers against the coming of the revelation.[18] The revelation itself is *sui generis*.

Heim's apologetic can be clearly seen in his latest work, his three volumes on natural science and the Christian faith, which are volumes four to six of his *Evangelical Faith and the Thought of the Present*. Following a lead from the German physicist Pascual Jordan that the language of today is the language of the natural sciences, Heim has gone to the trouble to think through the faith as it relates to the latest sciences and to communicate the faith in juxtaposition to scientific questions. Motifs in contemporary thought, inspired by classical materialism and Newtonian mechanism, attributing absoluteness and causal necessity to the objective world, do not need to be attacked by theology. The newer science has already discredited them. Physics, it seems, has been forced to become more philosophical by its successive reduction of matter to an indeterminate element, of space and time to relativity, and of mechanical necessity to acausality. The theologian in this context does not ask science to listen to the dogmatic conclusions of faith but simply to the wistfulness of science itself. After science has been allowed to interrogate itself, the faith introduces the meanings which are essential but inaccessible to science. The universe is sustained by a living God who relates Himself to the ongoing process as He will. That, roughly, is the thesis of volume five, *The Transformation of the Scientific World-view*.

Volume six, *Weltschöpfung und Weltende* (*Creation and Eschatology*), takes up the problem of the origin and end of the world. Here again the new science has destroyed the Laplacian and Newtonian concepts of a universe that is closed and self-existent. The universe is open at both ends. It has its beginning in an indefinable fog and its ending in what the scientists themselves call a "natural science eschatology," such as the notion of the heat death of the universe. The interpretative value of natural science in these instances, however, is candidly negative. It clears the air for what we need desperately to know about our universe but cannot know even from science. God is at the beginning and at the ending of time. While this affirmation cannot be made on the basis of a scientific method, it shockingly corresponds to the deepest though unanswerable questions of science.

There is a vast difference between apologetic in this sense and natural theology. Natural theology, as Karl Barth has rightly called it, is a species of intellectual works-righteousness where the mind arrives at the truth of God, not independently of God, perhaps, but independently of God's revelation in Christ. It is, therefore, a kind of theological peeping-tom act which spies on God independently of the manner in which God wishes to reveal Himself. It may succeed in finding out God's hands and feet, but, as Calvin has said, it will not find His heart. The heart is the sole master of its secrets.

Why, then, an apologetic? Why not simply a quiet, patient waiting for God to break into our perception when and where He will? Apologetic proceeds neither out of scepticism of God's ability to make Himself known independently of apologetic nor on the basis of a theory of natural revelation. Apologetics answers to the call of Christ to preach the Gospel to the world. It is not difficult to be a man of the world to the men of the world if one is a Christian, for a Christian is always at the same time a worldling. Apologetics simply calls upon a man to do earnestly what comes quite naturally—to talk to one's neighbor in the terms of one's neighbor about the matter of our life and death. A man in Christ knows much more about his neighbor than the neighbor knows about himself, not by virtue of his neighbor-relation but by virtue of the transcendent perspective of the Christ-relation.

A man is never asked, however, to step from his false though orderly world view into an esoteric faith-relation whose contacts with the rest of reality are allowed to remain amorphous and chaotic. The Christian man has the privilege of living within a church which is constantly developing "an honest theology of cultural high standing," to use Paul Tillich's phrase. This is no longer apologetics in the sense of establishing a bridgehead on enemy territory. It is the consolidation of gains. Nor is it simply dogmatics or systematic theology in the sense of the exposition of the faith of the Church. It is avowedly secondary to dogmatics, but not thereby without importance. It is a frankly bifocal enterprise which, while informed by the substance of Christianity, is patterned by the dominant issues in the culture of the time.

Despite my valiant effort to keep Heim's most respectable side forward, I must confess that I find his more popular later writings theologically inferior to his earlier work. Some might explain this apparent decline by the fantastic manner in which Heim wrote these books. Confined to bed with a heart ailment, he was permitted to dress and sit at his desk for but one hour daily. Whatever the reason, this later work deviates from his self-announced apologetic method. Until this time he had created categories which had theological and existential durability. Except for the first of his six volumes, these works abandoned categorical and analogical reasoning for sheer homily and illustration. The second volume, *Jesus der Herr* (*Jesus the Lord*, 1935) adds little to the understanding of Christology and soteriology except sermonic lessons drawn from the feeling of need for a strong leader which National Socialism inspired. *Jesus der Weltvollender* (*Jesus the Fulfiller of the World*, 1937) adds even less to eschatology and supports a rather traditional view.

Most vulnerable of all are the three volumes on natural science. Due to his serious illness during the time these volumes were composed, Heim's publisher kept negatively critical reviews from him.

Thus the benefit which comes from vigorous challenge was lacking to this process of composition. The most manifest difficulty is that the latest insights of natural science are used by Heim to justify traditional views of creation, miracle, and eschatology, views which many exegetes and theologians are no longer able to purvey as either mandatory or meaningful. An apologetic method which began with the capacity to sting the life of man with the sense of his inadequacy and to illuminate his life with the realization of God's adequacy ended in defense of doctrinal forms which had already begun to lose their meaning.[19]

How, then, does Heim stand up alongside the giants of the contemporary theological scene? A detailed comparison of the apologetic emphases of Barth, Bultmann, and Heim would be highly instructive. Suffice it here to make several generalizations.

Barth dismisses Heim's apologetic as a scholastic residuum in Protestant theology. Heim, however, believed that Barth defaulted in his leadership in the Church's conflict with the unbelieving world. There is no disputing the fact that Barth has warmed the heart of the believing community. For that Heim recurrently professed his personal debt to Barth. Whether Barth has chilled the life of modern man with a "sublime monotony," as Heim has claimed, is a serious charge whose validity the future must appraise. At the same time there is already impressive evidence that a strategy such as Heim's could lead the Church "out of the stuffy air of a closed space in which it spoils miserably, into the full expanse of world events."[20]

In the last years of his life Heim felt he had to choose between two projects, his memoirs or a critique of Bultmann. He wrote his memoirs. Bultmann was an enigma to Heim. That fact may indicate that Heim never really learned his lessons well from Heidegger. For Bultmann, hermeneutics is the sum and substance of the theological task. In that single discipline are embraced all the tasks which other theologies splinter into exegesis, dogmatics, apologetics, and preaching. Bultmann would not have criticized Heim, as Barth did, for flirting with natural theology; he would have recognized the thoroughgoing Christocentrism of Heim's position. Bultmann would have criticized Heim for developing Christian world views which had no necessary relation to man's self-understanding and which, therefore, amounted to nothing but cosmological speculation. Barth is just as disconcerted as Heim by Bultmann's disavowal of apologetics. In his little writing on Bultmann, Barth says that every time one mentions apologetics in Bultmann's presence, Bultmann "hits the ceiling." Barth cannot understand that, and says "in some one sense all theologians in all times have been and even must be apologists as well."[21] What Bultmann means, however, is that the method of theology is no different from the tactic of exegesis or of apologetic. It is simply in the light of the Scriptures to understand the meaning of human existence.

Barth, by his exclusive preoccupation with the Christian Gospel in its own terms, has run the risk of moving parallel to modern culture, although he himself understands that the connection between God and the world is a circuit which God, not the theologian, completes. Bultmann, with his concern for the meaning of human existence, has run the risk of changing the traditional form of the gospel, although not the gospel itself. Heim has run no risk. He has attempted to reach the world without jeopardy to the traditional form of the Christian gospel. Not even the pietistic community of Württemberg questioned his orthodoxy. He moved with no noticeable sense of intellectual agony back and forth from the existential needs of the modern world to what he took to be the historical facts of the first-century gospel. Behind the appearances of dialogue with the world, he has come close to maintaining a parallelism as sharp as Barth's while at the same time pursuing the interpretive task less courageously than Bultmann.

The great merit of Barth is that he has developed in theology today a conscience about the unique source of the Christian faith in the reality of God and His revelation. The merit of Bultmann is that he has been willing to lose his faith in its traditional form in order to find it as a meaningful reality. It may well be enough to say of Karl Heim that he stood at a point of transition between these polar passions.

FIVE

Demythologizing and the Meaning of Faith —Rudolf Bultmann's Theology

Faith occurs when the conditions of human existence are embraced by the historical message of the Bible. By "conditions of human existence" is meant what the eighth-century British monk, the Venerable Bede, must have had in mind when he said that the life of a man is like the flight of a bird. The bird flies out of the darkness through an open window into a lighted room. He flies around in the lighted room for a time, then darts through an open window back into the darkness. Man's life is like that. He comes from he-knows-not-where. He goes to he-knows-not-where. But his capacity to live life with meaning in this lighted space we call "the world" depends upon his getting answers to these fundamental questions about origin and destiny.

By "the historical message of the Bible" is meant that according to the Bible history begins in an act of God called "creation," and history will one day end in the fulfillment of the implications in that originating act. If a man lets his life be embraced by this message, he gets answers to the fundamental questions of his existence: God is at his beginning, and God is at his ending. With that understanding, a man has the moral energy to live in the present.

According to the New Testament, Jesus of Nazareth is the

center of the Biblical history. Because of him, the intention of God at the beginning, in his creation, is made quite explicit. As the prologue to the Gospel of John says, Jesus is the word by which God created. Likewise, according to the Book of the Revelation, Jesus will one day come "riding on a cloud." That is not a meteorological judgment. "Cloud" for the Bible is not a cumulus formation in the skies. "Cloud" for the Semitic mind is a symbol of God's leadership. God led his people in the wilderness by a cloud. At the end of history, God will still be leading his people. Even if he were to lead his people by a cumulus formation in the skies, or by a mushroom formation, the point about the Biblical message is that Jesus will be in that cloud. That means that now, because of Jesus of Nazareth, we can discern the meaning of history up to its very ending. Thus, if a man allows his life to be embraced by the Biblical message, as it is made concrete in Jesus of Nazareth, he will see, as the Epistle to the Hebrews has said, that Jesus is the pioneer and perfecter of our faith and that it is this understanding of the conditions surrounding our existence which gives us the perseverance to live in the present.

I

This comprehensive summary of how our Biblical history interprets our lives, bringing them to faith, has locked up in it a number of important elements which are not immediately evident. Therefore, in order better to grasp the dynamics of faith, I must elaborate some of the understandings of reality which are at the base of modern ways of thinking and speaking. At the center of these is Rudolf Bultmann's project for demythologizing the New Testament faith. What needs to be shown is how demythologizing is a method of interpretation or hermeneutic, and how from this procedure there proceed understandings of language and history which bear significantly upon the focus of Christian faith today. These understandings are providing an opportunity for the reconception of faith which, in many cases, means the virtual renewal of faith.

A. Basic to these is *hermeneutics*. Hermeneutics is the science of interpretation, especially the interpretation of a written text. Considering that a book, the Bible, is at the center of Christian faith, a science of the interpretation of the text has been indispensable. The word hermeneutics is a simple transliteration of the Greek word meaning "to interpret." Recently it has been suggested that the word may derive from the name of the Greek god Hermes, whose duty it was to deliver the messages of the gods. From that clue, it may well be that hermeneutics is not simply responsible for interpreting the meaning of a text, but for getting the meaning of the text across to the interpreter and through the interpreter to others. That is to say, interpretation has not occurred simply when the interpreter has explained what the text means. The text must be allowed to interpret the interpreter. Only then can it be said that the message of the text has been delivered.

Three basic principles are involved in acts of interpretation which are applicable to the reading of the Christian's text, the Bible. First, one must read the text intelligently. Every schoolboy knows that the intelligent way to read a book is to find the questions to which the book is speaking and to determine what the book's answers are to these questions. To read the Bible intelligently, one would let the Bible answer the questions that the Bible is asking and answering. In that sense, reading the Bible is the same as reading any other kind of book. One does not look for the answers to mathematics questions at the back of French grammars. One does not look for answers to scientific questions in the literature of Shakespeare. Every book must be read from the standpoint of that book and its intentions.

Second, one must take to the reading of a book some concern of one's own, some prior interest, some question of significance to oneself. As the French novelist Stendhal has said, "I have an absolute lack of memory for what does not interest me." Horace Bushnell once wrote in a similar vein to his daughter: "The Bible is dull to me when I am dull." An uninterrogated book is as unproductive as an uncultivated field. Television is a curse to passive viewers, and the Bible is voiceless to readers who really have no "interest" in what it is saying.

Third, faith itself is a hermeneutical affair. That is to say, faith occurs when the reader hears the answers of the word of God to its questions as the answer to the questions which he is raising.

B. One form which hermeneutics is taking in today's church

is called *"demythologizing."* When applied to the reading of the New Testament, it is a way of interpreting the Bible so that faith can occur, so that the interpreter can be interpreted.

How does "demythologizing" accomplish this purpose? The New Testament is found to be asking one kind of question: "What must I do to be saved?" "What wilt thou have me to do?" "What is man that Thou art mindful of him?" These are all questions about the fundamental meaning of human existence. But the New Testament appears to be giving two kinds of answers. One kind of answer is called myth. Myth in the connotation currently given it in theological studies is not the same as falsehood, but neither is it the same as speaking the truth in a higher form than ordinary literal prose can do. The myth-making of the poet expresses spiritual truths in a way in which literal speaking cannot do. But the myth-making referred to in New Testament studies is a device for securing spiritual truth in literal ways of speaking. Myth is a way of speaking about God as if his activity in the world were like any other object in the world, subject to touch and sight.

But myth is not the only way the Bible has of speaking. There is also *kerygma.* "Kerygma" is simply a Greek word transliterated into English and meaning "proclamation" or "preaching." Kerygma is a way of speaking about God where God's word can be heard as the answer to the question of the meaning of man's existence. Myth evokes curiosity and protracts decision. Kerygma illuminates the situation and precipitates decision. That is why one ought not read the New Testament without demythologizing, without reducing the myth to its kerygmatic intention. New Testament myths are not "cunningly devised." They are the way the Apostolic faith had of attempting to express the faith, usually with the expectation of making it more believable and less subject to doubt. Demythologizing, then, does not cut myth out of the Bible, leaving only a remnant of the original text. After all, the Bible as it stands is the canon of the church, the official text, the constitution of the faith. It must be left intact, not torn apart. In that sense, however, the Bible asks for no immunity that is not given any other text. Shakespeare's plays must be left as they are. Interpretation of the Bible, like the interpretation of Shakespeare, searches for the answers to the questions which the text is raising. If the myth is not answering the question of the meaning of human existence, but the kerygma is, then one ought to give the kerygma a precedence which is not given to the myth. And, if one selects myths as the basis for his preaching and teaching, then he ought to get at the kerygmatic intention of those myths, and not perpetuate the literal, quasi-scientific drive of the myth.

Three things are at stake for the church's faith in demythologizing. One is the church's message to modern man. The New Testament message is often expressed in the cosmological myths of the first-century man. That cosmology, being pre-Copernican, viewed the earth as a saucer floating between heaven above and hell beneath. To this day, interpreters of the incarnation, which is the story of God's birth in Christ, find it difficult to account for Jesus apart from stories which picture some kind of movement from heaven above to earth below. Interpreters of the resurrection and ascension are puzzled to account for them without some spatial imagery based on a pre-Copernican cosmology. But we no longer have a pre-Copernican cosmology. Jesus cannot be thought to ascend in the way an astronaut goes off into space, as if from his launching pad there in Palestine. And Jesus must not be thought to return one day with some kind of fireball re-entry into earth's space, which would dwarf Gagarin's re-entry the way the atom bomb dwarfs the firecracker. The contemporary Christian interpreter must not put the Christian faith in the position the Shinto priest in Japan is in today. One of the main liturgies of Shintoism depends upon the use of two feathers from the Ibis bird. But the Ibis bird is nearly extinct. A pre-Copernican cosmology has long been extinct. To tie the faith to an outmoded view of the world guarantees that faith will be driven out of existence.

A second thing at stake in demythologizing is the principle of justification by faith alone. Myth is a way of treating the realities of faith as if they were as demonstrable as the realities which science isolates. Myth-making is a quasi-science. When the Apostle says in I John 1:1, "What our eyes have seen and our hands have handled declare we unto you," he is engaging in a myth-making tendency. By the very way in which he attempts to establish faith as something that can be proven, he blocks the coming of faith. The Gospel of John speaks against that tendency when it has Jesus say to his disciples in Chapter 14: "I must leave you. Henceforth the world will see me no more." For faith to come, Jesus must be removed as an object. An even more classic illustration of the conflict of myth and kerygma is to be found in the resurrection narratives. Two types of narrative had developed in the early church regarding the resurrection. The Thomas story participates in a myth-making tendency. Jesus allegedly shows Thomas his hands and feet as proofs of his resurrection. But the Mary story has Jesus saying to Mary, "Touch me not!" What is happening there? Did Jesus discriminate against Mary? No, the author of the Gospel has found that in the materials available for writing his Gospel, some stories have a mythological tendency, such as the Thomas story. Other stories are being told in the church to refute the mythological stories. The Thomas story is retold in the Gospel not as a basis for faith but in order to attack it as it was being attacked in the early church, by the Mary story. The Mary story is a refutation of the Thomas story. We are not left in doubt about the Gospel's attitude toward the Thomas story, when it is said at the end of that story, "It is better to believe not having seen." In the early church, myth is to kerygma what law is to faith. Law was a worldly way men had of gaining security before God. That is why Jesus came to end the law and put life on the basis of faith, which is trust alone in God. Myth is just as worldly a way of attempting to make faith secure by acting as if there are psycho-physical evidences for it. What was meant to occur as insight into the meaning of human existence, myth turns into objective evidence. What was meant to be a life based on trust in God alone, myth turns into a way of seeing things which makes it unnecessary to trust. But a worldly faith does not exploit the world for religious purposes, either moral or mythological. A worldly faith is a faith which by virtue of its trust in God alone brings the reality of the world to light.

A third thing at stake for faith in demythologizing is the very uniqueness of Christ. Some interpreters of the demythologizing method believe it should relinquish its last myth, the claim that God reveals himself uniquely in Christ. That understanding is a miscalculation of the importance of demythologizing to faith. For demythologizing, instead, calls attention to Christ's uniqueness. Myths are stories about the activity of the gods applicable widely in religious circles beyond Christianity. When these stories are applied to Jesus of Nazareth, it may be with the intention of dignifying him; but the effect is the opposite. The effect is to blunt his uniqueness. Jesus is called "Son of God." But the Gnostics had applied that language to their religious phenomena. Jesus is called "the dying and rising saviour." But the Hellenistic mystery religions had applied that title to their gods. It is said that Jesus will one day come riding on a cloud. But that story was used by Apocalyptic Judaism with reference to its promised Messiah. Jesus is said to speak the word of God. But the Old Testament prophets did that. All these efforts to apply to Jesus stories about the activity of the gods in other religions tend to blunt the uniqueness of Jesus. But what, then, is so unique about Jesus? Jesus is unique in that when he speaks, God's word is heard by men as the meaning of their existence.

C. What might seem to be an unusual concept of *language* is at work in these references to Jesus as "the word." People customarily think that the meaning of a word is exhausted in its function of pointing to a thing. Thus if one had the things, he would need no words. Jonathan Swift writes in that vein in *Gulliver's Travels*. A diplomat who wanted to go to a foreign country could avoid learning a new language. He could simply collect all the things to which he hoped to refer, pack them in a sack, carry them across the border with him. Then, when the occasion for communication arose, he would simply open up his sack and point to the things. Horace Bushnell observed a similar thing happening in the early church. A great spiritual event had occurred in the ministry of Jesus of Nazareth. When the apostles looked around for a language in which to express this spiritual reality, they found only the language of things. They made that compromise. They expressed the spiritual reality in the language of things. Subsequently, however, the church has forgotten that compromise and has treated its spiritual reality as if it were a thing. That is the meaning of mythologizing. We are now required to come clean and re-appropriate the Christian message in the dimension of reality appropriate to it.

Is it any advantage, for instance, when one says a word like "Bible" that he has a book to point to? Or "pulpit" that he has a wooden desk to rap? Or "layman" that he can point to some unordained thing beyond the chancel? What then will one do when he wishes to say the word "God"? Where will he point? What would Swift's recommendation have been for the training of a missionary? How do you carry God across borders in a sack?

But it is no necessary advantage to have a thing to point to when one uses a word, because words are not necessarily surrogate things. "Bible" is not a book, but the whole realization that "God hath not left himself without a witness." "Pulpit" is not a wooden desk, but something such as Herman Melville had in mind when he said, "The world is a ship in its passage out, and the pulpit is the prow of the world." The word "layman" is not a reference to a thing. It is a summons:

> Rise up o men of God,
> Have done with lesser things!

And the word "God" means "man can learn to receive his life from beyond himself."

The function of a word is not to point to a thing but to change the situation. When a young man says to a young woman, "I love you," he is not describing his emotions. He is changing the situation. When the church says to the world, "God loves you," it is not engaging in some detached study of the attributes of God; it is calling the world to repentance.

The meaning of "word" in Biblical faith is so powerful and originating that when God wanted to create a world he did not foment a big technological miracle. He simply said, "Let there be." "And there was." The creation of the world is an event of speaking, as the poet Dylan Thomas knew when he described creation in the line, "When the world was said . . . !" When God wanted to incarnate himself into human history, he did not perpetrate a big genetic irregularity. He simply whispered in the ear of Mary. And when God wished to perpetuate his word in human history, he raised up the church. Henceforth, "ye are ambassadors of Christ, God making his appeal through you." So powerful is the word of God that Origen, the first systematic theologian of the Christian Church, said of it, "The word of God is like the trumpets of Joshua at the battle of Jericho."

D. How can a word uttered so long ago and now become *history* be heard again today? Oddly enough, that is the only kind of word that can be heard again. For history is not a mere fact of the past. History is what has happened with such meaning that it can continue to support our lives with meaning. Think of all the facts of the past that no one any longer remembers. Are they history? Not in any adequate sense of the word "history." What is the historicity of the Bill of Rights? That it once was written in the past, or that it continues to supply Americans with guidance for their collective life? As the Italian playwright Pirandello has one of his characters say, "A fact like a sack cannot stand up unless it is filled." The words of Christian faith are historical, not in the way in which they point to the facts of the past, but in the way they continue to create our meaningful life in the present.

Almost any Christian would want to say that the Christian faith is historical. Where Christian interpreters divide, however, is over what is meant by history. The division is not innocent, for it seriously affects the church's understanding of itself. Probably no concept has come under closer scrutiny in theology today than this one. The importance for us is the bearing the discussion has on the way we do our thinking in the church and on the very structure of our lives as Christians.

Three meanings of the word "history" are current. When one hears today that the Christian faith is historical, therefore, three different things can be meant: 1) it is based on facts; 2) it is the basis for our meaningful life; 3) it is the interpretation of facts in such a way as to supply the basis for our meaningful life.

A referendum on these alternatives would probably poll most heavily for option three. There the virtues of the others seem to be combined, without their vices. Facts without meanings seem blind; meanings without facts seem empty. Thus when one interprets facts in such a way as to provide the basis for a meaningful life, the blindness of facts is overcome by meaning, and the vaporous quality of meaning is contained in solid fact.

Contemporary theology is in ferment, however, because it is now being urged that the truth rests with option two: the Christian faith is said to be historical because it is the basis for our meaningful life. For that view, there are no facts in history. The reality of history is not fact but meaning. History is not fact plus interpretation. The reality of history *is* its eventfulness. Eventfulness does not refer to factuality but to significance. But why is it not possible to establish history's factuality, then go on to talk about the meaning of the fact? Because history is not facts with meanings. History is meaningful events. One does not get history by adding meaning to fact.

There is one good reason for that: *the factuality of an event cannot be established without suspending its meaningfulness.* One cannot simultaneously examine an eyeball and discern the meaning which that eye is embodying. One cannot at one and the same time look at and through a window pane. One who insists on looking at it, therefore, sacrifices the scene beyond it. In a similar way, to establish historical factuality requires one to stand in clinical detachment, outside the very meaning which gives the history its status as history.

That does not mean that the question about fact has no bearing at all on meanings. Art-lovers are in some important way dependent upon the chemistry of pigmentation. But the most naive art-lover knows the difference between the question about pigmentation and the question about beauty. Theologians are in some important way dependent upon archaeologists, but the simplest believing Christian knows the difference between the blistered hands of a pickman and the stigmata of a saint. Statements of fact may throw light upon historical questions but they are not themselves genuinely historical statements. History vainly feeds on facts as a character in an Ionesco drama vainly devours crusts of bread to fill the gaps in his memory.

Devotees of option three, above, are not generally moved by this kind of analysis. They concede that one does not live by facts. Yet, while one lives by the meaning in facts, are not facts the necessary antecedents of meanings? That is what is being denied today. A distress signal flashed from a mountain is decoded as a message about some human emergency. Obviously the light is not the sufficient cause of the message. But is it not the necessary cause? On the contrary—why is it not truer to say that the fact of the light is a derivative of the meaningful message? The meaningful message is the necessary antecedent of the factual light, and not the other way around. Likewise in the Christian faith, the antecedent of the cross is not some geological formation called Golgotha, but Jesus' obedience to the word of God. The antecedent of the resurrection is not the empty tomb, but Jesus' obedience, victorious over the powers of the world. The antecedent of the divine sonship of Jesus of Nazareth is not some genetic irregularity, but God's word to his people fulfilled in the ear of Mary. The historical lightning which drove Martin Luther into a monastery was simply not the same kind of reality as the factual lightning which led Benjamin Franklin to the discovery of electricity. Why, then, should the church nurture the supposition that the historical solidity by which God illuminates our lives in Christ is its quality as fact?

Implicit in history, insofar as it has a dimension of the past, are acts of translation by which what was vital there continues to be brought forward. The Christian interpreter resembles a character in a Samuel Beckett play, *Krapp's Last Tape*. Krapp sits there listening over and over to the old speeches he had taped years ago, and he is unable to puzzle out any meaning in them. He is cut off, even from his own past. Is the Christian interpreter able to play back the Biblical message with any greater likelihood of its coming to life for him today? Interpreters of Bach sometimes try to reproduce the conditions under which Bach originally played his music, so they recreate clavichords of the vintage of Bach, forgetting that Bach himself deplored the limitations of the instruments he was forced to use. Others attempt to hear Bach's music as he heard it, forgetting that in three centuries the human eardrum has evolved in such a way that twentieth-century man can no longer hear as the sixteenth-century man did. Students of Bach have noticed that Bach provided no dynamics marks on his musical scores. Sometimes they are tempted to write them in, publishing them once for all as a permanent guide for other interpreters of Bach, forgetting that Bach intended directors to play the music as they, the directors, heard it, and not in imitation of Bach.

The history of Jesus of Nazareth is conserved in much the same way as Bach is heard, in the way in which his proclamation comes to fulfillment in our hearing today, through acts of translation and interpretation. This responsibility toward the past was first noticed in jurisprudence. How do the laws of the past remain valid in the present? By acts of interpretation. Therefore, political slogans like "back to the Constitution" are either ignorant of hermeneutical responsibility or cunning efforts to exploit the ignorance of the people. "Back to the Bible" has the same hermeneutical perils. In history one does not "go back." History is what is brought forward as the basis for one's meaningful life.

History, however, is a reality more like art than like science, and Christians who wish to embrace their faith in its full historicity must be prepared to embrace two by-products of this alliance.

For one thing, history like art creates a meaningful world for us. The Acropolis at Athens does not stand there as a relic from the past to be admired as an object. It emerges out of the Athenian hills in such a way as to blend the earth with the sky and the sea and men with their gods, in one habitable world. The message of the church is like an art work that assembles our life in a significant way and gives us a sense of a new age of meaning, a new creation in which to live.

At the same time, history like art is filled with ambiguity and suggestiveness which leaves no guarantee that anyone will really "get" it. Pose the formula $2 \times 2 = 4$ to as many people as you wish. Some may not like it, but none will reject it, at least not as a practical base of operations a man would expect his wife to employ in using the checkbook. But stand before a Picasso in your local gallery and listen to the comments of the people as they go by. Some will say, "Tremendous!" Others, "I don't get it!" History has that ambiguity in common with art, and that ambiguity is one feature which distinguishes history and historical faith from both science and mythological faith.

But "don't we know that God exists?" We do not *know* that. If he is our father, we *love* him. "Don't we know Jesus is the son of God and the Lord of man?" We do not *know* that. If we are his servants, we *obey* him. "Don't we know God raised Jesus from the dead?" We do not *know* that. If we are his witnesses, we *worship* him. "Don't we know that the church is the body of Christ?" We do not *know* that. If we are its members we *serve*. "Don't we know that the future is on God's side?" We do not *know* that. In history we are pilgrims. We live in *hope*.

II

Rudolf Bultmann's major contribution to hermeneutics and the focusing of faith has been his emphasis upon pre-understanding (*Vorverständnis*) in every event of interpretation. One of the best ways to discern the meaning and importance of pre-understanding for faith is to see what has been his analysis of the role of the Old Testament in Christian understanding, for while he holds that the Old Testament is not revelation for the Christian, he nevertheless attributes to it a very important position in the Biblical canon and in the interpretation of faith. It is pre-understanding for the New Testament.

The most important of the problems Christians had to face in the early centuries was the question of the significance of the Old Testament.[1] Yet the rise of the modern historical method still has not contributed substantially to a solution of those early problems. One sign of that fact is the continual oscillation between claims to the continuity of the Testaments and claims to their discontinuity. Indecisiveness about the significance of the Old Testament relative to the New is as evident today as it was in the days which antedated historical science.

Rudolph Bultmann calls for an end to that vacillation by refusing to regard the Old Testament as revelation for the Christian. The New Testament and not the Old expresses the form in which God is now calling his people into existence. Therefore, for a Christian to take the Old Testament as revelation would require either exegetical anachronism or exegetical guile. What he means by the Old Testament as *Vorverständnis*, however, separates his decision from Marcionism. For while he keeps the discussion strictly within the historical discipline, he finds a way of maintaining the Christian relevance of the Old Testament. Of course, historians have always been able to abandon their academic tools while ascending to the pulpit; but they have not found it easy to live with the dualism in that procedure. For example, is it theologically defensible to select one's Easter text from a Psalm? If it is, ought one claim of this text, as Wilhelm Vischer once did, that "we do not understand a single word in the whole Bible if we do not find Jesus Christ in this word"?[2] This may be called an extreme example. Yet, is it any more acceptable for an Old Testament scholar to announce that the exegesis in the commentaries he is editing will bear in mind above all else, as Martin Noth has proposed, that "the New Testament preaches Christ as the end of the Old Testament acts of God"?[3]

Canonicity makes one book of the Bible. Not having supplied a rationale for that decision, the church has accustomed itself to finding Christianity in these pre-Christian texts. Historical method up to this time has not seriously challenged that primitive procedure. Bultmann, however, proposes a revision which makes historical method more fully historical, yet without violating the interests of Christian piety. The clue to his proposal is in the understanding of the Old Testament as *Vorverständnis* or pre-understanding to the New Testament. The force of his suggestion is in the way it transcends the subject-object structure which up to now has prevailed in the historical sciences, even among theologians.

An historical method which does not deliberately employ a pre-understanding tends to handle its data from the outside. The past is reconstructed from a spectator's viewpoint. Battles are reported by those who have never fought in one, love and death by those with no personal inclination for either. An historian in this tradition is "the great eye-piece," as Count von Yorck identified Leopold von Ranke. He examines his data at a distance. But as Samuel Beckett once observed, the eye is hard of hearing. The historian whose materials will speak is the one who adopts a procedure beyond the limits of mere voyeurism. *Vorverständnis* is Bultmann's alternative to hermeneutical voyeurism.

The examination of the Old Testament as a body of knowledge which can be held in separation from one's commitments has, of course, contributed enormously to the understanding of the subject matter. Has it, however, resolved the traditional problems of the significance of the Old Testament for the Christian faith? Within the subject-object framework, where questions are raised from the outside, historical method has found no consistent way of determining the relation between the Old Testament and the New. For instance, history like nature proceeds developmentally, so that what is old always bears some genetic relation to what is new. In that sense there is undisputed continuity between the Testaments. By the same rubric, however, movements in other parts of the East and in Greece are also in continuity with the New Testament. Moreover, when the doctrinal content of the two Testaments is considered, there are grounds for continuity as well as for discontinuity. The New Testament retains the historical consciousness of the Old Testament and its accent on the transcendence of God. Yet, judged by content, the Old Testament is a book of prophecy simply, while the New Testament is a book of fulfillment. As Bultmann points out in his essay on "Prophecy and Fulfillment,"[4] the concepts of covenant, kingdom of God, and people of God, whatever their verbal similarities to New Testament concepts, are so fundamentally different as to illustrate discontinuity between the Testaments.

Pre-understanding, however, is the key to overcoming the

material considerations of this subject-object framework. In so doing, it provides a consistent pattern for discerning the relation between the Testaments. In respect of its being a pre-understanding to the Gospel, the Old Testament is always in continuity with the New. If one knew what that claim means for Bultmann, one would readily understand why it is wrong to classify Bultmann with Marcion and Harnack who proposed the elimination of the Old Testament from the canon on the grounds of its discontinuity with the New.

What, then, is a *Vorverständnis*, a pre-understanding, and in what sense can it be said that the Old Testament plays that role in relation to the New? Pre-understanding is the historical procedure which overcomes the external approach to historical data by a method of appropriating history inwardly. It does not function as an elite form of historical understanding. It claims rather to be the method but for which much of history remains dumb. Pre-understanding is a method of putting questions to a body of historical material where the questions originate in one's own concern for living. Where that occurs, the material cannot be an indifferent object of investigation. It involves the question of the very meaning of one's life. According to this method, there is no understanding of history which is not also an understanding of one's own life.

What occurs in this way of understanding history is often referred to as existential hermeneutic. The truth is that it was developed by Bultmann long before existentialism became articulate in Martin Heidegger. His Marburg professor, Wilhelm Herrmann, had taught Bultmann that the Christian faith always expresses itself in relation to "what concerns us, what is problematical for us." As Karl Barth, another pupil of Herrmann, has said, "We learned theology from Herrmann through our pores." But Bultmann learned this particular lesson better than Barth, and therefore has never deviated from the claim that the understanding of God always involves an understanding of man. A man who speaks about God always does so on the basis of some particular understanding he has of himself.

Wilhelm Dilthey helped Bultmann to turn Herrmann's intuition into historical method. Dilthey had learned from Schleiermacher that exegesis and understanding are not two stages in a process of interpretation. They are identical. One does not first examine the text and then understand it. Understanding is immediate to a proper method of examining a text. The crucial presupposition for understanding historical materials is, according to Dilthey, "the interpreter's relationship in his life to the subject which is directly or indirectly expressed in the text."[5] Therefore no interpretation can be said to be presuppositionless. Proper interpretation presupposes prior understanding, *Vorverständnis*, the putting of a question important to the interpreter. One cannot understand political history without some appreciation of the state and of law, or economic history without some concept of economics and society, or religion and philosophy without some understanding of what they are. One cannot assimilate Luther's Wittenberg theses without an actual sense of the protest prevailing in his time against Catholicism.[6] Joy is not understood in history by one who has had no personal anticipation of it. Discussions of gratitude and responsibility, love and hate are abstract apart from some inkling that these are in some sense "my own possibilities." Similarly, "I must have a *Vorverständnis* for sin and forgiveness if I shall understand, if they are spoken to me."[7] "The fact that when Christian preaching meets a man it can be understood by him indicates that he has a *Vorverständnis* of it."[8]

> "A particular understanding of the material on the basis of a life relationship is thus always presupposed in the exegesis, and to that extent there is no presuppositionless exegesis. I call this understanding the *Vorverständnis.* . . . If we interrogate history . . . it really begins to speak to us. The past becomes alive in the discussion with it and through history we become acquainted with our own present; historical knowledge is at the same time self-knowledge. The understanding of history is possible only to one who stands over against it not as a neutral, non-participating observer, but to one who stands in history and assumes responsibility for it. This understanding of history which develops out of our unique historicity we call the *existential encounter.* . . . It means that the subject-object scheme which has validity for the observations of the natural sciences does not hold for historical understanding."[9]

The significance of the Old Testament for Bultmann is precisely in this role as pre-understanding to the Gospel. As the treatise before us expresses it, the Old Testament helps us "grasp our own historical situation." The Old Testament's consciousness of the historicity of man supplies the prior understanding which makes it possible for the New Testament message to be heard. The historicity of man is the consciousness that "the concrete answer to man's question about the future springs from his own concrete history." On this ground, Bultmann can appropriate the traditional Lutheran model of the relation between the Testaments as the relation of law to gospel. The prophecy-fulfillment model he cannot accept because it encourages the comparison of bodies of doctrine which one may consider without involving himself. On the prophecy-fulfillment model one is more impressed with the discontinuity between the Testaments than with the continuity, as we have seen, unless from a stance within the New Testament he typologizes or allegorizes the Old Testament faith after the historiographically loose manner of the early church. But when one enters into the Old Testament as a condition of being under the law, the existential groundwork is laid for hearing the message of justification by faith communicated through the New Testament gospel. When one enters into the Old Testament effort to realize the covenant of God within history and appropriates as one's own the "inner contradiction" and "miscarriage" of that method, he is prepared to receive the news that God has brought this method to an end through Jesus of Nazareth.[10]

Are there concrete illustrations of how this method is put to use in an exegetical situation? There are, and they illustrate the claim that the Old Testament is a pre-Christian text in which one must not find what was not there for those who wrote it. Historical method is honored. What then is the Christian significance of these pre-Christian texts? Their Christian significance is in their ability to evoke the *Vorverständnis* to which the Christian faith can speak. In Bultmann's *Marburger Predigten*[11] there are only two sermons based upon Old Testament texts. But then Luther, who devoted twenty-eight of his thirty-two Bible-teaching years to the Old Testament, preached five times as many sermons from New Testament texts as he did from Old. In fact Luther is even on record as asserting that "the Old Testament is not to be preached."[12]

One of Bultmann's sermons draws on the promise to Noah following the flood. "While earth remains, seed time and harvest, cold and heat, summer and winter, day and night shall not cease." (Gen. 8:22) It takes no great access of inventiveness to calculate the response when it is known the sermon was preached in Germany on May 9, 1937. The question of the revelation of God in nature is lifted at a time of year when nature is most suggestive of God's beneficence and in a political climate which is eager to endorse what comes naturally. "In the susceptibility of man for the fulness and splendor of nature is hidden a susceptibility for God." Yet, nature is full of riddle and ambiguity. Therefore, devotion to the powers of nature is a risk. A sinister power is at work there which cannot reveal itself to our hearts. In fact, faith in nature fails to understand the properly *human* nature. For man is not simply nature but spirit, image of God. "If he forgets that he has his life to live in responsibility to God, his life is a riddle and his death is hideous." God is present in nature, therefore, chiefly in the sense that nature "compels man to ask about God."

The other sermon was preached under even more dramatic circumstances, on June 23, 1946. The text is from Lamentations. "The goodness of the Lord is that we are not cut off. His mercy has no end." Bultmann raises this question with his congregation: "Is the world of the Lamenter different from the one in which we live?" The consolation he offers to the depressed people of Germany is in the conclusion that "God is our portion." That means "we stand before a choice—God or the world. I choose God—he is my portion, even though I build only on faith and hope and have nothing visible and concrete at hand." We must "wait quietly," "be patient," and "make each decision by confessing the Lord and turning away from the world." "Why should a man complain about the punishment of his sins?" (Lam. 3:39) The answer? "Only the patient have the inner calm to adjudicate the guilt question. But we stand before God, and before him none of us is pure." Is not the choice for God rather than the world the abandonment of human hope? Yes, but for a hope which is beyond human hope. But is not the Christian preaching concerned with the grace of God? Yes, but "the gospel of grace says not that we are spared the cross but that the cross is itself grace, that God kills in order to make alive." That is the true patience—to be prepared to hear in God's "no" to our wishes his secret "yes!" The way into the darkness of death is already the beginning of the life of resurrection. Not that we hope only in "the future glory which God shall give." Rather, as the Apostle Paul says, "We rejoice in our sufferings." (Rom. 5:3–5)

In this handling of the Old Testament text is discernible a

continuity with the New Testament based purely on the role of the Old Testament as pre-understanding to the New. In identifying with the structure of the experience of the Old Testament, one is prepared to hear the truth of the New Testament. One of the most widely applauded of the preachers who has majored in the use of Old Testament texts is the Basel pastor Walter Lüthi. Prior to the last war he impressed the German people deeply by what one has called "the unerring aim" of his preaching. "Without engaging in politics, he clarified the situation of those days from the scriptures," especially from Daniel, Habakkuk, and Nehemiah. Consider, for instance, the rule of Habakkuk over a situation in which law was impotent and the Chaldeans stood at the gate. Nowhere does Pastor Lüthi say in his sermons, "these are the Germans!", "That is Hitler!" In fact, the sermons are directed to the Swiss, and particularly to the people of Basel![13]

Gerhard Ebeling reports his own use of an Old Testament text to illustrate how a modern may enter into the Old Testament. Toward the end of the war when the report of Hitler's death was circulated throughout German army installations, Ebeling asked his "entirely non-churchly comrades" to let him read something from the Bible. He chose Isaiah 14, which is a song of triumph over the demise of the King of Babylon. As he reports, "the silence which followed the reading impressively testified to how readily it was heard."[14] According to Ebeling, "The immediacy with which the text is heard rests on the actual or intended correspondence of the present situation with the one in which the word had its original locus."[15] I believe Bultmann presses this hermeneutical case a step further, however. The Old Testament does not simply presuppose in its hearer an existential correspondence. It helps to create that correspondence by evoking a pre-understanding which in turn contributes to the hearing of the New Testament.

In the early church the Old Testament was regarded as the sacred scriptures to which the New Testament was the exegetical appendix. Bultmann has completely reversed that arrangement. However, he should not for that reason be linked with Schleiermacher's project to make the Old Testament an appendix to the New. The New Testament is the sacred scriptures for Bultmann; but the Old Testament is its exegetical preface. One might respond that it is consistent with the intention of Christianity for Bultmann to elevate the New Testament to prominence as sacred scriptures, or even to reduce the Old Testament to exegetical preface. But the plain fact is that the Old Testament for Bultmann is not the *indispensable* preface. Other literature may substitute as pre-understanding to the New Testament. In his incautious way Kierkegaard anticipated Bultmann's position:

> This is the reason my soul always turns back to the Old Testament and to Shakespeare. I feel that those who speak there are at least human beings: they hate, they love, they murder their enemies, and curse their descendants throughout all generations, they sin.[16]

A Protestant need not become alarmed about that position, however, for three reasons. First, the Biblical canon is not closed, so that one need not concede grudgingly that extra-canonical literature is often productive of faith. Second, the Protestant principle of *sola scriptura* refers to a Biblical mode of understanding and not to the Bible as a book. Third, for Christians the Old Testament will always be an indispensable preface to the New just because in the New Testament the Gospel has been interpreted through the texts of the Old Testament.

A major value in the association of *Vorverständnis* with the Old Testament is the way it clarifies Bultmann's much debated hermeneutical method. I have in mind several of the most popular objections to his method.

(1) Do not historical procedures require the historian to abandon all presuppositions? Yet Bultmann standardizes pre-understanding. For Bultmann *Vorverständnis* is an indispensable presupposition for historical understanding. But culturally or psychologically conditioned prejudice is something utterly different. Pre-judgments disfigure historical reality; pre-understanding delivers it from latency to life. Objective historical data which have not been brought into correspondence with personal existence often function as prejudice, thwarting historical illumination. In Jesus' time, for instance, some held the dogma regarding the expected Messiah that "no one will know where he comes from." (John 7:27) That was a pre-judgment in terms of which Jesus could not have been received as the Messiah, for everyone recognized him as "the son of Joseph, whose father and mother we know." (John 6:42)[17] Pre-understand-

ing does not, unlike prejudice, screen out the future selectively. It holds existence open to the future, receptively.

(2) Is not the knowledge of *Vorverständnis* a species of natural theology which comprises the element of uniqueness and surprise in the Gospel? True, some of the motives in existential hermeneutics correspond to some of the motives in natural theology. New revelation would be incomprehensible to persons living in the age prior to that revelation if there were not some general preparation for it. However, a pre-understanding is not to be confused with a religious *a priori* which makes religion a universal possibility. Universals, like objective historical data, exist outside the understanding. The realities of faith, on the other hand, exist in and for the understanding. This is the meaning of Bultmann's alleged individualism. Existential individualism is not in conspiracy against community, such as a people or church constitute. It is against communities based on universals which rule like axioms or fates, independently of the decisiveness of the participant.

The customary objection to natural theology is that by contributing positive knowledge to the moment of revelation, it engages in a form of intellectual righteousness-by-works. This charge cannot hold against the strategy of *Vorverständnis*. Pre-understanding is not a positive knowledge; it is wholly negative and questing. It is composed not of answers at all, but only of questions. When the exegete takes his *Vorverständnis* for final understanding, he falsifies. When the existing man allows his pre-understanding to become "an assured state of affairs"[18] he has fallen into sin. Sin is not a destruction of man's ontological structure, but a perversion in his hermeneutics. Sin is what makes it possible for man to ask questions about God in any but a perverted way.

The bearing of this analysis upon the significance of the Old Testament is most provocative. Traditionally the church has tended to regard the Old Testament as a prefiguration of the New, a foreshadowing, an *umbra veritatis*, a shadow of the truth. For Bultmann, as for Luther after 1519 (the year of his break with medieval hermeneutics), the shadow of the Old Testament is not a mysterious twilight from which Christians may derive positive allegorical or even typological meanings. The shadow is a condition of real night.[19] The knowledge of the Old Testament as pre-understanding is not-knowing knowledge, as different from New Testament knowledge as night is different from day. Yet, it is continuous with New Testament knowledge. Continuity here obviously cannot be analogous to the smooth continuity of water and milk. The relation is not that homogeneous. Nor is it, on the other hand, as discontinuous as water and oil. The relation is not that dichotomous. It is a continuity, however, such as exists between thirst and water.

(3) What, then, is the significance of the much vaunted "hermeneutical circle" in which textual answers and interpreters' questions presuppose each other? Does not the very form of the question determine the substance of the answer? Do Old Testament, existential type questions really deliver the full-bodied Christian message from the New Testament womb? Here two things should be observed on Bultmann's behalf. First, the purpose of the hermeneutical question is not to change the text, not even to modernize it, but to understand it. Karl Barth, in his little writing on Bultmann, has complained that he does not see how by Bultmann's method he would go about interpreting the Bible to his children, let alone to modern man. Bultmann replied to Barth in a still unpublished letter that the primary test of hermeneutics for Barth should be whether he can interpret the Bible to himself.

Second, Bultmann candidly admits that the form of the question does tend to pervert the answer of the text. That fact, by itself, would be calamitous, were it not for the additional fact that the text has an integrity of its own which asserts itself over against the interpreter, challenging the form of his questions. Everyone knows that in Bultmann's thinking the interpreter is not a *tabula rasa*, a passive receptacle upon which history writes its answers. Equally true in Bultmann's thinking, however, is that neither is the text a passive object. The interpreter does not simply wrest from the text the answers to his prior questions. "The new affects my old understanding like a benign or shattering destiny, putting the old in question, breaking it down, and making it new. Thus the old can understand the new if the new is its negation."[20] The work of an exegete is a theological work not by virtue of the hermeneutical method but by virtue of the text being interpreted.[21] The decisive thing in a Biblical hermeneutic, then, is not the possibility of an understanding which is accessible to the interpreter in such a way that he can choose at will or even decline to choose. The decisive thing, rather, is that the interpreter is confronted with possibilities he cannot grasp as his own.[22] Therefore, the Old Testament in Bultmann's view is not simply on call to the interpreter's interrogation. That would be to miss the major point in the Old Testament as pre-understanding. Rather, the Old Testament quickens the historical consciousness of man, evoking his questioning spirit. These questions, in turn, become his threshold to an understanding of the New Testament, but not without the opportunity for the New Testament itself to reshape the question of the Old more closely to the image of its own intention.

The medieval cathedrals of Europe are veritable mirrors reflecting in their portals and windows the stories of the Bible. The Old Testament story preponderates. In Sainte-Chapelle the entire Old Testament seems unfolded in its windows, but the story of Christ is limited to two windows. That ratio does not seem unfair to the New Testament, however, for in these cathedrals every Old Testament story seems to have the New Testament consummation stamped upon it. When Samson rips the gates of Gaza from their hinges or Elisha raises the widow's daughter, the resurrection of Christ is clearly prefigured. When Isaac carries wood for sacrifice, he prefigures Christ carrying the cross. The history of Christian art like the history of the church is the history of the exegesis of the Scriptures. But Old Testament themes treated as prefigurations of the New Testament are the exegesis simply of the New Testament. The church art of the future need not perpetuate that mono-testamentalism. That would be Marcionism in a very deceptive form. Marcionism is mono-testamentalism which calls for the rejection of the Old Testament. Ironically, the church from the very beginning has sponsored creeping Marcionism by exegetically absorbing the Old Testament into the New. Historical criticism developed the first effective block against this exegetical deception, but provided no theological rationale for reading the Bible as one book. The importance of Bultmann's analysis of the Old Testament as *Vorverständnis* to the Gospel is in showing one possible way to terminate creeping Marcionism in the church. The Old Testament has a right to be represented on its own, according to its own intention. What, then, would be its justification in a Christian setting, reminding one as it does of the days before God's covenant in Christ? Samson, Elisha, and Isaac would still be there, but now as figures of real historical life, undergoing real moral crisis, real human pathos, real trust in the faithfulness of God. That figuration is not prefiguration but pre-understanding. If it leads the worshipper to the message of cross and resurrection, it will do so free of dogmatic prejudices which distort. It will do so by opening life to gospel possibilities through the evocation of sheer humanity.

SIX

Being and the Event of Faith
—The Later Heidegger
and Heinrich Ott's Theology

A picture of the later Heidegger is important for its double exposure of the contemporary theological scene. In the foreground is brought to light the shape which theology is taking at present. More importantly, although indistinctly in the background, there appears a defensive reaction to the threat to systematic theology which the hermeneutic of the earlier Heidegger inspired. Rudolf Bultmann, in employing the existential insights which Heidegger's *Being and Time* developed, advanced a method of interpreting the Scriptures which so thoroughly articulates the Christian faith that it has put in question the need for a systematic theology. Meanwhile, however, Heidegger has elevated other elements in his position than those which Bultmann found useful. May there not be some basis in this later, non-Bultmannian Heidegger for countering the threat to systematic theology which Bultmann's position represents?

I

The theologians who profited by dialogue with the early Heidegger were primarily influenced by his understanding of what history is. In philosophy classically conceived, thinking was always in some direct relationship with being. Reason always had some immediate rapport with ultimate reality. Immanuel Kant was the first major philosopher to separate thought and being. That was the end of ontology in its classical form. But Kant nevertheless allowed man's reason to stand in harmony with man's own being. That was the open door to ontology in its modern, anthropological form. Hegel subsequently revealed a separation within the nature of man, showing phenomenologically that reason is not simply alienated from reality; it is alienated within itself. The only cure for this alienation, according to Hegel, is to be found in history. One cannot relate to "Being itself" without historical mediation. Hegel's phenomenology, then, is the source both of modern historicism and of existentialism. To historicism truth appears in history alone. But to existentialism history appears as an *aporia*, that is, a reality upon which man depends for his reconciliation to ultimate reality, yet a reality which records only alienation.

The early Heidegger was existentialist, phenomenologist, and historicist. Søren Kierkegaard supplied the basic existential formula, largely through the inspiration of Hegel: "Existence separates thought and being," so that nothing of being can be in thought without the mediation of existence. Edmund Husserl's phenomenology supplied the logical rigor for working philosophically within that formula: man must live by what appears in human existence. Wilhelm Dilthey supplied the cultural materials, the specifically human substance of history, in his historical science of hermeneutics. Heidegger's *Being and Time* drew these three rays into focus. Rudolf Bultmann and Friedrich Gogarten pre-eminently have done their theology within that focus.

For Bultmann, the focus revealed why one could read the New Testament as history. But the term "history" no longer meant what it had before the days of Kant and Hegel. History was now the sole medium in which reality appears and in which thought struggles to overcome its emptiness. In that setting, the New Testament was no longer a record of first-century facts which one had only to interpret in a twentieth-century language. The New Testament was history's way of submitting what reality there is in it as the basis for the meaningful life of the existing man.

Probably Gogarten among contemporary dogmatic theologians best saw the implications of this method for systematic theology, for he is the only major dogmatician who, on principle, has not attempted a system. As early as 1921 Ernest Troeltsch anticipated this future for Gogarten when he called him "an apple from the tree of Kierkegaard."[1] When one understands history as the medium in which reality appears, concedes that one's own rationality is fully historical, and appreciates the Bible as the history of the appearance of reality in its ultimacy, dogmatic theology seems to have nothing to add to the exegesis of the Scriptures. Dogmatic theology could even be said to be a distraction, for it treats its statements about reality as if these statements were true independently of the history in which reality appears.

Meanwhile Heidegger seems to have effected one of the most stunning shifts of emphasis in the history of philosophy. Where classical philosophy from Socrates to Descartes had operated on the assumption that thought and being are always in continuity, and where modern philosophy had held that it is history which mediates being to thought, the later Heidegger has been promoting a third possibility. It is a matter of indifference to theology that this position was already present in his early work, because it has only come to prominence and thus begun to influence theology through his later works.

In the later emphasis of Heidegger, questions of history surrender their primacy to questions of being. But they do not do so in the classical way where being is in continuity with thought. Being now becomes the unthought but necessary mediator between thought and existence.

For Heidegger's phenomenology, this new position was no radical change, since being is still encountered only as it appears in existence. For his historicism, the shift was quite significant, since he no longer looks for being *as history*, but only for being *as historical*, that is, for being *as the possibility of history*. For his existentialism, it was calamitous, for two reasons. First, one no longer thinks in the face of death, which is the rudimentary *aporia* of historical existence. One thinks in the presence of the something without which history would mean encounter with nothing, that is, in the presence of being. Thus, in the later Heidegger poetic calm and rational ineffability supplant existential anguish and the quest for a concrete historical articulation of meaning.

The second notable occasion for Heidegger's retreat from

existentialism was his suppression of subjectivity in the determination of meaning. Hence, where the early Heidegger emphasized the mediation of man in the realization of meaning, the later Heidegger criticizes this emphasis as a remnant of idealism, of Nietzschean self-assertion, holding it responsible for subjectivistic fragmentation and for manipulation of the wholeness of reality. In the later, more ontologically disposed position, the self has learned submission to being, which is revealed without the self's transforming activity. One sign of Heidegger's resoluteness in this turn away from subjectivity is his restoration of *things* to a place of centrality.

This turn in Heidegger's philosophical development like a flare above the battle clearly exposed the relative positions of the main theological strategists of Europe today. Ordinary information, of course, already had the general picture. It was widely known through the ranks that Barth lay to the right and Bultmann to the left, and that to the right of Barth were flanked his cautious codifiers, like Otto Weber and Hermann Diem, and to the left of Bultmann his incautious advance patrol, like Ernst Fuchs and Gerhard Ebeling. The Barthians were identifiable by their concern for the priority of the being of God in himself and the Bultmann contingent was known for its existential interpretation. But a large body of theologians eager to see service found it difficult to join forces with either side. The Barthian dogmatics was held to be too traditional, too easy to reduce to orthodox patterns, too trinitarian to be adequately incarnational or cruciform. The Bultmann method of interpretation was held to be too indifferent to the broader demands of theology as a systematic science, remaining silent about anything that did not have meaning for man as man, and being satisfied to substitute expositions of Biblical texts for comprehensive outlines of Christian belief.

The value of the sudden illumination from the Heidegger turn was not that it exposed these positions but that it disclosed a corridor between them. On the basis of his own reconnaissance in the light of the later Heidegger, Heinrich Ott, Barth's youthful successor at the University of Basel, has called for a third front in the development of systematic theology. It is based neither upon the *being* of God, which is the Barthian trend, nor upon *hermeneutics* as the analysis of human existence, the trend of Bultmann, but upon *hermeneutics* as the analysis of being.

Systematic theology as the hermeneutical analysis of being means two things above all. First, systematic theology is not a science in the customary modern understanding of the word. According to Heidegger, "science does not think," because it does not know what it means by what it does. Systematic theology is a non-scientific form of thinking as a discipline which is oriented to the question of fundamental meaning. If it is a science in any sense, it is a hermeneutical science, which by definition must know what it means in what it does. It is thinking, disciplined for the purpose of interpreting meaning, to the end that being itself, and thus God in respect of his being, may be revealed. Thinking in this sense is not proving but pointing. That kind of thinking, as Ott believes, classifies systematic theology more closely with prayer than with science.

In the second place, systematic theology is necessary as one phase of the generally accepted hermeneutical circle. According to the strategy of the hermeneutical circle, before one can understand a reality—a work of art, a writing, a conversation—he must bring some understanding to it, even though only in the form of a question. Systematic theology in Ott's view has the function of helping the exegete interpret the text of the Bible by supplying him the proper questions to ask of the text.[2] Hereafter, what systematic theology intends by its outline of doctrines—incarnation, atonement, eschatology, and the like—is not a description of reality, and least of all a body of right teaching which is synonymous with faith, but a series of right questions to be asked of the text. The doctrinal framework of systematic theology is the handmaiden to the interpretation of the Scriptures, a deductive moment in theological reflection which facilitates the more inductive process of exegesis. Systematic theology is a unity of vision in a discipline which might otherwise be content with fragmentation. It is a trans-scientific kind of thinking without which Biblical interpretation might never rise beyond the scientific level, which is the level of philology and textual criticism, not knowing what it means by what it does.

Ott's point of view as expressed here was originally presented to an audience composed largely of Biblical scholars. Their immediate reaction was that Ott had made exegesis an auxiliary science to systematic theology. Whatever Ott's intention, quite the oppo-

site is implied. Ott is a systematic theologian who, after encountering Rudolf Bultmann's exegetical method, was left wondering what
work was left for him. This twofold proposal for a systematic theology is not the ostentatious and indulgent offer of succor from a
queen of sciences. Rather, systematic theology is now in the position of being required to supply a reason for its existence. It is in
the process of being kidnaped by New Testament theology and
of offering a ransom for its life. Ott believes the ransom is subscribed
by the later Heidegger.

If this analysis of the situation is accurate, two questions need
to be answered. (1) What is there about the historical hermeneutic
of Bultmann that makes it such a threat to systematic theology?
(2) Is Ott's alternative of ontological hermeneutics able to achieve
what he projects?

II

Bultmann has always contended that the interpretation of a
Biblical text is not only exegesis but dogmatics, preaching, and apologetics as well. No one has ever paid much attention to this claim.
In one way, it was too obvious. These four operations have always
been able to occur in any single individual, successively. In another
way, it was too unrealistic. These four functions are already structured into theological institutions today. Is it not enough that they
interact without having to deny them some measure of autonomy?
However, either of these ways of looking at the matter has mis-
judged the rigor in Bultmann's method. The four theological functions do not occur successively, whether in the same person or in
four different departments of theology. They occur simultaneously
when one exegetes the Scriptures properly. A proper exegetical
contact with a text will *be* dogmatics, preaching, and apologetics
because it will *do* what every one of these disciplines is designed
to do. The act of understanding a text (exegesis) is the act in which
the significance of the faith appears (systematic theology) in such
a way as to become significant for the interpreter (preaching),
despite all his prior resistances (apologetics).

How can exegesis bear so heavy a burden? The key to that is
in what Bultmann has meant by hermeneutics as the science of
history. Traditionally it has been supposed that the exegete is an
historian oriented to the past. He will determine, for instance, what

the apostles believed. The systematic theologian is oriented to the present. He must say what we can mean by what the apostles believed. In the hermeneutics influenced by existentialism, however, the science of history stands in the present. It is absolutely cut off from the materials of the past unless they are addressing questions which the man of the present is asking. The capacity for the past to survive in the present is a direct attribute of the interest the past holds for the present. One does not seek in ancient manuscripts what does not interest him. Therefore, the old understanding of history as a river flowing out of the past into the present is misleading and false. In hermeneutics as the science of history, the systematic theologian is no longer needed to bring the Biblical faith up to date. The exegete, for whom nothing can be delivered from the past which does not present itself meaningfully, is already engaged in that operation, and within the general procedures of historical method.

Again, traditionally the preacher has been the one who takes the results of Biblical scholarship and makes them edifying to the hearer, appealing to the hearer to believe this faith. According to Bultmann, faith is an historical reality. That means faith is part of the structure of history itself. One does not hear a meaningful statement, then decide to accept it. Believing is ingredient in the structure of meaning. Thus, the exegete asks of the text those questions the text is asking which are also the questions he as an existing man is asking. When the text answers these questions, to say the exegete understands the answers is to say he finds them answering his questions. In that moment, exegesis is identical with preaching. Preaching is primarily the hearing of the word and only secondarily the declaring of the word. The act of preaching presupposes that a word which has been heard will make possible the hearing of the word. Hearing implies that the word has been received as the answer to the question of one's existence as a man.

Now it can be understood why exegesis, seen in this thoroughly historical way, also absorbs the functions of apologetics. Traditionally, apologetics was a way of convincing the incredulous of the rightness of the faith. Bultmann knows no way of doing apologetics which is not simply preaching, and thus exegesis. The faith, being history, carries its own power to convince. There is nothing magic in this liaison. History occurs when an event which was meaningful for others becomes meaningful for me. There is no way of establishing a meaningful connection with an event from outside the event. Yet, when the event does become meaningful through one's interior connection with it, it does so with a suddenness and illumination which dispels resistance and thus dispenses with apologetics.

Considering this omnicompetent exegetical procedure, is there anything distinctive left for systematic theology to do? For Ott, two things remain: (1) an interpretation in which *being* and not *human existence* is the horizon for hermeneutical interrogation; and (2) a deduction of the relevant questions to which being will reveal its secrets in the exegetical moment. In the face of Bultmann's historic hermeneutic, are Ott's proposals really able to save the relevance of systematic theology?

III

The issue between Ott and Bultmann is not whether systematic theology will be a hermeneutical science but whether this hermeneutics will finally be oriented to ontological questions or to historical questions. Because of his preoccupation with historical questions, Bultmann found the early Heidegger's existential concerns helpful to theology but declined to give his ontological concerns the kind of priority which Heidegger sought for them. In the later Heidegger references to history have virtually dropped out of his language, and the materials upon which he exercises his hermeneutical analysis of being are not historical materials but the verbal medium often considered to be the furthest removed from history, namely, poetry. Ott now proposes to develop theological hermeneutics as an ontological enterprise. The suggestion is ingenious, because New Testament scholarship, bound as it is to historical method, could not employ this form of hermeneutic without in some sense becoming ancillary to a discipline other than historiography. Thus, Ott appears to have come upon an invulnerable method of saving a place for systematic theology among the theological disciplines.

The struggle between ontology and historiography as bases for a theological hermeneutic is reflected in every one of the major questions suggested by Ott's proposal. Three such questions deserve examination.

A. *Is the analysis of being properly a pre-understanding which delivers the meaning of an historical text such as the Bible, as Ott believes it can, or is it a pre-judgment which thwarts the emergence of such meaning?*

Paul Tillich, for instance, long ago decided that the question about "Being itself" was the fundamental question, because he believed "Being itself" to be the only non-symbolic way one has of referring to God. Tillich learned this title for God when he was Heidegger's colleague at Marburg. Meanwhile Heidegger has insisted that "being" is not "God" just as Samuel Beckett has insisted Godot is not. While he is willing to entertain the possibility that there is some analogy between theological thinking and ontological thinking, Heidegger has not endorsed what medieval theology called the analogy of being, which is the method of arriving at the truth of God by asking the question about being. Yet, in his book on the later Heidegger, Ott has made the point several times that in view of Heidegger's ontology, Barth's objection to the "analogy of being" is overcome. By that he meant that being, for Heidegger, is not an ultimate reality accessible to human reason, as it was in pre-Kantian, scholastic theology. Being makes itself accessible in an unthinkable language.

Should Barth be satisfied with the analogy of being done on this basis? I believe he should not. The revision in ontology which Heidegger sponsors has not affected the grounds of Barth's objection. Barth was not interested in denying either God's power to reveal himself or man's power to intuit God's nature. He was interested in availing himself of the concrete understanding which the triune God chose to make available in history, in Jesus of Nazareth. *Analogia entis* for Barth is not countered by *analogia fidei* of the sort where the truth of God can only be revealed to a modest and receptive intellect. *Analogia fidei*, Barth's alternate to *analogia entis*, means *analogia relationis*, the relation of faith. The relation of faith is man's relation to God's self-relation, to God as trinity. But this relation is mediated by Jesus Christ, who is the form in which the trinity communicates itself in history. Hence, the *analogia relationis* involves the relation of the concretely existing man to the concrete history of Jesus of Nazareth. This analogy of relation is currently being conserved in the "new quest of the historical Jesus" where faith is illumined not by the question about being but by the question about the historic form in which God has made himself present in human history. That quest is in the tradition of historicism where historical questions are prior to ontological questions. The discussion which followed the oral delivery of Ott's paper on systematic theology was so preoccupied with references to being that Heidegger himself took the floor to ask, "What has all this to do with Jesus Christ?" He was not being pious. He was suggesting that for a theologian there may be only one thing worse than forgetfulness of being, and that is forgetfulness of history.

Theologians oriented to ontological hermeneutics are fond of saying that if there is such a thing as being, theology must deal with it. Since the days of Edmund Husserl and the advent of phenomenology, that simply does not follow. Husserl showed how it is possible to bracket out the question of being in order to give the question of meaning priority. In that sense Husserl's phenomenology is closer to the historical science of hermeneutics than it is to the later Heidegger's phenomenological ontology, for as Dilthey said, "Man is there not to be but to act." Heidegger, in putting his kind of ontology as a discipline beyond history as a discipline, classifies history as a descriptive enterprise. The subject matter of history is thought to be merely a qualification of man's being. For him, the methods of history do not determine one's relation to history but presuppose such a relation, which is ontological and therefore best explored and renewed by ontology.

If that were the whole truth about history, it would be convincing to observe that ontology, transcending adjectival qualification, is necessarily prior to the methods of history. That attitude toward history is quite appropriate with reference to historical positivism, but it tends to by-pass modern historiographical gains. History in contemporary thinking is man existing in his acts, not simply describing them. In contemporary historicism, man is his history, and where he has no history, he has no being. History is both the creation and the revelation of man's being. Therefore, ontology, while it may well be a kind of pre-philosophy, as Heidegger claims it to be in his new view, is itself dependent upon historiography, which defines man where he really is.

Two things of importance follow for theology in relation to the later Heidegger. First, history cannot be treated, as Heidegger does, simply as one more regional ontology. History is not one among several areas but the horizon of every area of investigation.

From this the second thing follows. Historicism, the philosophical position which orients all questions to the question of history, ought not be classed as a species of ontology just because it happens to define being as historical. In asking the question about the meaning of reality through the medium of history, historicism constitutes a way of being which does not emerge when the question of being is raised. History is an horizon so inescapable that being is itself a derivative of history.

The Bible, for instance, does not ask the question of being but of historical meaning and act. To be sure, Exodus names God the "I am that I am." But, the Hebrew expression "to be" (*hāyā*) embraces the connotations given it not by ontology but by the history of Israel's responses to the acts of God. Thus the Hebrew Scriptures respond not to ontology but to what the Japanese theologian Tetsutarō Ariga calls "hayatology," or what the western world knows as historiography. The question of being raised from the standpoint of the question of meaning for man (historiography) is a completely different question from the question of meaning raised from the standpoint of the question of being (ontology). Does the New Testament raise the ontological question when it cites Jesus as saying, "Before Abraham was, I am"? To say that this is a question of being is to attempt to go behind what for the New Testament is final, namely eschatology—the redemptive presence of God in Jesus of Nazareth. In the eschatological faith of the New Testament, being cannot qualify history because it is history which qualifies being, giving it its end. Therefore, to ask the question about being is to engage in a hermeneutics of pre-judgment, bringing to the text concerns which are not prior for it.

New Testament faith is eschatological and not ontological. That is, it is an *answer* to the question of the meaning of history where the answer is given within history *as* history and not at the horizon of history as "Being itself." Even if "Being itself" were identical with God, one would have to say that the New Testament is not oriented to God in his being but God in his act of self-revelation, God giving history its end in the form of Jesus of Nazareth. The ontological theology of Paul Tillich is innocent compared to Ott's project because Tillich has not attempted systematic theology as the deductive phase of Biblical hermeneutics, as Ott has. In Ott, however, the deductive pre-understanding collides with the nature of the text. If put into operation, it would convert his proposed hermeneutical system into a system of pre-judgments.

B. *Is there sufficient guarantee in Ott's method that the doctrinal questions by which he proposes to inform exegetical work will be continually subject to revision from the initiative of the text itself?*

Implicit in a hermeneutical circle is the subordination of the deductive phase (the question of the interrogator) to the inductive phase (the question of the text). Ott's fondness for such traditional, ontologically weighted questions as doctrine of God, Christology, sin, and justification inspires scepticism regarding his outcome. In Europe more than in America, of course, dogmatic theology is built upon the ecumenical creeds and particular church confessions. For instance, when Karl Barth left the pastorate to teach theology at Göttingen (in the pay of American Presbyterians), he was forbidden to name his course "Dogmatics," for the only dogmatics admissible there at the time was Lutheran. That condition existed in the twentieth century.

Biblical theology, however, originated as long ago as the seventeenth century as a reform within dogmatic theology itself. The reform was brought on by the necessity for historical honesty in handling the Bible, combined with the unwillingness of systematic studies to accommodate to the same necessity. Exegetes ought never let dogmaticians forget that day of their liberation from dogmatics. Exegesis as a New Testament science which, thanks to the rise of the historical consciousness in the modern world, has so recently won the right to allow the Bible to speak for itself, is justifiably cautious about entering into liaisons with a discipline which does not usually submit itself to the same kind of historical dialectic.

There are evidences in Ott's discussion that he is not prepared to protect the gains which have been made by Biblical studies in their independence from dogmatics. One is that he seems willing to give the Bible as canon priority over the Bible as history. In so doing he supports a medieval position which the Reformers denied by their willingness to change the canon. Ott clings to the canon because on this basis systematic theology can be to Protestantism what the *magisterium* is to Roman Catholicism, the agency which interprets the intention of the church in holding the Bible as its constitution. Thus Ott claims that theology must integrate the Old

Testament into its consideration, but, consistent with the official dogma of the church up to the present time, he does not give a rationale to support his demand.

As an illustration of how his method would work, he offers an exegesis of Psalm 1. But his hermeneutical presuppositions are New Testament presuppositions, as Wilhelm Vischer's are when he looks for Christ in the Psalms. Presumably that would be possible on the basis of a hermeneutics of being if being were a continuous reality within all its historical manifestations, bridging the gap between the Testaments, although that would be to conceive being in its pre-Heidegger sense. Presumably that would be possible as well if being were, as in Heidegger's understanding, the event in which some primal word gathers the realities of earth into a world. But the Biblical faith testifies to a God who binds his people through historic covenants. Now that the new covenant has occurred in Jesus of Nazareth, is it historically justifiable to interpolate that covenant into the record of God's old covenant? Theology is unwarranted in affirming that the God we meet in the Old Testament is the same God we meet in the New Testament. That is not to say there are two Gods but only that the Testaments are conceived not on the basis of one being of God or of one primal word of God but on the basis of two historically distinct modes of relationship to God. Inasmuch as Christians are those related to God on the basis of his covenant in Christ, the Old Testament does not have the same status as revelation as the New Testament, the analysis of being notwithstanding.

Ontological presuppositions are also employed by Ott to provide unity within the New Testament. It is true that the New Testament is a highly diversified account of the meaning of Jesus Christ and his impact upon the early church. However, such diversity is utterly characteristic of historic reality. To go beneath it is to jeopardize its status as history. To attempt to smooth over its ruggedness by ontological unities which exist only at the limit of history, as does Ott's use of Heidegger's being, is alien to history's intrinsic structures. A science of history ought to win its sense of unity and continuity by thoroughly historical means. The variety in the accounts of the resurrection, for instance, must not be unified, as Ott proposes, by participation in what he calls the Christ-being. But, then, what is the alternative? What the resurrection means ought to be found in the historical materials themselves, inclusive of the records of the witness of the pre-Easter Jesus to his own mission.

Ott illustrates unity in variety from the experience of friendship. It is difficult to understand how by that analogy he is faithful to Heidegger's view of being where being is not some unitary reality at the base of particular phenomena but the essence of every particular occurrence. Friendship, he says, is a silent being beneath all friendly conversations. Analogically, is the God-relation a continuous reality beneath all verbal witness to it? Is the God-relation reflected, like Martin Kähler's morning sun, in every scattered dewdrop of historical witness, giving the diverse witness a common being? Tempting as the analogy is, it depreciates the historical character of faith for which the God-relation of a Christian is always mediated by an historical word—the word God speaks in Christ and renews in the witness of the church. Beings are related not on the basis of their being but on the basis of their acts, their covenants —uttered, remembered, and renewed.

C. *Is it theologically justifiable to separate the Christ event from the message about the Christ event?*

Ott's desire to do so shares the fundamentally positivistic and common sense drive which operates to some extent in every Christian thinker. The difference for Ott is simply that he illuminates his conviction by Heidegger's very sensitive and sophisticated ontology. His explicit justification manifests two main concerns.

1. *Christ is at work even where he is not preached.* What does that mean? Presumably for Ott it means that the preaching of the church like the apostolic witness derives its validity from its participation in the Christ-being, which is the ontological event continuous in all historic witness to the Christ. The Christ-being is there, *extra nos*, independent of the contingencies of witness. In historical hermeneutics, on the other hand, exegesis is not a reflective relation to an event which is there without that relation. As Ernst Fuchs has said, exegesis is standing in the event. Heidegger prepared for that understanding in paragraph 44 of *Being and Time*, where he asserted that before the laws of Newton were discovered, they were not true. But he did not add that once the laws were discovered, one had only to relate reflectively to their truth. Truth, he said, "is in the discourse." One might ask, "Where is the Christ

now?" just as one might ask, "Where is Beethoven's Ninth Symphony?" In the light of the earlier Heidegger he might answer, as indeed the late Maurice Merleau-Ponty did,[3] that the Ninth Symphony appears only in the different renditions one gives of it, although the symphony is not reducible to the rendition.

The theological significance of this phenomenological suggestion is patent. Heidegger knows that in the phenomenological method of Husserl and in the historical method of Dilthey subjectivity is not a distortion of reality but an aspect of its structure, an aspect which does not emerge without one's deliberate subjective penetration into that subjective structure. Yet, even with that subjective initiative in the discernment of who Christ is, Christ remains a reality *extra nos*. Subjectivity does not reduce him to a psychological state of other men. He is significant *extra nos*, yet only in his disclosures. His disclosures occur in the witness which is made to him. But the witness is always an interpretation which is made of him. Disclosure is an event of historical mediation, mediation through human existence, in which a man's life is embraced by God's meaningful claim.

The urgency of the theological task is directly related to this historicity of the Christ event. What is in history survives in the witness which is made to it. What is in being, on the other hand, can be said to happen, but if it happens without such witness, it does not happen meaningfully, that is, historically. To suppress subjectivity in hermeneutical work, as Heidegger and Ott now do, is hazardous, for nothing happens meaningfully which does not involve a human interpreter. Not that meaning originates with human understanding, but that the question of meaning is nowhere raised nor the answer given except as mediated by the historical form of existence.

Does not that claim tend to by-pass nature as a meaningful reality? Ott believes that the ontology of Heidegger could overcome the dichotomy between nature and history which seems so prevalent in existentially influenced theological thought. He will probably evoke the appreciation of sacramentalists and devotees of natural theology, as Tillich has with his ontological version of these concerns. But there will be an equivocation at the base of this achievement. Nature for historical hermeneutics is the structure of reality where the question of meaning for man is not asked. History, on the contrary, is the structure of reality where the question of meaning for man is asked.

The equivocation of the ontologists appears in their saying that Christ is at work in nature, especially when they invoke the Johannine logos doctrine of creation in support of their claim. When the prologue to the Gospel of John identifies the Christ as a participant in the act of creation, it is not saying that nature has the Word of God hidden in it. Nature is reality where such humanly meaningful questions are not raised, as they are not in the scientific measurement of the exterior world, or in the historical effort to establish facts without regard to their fundamentally human, historical significance. Creation, therefore, cannot be confused with nature, inasmuch as creation is the act in which man receives the world from God. Sacrament cannot be confused with nature inasmuch as a sacrament is the seal of God's promise that the world is there redemptively, that is, in the best interests of man. In this definition of terms, if one treats the world as nature, one ceases to regard it as creation and it becomes demonic, as Paul said to those who made the world their object rather than their responsibility. If one treats a sacrament as nature, that is, without participating in its fundamental intention, one receives it unworthily, and ceasing to be a sacrament, it becomes an instrument of wrath.

Ontology as Heidegger conceives it does not support the naturalizing of creation and sacrament. However, it does give courage to such efforts, because it allows one to refer to what is real in being without relating to the historical frame of reference out of which such realities are founded. This danger is revealed in Heidegger's equivocal response to attacks upon the a-historical character of poetry. Ott's discussion feeds upon this equivocation. Heidegger claims that poetry—in this case the poetry of Trakl—"does not need historical 'objects.' Why not? Because his poetry is in the highest sense historical."[4]

When *Being and Time* was written, this comment would have meant that scientific history, which looks for objects in history as if they were objects in nature, that is, without raising the question about their meaning for man, is not the sufficient cause of the history man lives. Appearing as it does over thirty years later, however, the comment means that a truly historical event manifests the power of destiny. The poet pre-eminently expresses that power found in events, but he does so without reference to any event in particular. This view was already expressed by Heidegger in his essay on "The Origin of the Art Work" in which he developed the position that historical truth comes into existence through art. "All art is in essence poetry" and "whenever art happens . . . only then does history begin."[5] That very creativity of a poet, as of any artist, makes him an exhilarating threat to all cultural structures which are oriented to prior historical manifestations of destiny. But this same creativity is also the reason poets, and ontologists as well, can be called a-historical without meaning simply to imply that they do not do history as a natural science. Insofar as poetry and ontology find meaning which is not an attribute of relation to some event in particular, they are a-historical "in the highest sense" of the term "historical." Preaching does not enjoy the luxury of poetic creativity, for while it creates "new being," it always does so "in Christ," that is, by reminiscence of God's historical act.

2. *According to Ott, there is a silence in faith which is deeper than expression.* One might say of the later Heidegger what Hegel once said of the German idealists, that their favorite text is Acts 17:23, "to an Unknown God."[6] Heidegger's being reveals itself as the "unthought." This suits the mystic mentality. And it is significant that in his early career Heidegger announced he would some day write a large study of the mystic Meister Eckhart. It also suits the Counter-Reformation mentality. I refer to the decision of Trent affirming, against the rising Protestant theology of the word, the hermeneutical inaccessibility of the Bible; and it is significant that Heidegger studied theology for three semesters in a Roman Catholic seminary in Freiburg, with some thought of preparing for the priesthood. Medieval theology was a theology of grace which emphasized the prevenience of God's activity. Protestant theology is a theology of the Holy Spirit which, without de-emphasizing prevenience, always holds God's activity in equilibrium with his Word. Grace operates effectively in silence, without being understood. The Holy Spirit works when the church interprets the Gospel in such a way as to be understood. That circumstance is not a proscription upon God's action but a promise of his action. Beyond that, the Protestant expression of the faith is not simply to be identified as a reality primarily verbal, as Heidegger and Ott are willing to do, with their accent on language as the house of

being. It specifies that language is constitutive of meanings which can be linguistically articulated without loss of meaning and without resort to the esotericism of poetry—that is, in the medium of history. The later Heidegger's emphasis on ineffability is edifying, inspiring one with a sense of the Holy. But the Protestant faith is unimpressed by signs of holiness which do not interpret themselves in continuity with the word in which God has expressed his intention for the world, which is a word inextricably historical.

Protestant faith is a religion of maturity in which man is oriented toward the world through the mediation of an historically illuminating Word. Ott, with Heidegger, tends to draw his faith back into the days of silent meditation on mysteries deeper than words. Heidegger's early writing expressed a certain sadness about man without God in the world. His later writing has overcome this sadness through a sense of the hiddenness of an unnamed being at the horizon of existence. Theologies like those of Bonhoeffer and Gogarten have no need to take this step with Heidegger into his later thought because the early Heidegger had already expressed in a secular way what the eschatological faith of the New Testament was saying. Man must learn precisely to get along without God in the world and to cease living in religious wistfulness for a silent mystery on the horizon. The good news of the Gospel includes God's act of making man his heir, turning the world over to him as his responsibility. The poetic mystification and ineffability of the later Heidegger is a wholesome corrective where philosophical and theological language claims too much. However, it courts the danger of gratifying modern man's immature religiousness rather than calling him to responsibility, because it fosters quests for the unknown even after those quests are terminated by the revelation, however modest, in which the unknown God is named.

What, then, is to be gained by turning to the later Heidegger? Ontological hermeneutics is unsuited to a radically historical faith. Theologians who are still being called "younger" do not enjoy resisting new possibilities, especially when they are proposed by still younger theologians. But there is some relief from that strain in the realization that the younger proposal is based upon the older Heidegger. It would be a pity if an older Heidegger were now to lead us away from possibilities which have not yet had a chance fully to be understood and developed. When they are developed, so that systematic theology does continue to exist as an independent discipline, they should take the shape not of an ontological but of an historical hermeneutic. That will mean that in theology the question of the meaning of God's word for man will have more power to invoke faith than the question of its being. That is to say, the question of the historical form of God's word will do more to focus faith than the question of its being.

SEVEN

Subjectivity and the Reality of Faith
—Søren Kierkegaard's Theology

During the period between the two World Wars, Christendom became aware for the first time of the writings of the nineteenth-century Danish thinker, Søren Kierkegaard. Of his vocation he had said, "My task is to revise the definition of a Christian."[1] Then, of his result he had commented, "It is clear that in my writings I have given a more precise determination to the concept of faith."[2] Contemporary Christianity, however, has largely missed Kierkegaard's point. We have skimmed the cream of his epigrams to fatten our ailing beliefs. Yet, he himself was not interested in beliefs, that is, in *what* Christianity is. One drive dominated his work and that was the question of *how* to become a Christian. At first that seemed very obliging, because it left Christendom's beliefs intact while providing new and more seductive tactics for communicating those beliefs. Was Kierkegaard, then, primarily an evangelist, not a philosopher or theologian? We have been most ready to seize upon him today as a nineteenth-century spokesman for the eighteenth-century conviction that if one's heart is right, one's hand may be grasped.

Karl Barth and Pope Pius XII stand almost alone in comprehending what Kierkegaard really was about. If Kierkegaard is right, they have observed, traditional Christianity is wrong. Being Vicar of traditional Christianity, the Pope had no alternative but to censor this existential threat in his 1950 encyclical, *Humani generis*, although leading Catholic theologians at the Vatican Council were among those influenced by Kierkegaard and censored by the Vatican. As far back as 1921, in the second edition to his *Epistle to the Romans*, Barth saw that he would have to decide between Kierkegaard's attack on Christendom and his own evolving project for theology as a *church* dogmatics, although many of his own lustrous theological interpretations have been sparked by Kierkegaard's insights. No pathological quirk determined Kierkegaard's refusal of the church's ministry at his death bed. Correspondingly, it is not theological hygiene alone which motivates a theologian to seal himself off from the philosophical contagion of Kierkegaard.

Kierkegaard had seen something which, if true, shattered Christendom's customary mold. Jesus of Nazareth had appeared in history as the occasion for faith. He came as the paradigm by which a whole new mode of existence was to be inflected. The paradigm evoked the question, "How do I become a Christian?", and the answer, "By faith." Hearing the answer, Christendom immediately began to enter into objective discussions of the question, "What is faith?" The history of theology is a history of the attempt to approximate Jesus' answer to that question. Kierkegaard, however, calls for an end to that history. The church has been attempting to answer a question which Jesus' advent did not put. Therefore, the church's falling short of Jesus' answer is not the result of any lack of diligence or talent or devotion on the part of the church. A long doctrinal highway has been built through Christian history but it is always only an approximation. It never arrives, because it may well be pointed in the wrong direction.

Jesus said, "I am the Way." The church had also heard him say, "I am the Truth." Believing it necessary to have the truth before choosing the way, the church then asked, "What is faith?" Kierkegaard understood, however, that for Jesus the way is the truth. Hence, faith *is* not a "What" but a "How," a mode of existing. Therefore, one does not ask "What?" but "How?" if it is the truth one seeks. Christendom is the story of man's refusal to ask "How" without first asking "What." That is why it is a miracle when anyone becomes a Christian in Christendom. It is also why it is irresponsibility to faith and insensitivity to Kierkegaard to regard his existential method as merely ancillary to the established doctrines of the church. Kierkegaard's understanding is rather an invitation to a more fundamental theology of faith. Kierkegaard often expressed the fear that his point of view would get into the hands of the professors, who are so vocationally disposed to detail truth in paragraphs. It seems strange he did not anticipate that his real enemies would be the preachers, who are so vocationally disposed to perpetuate vivid illustrations without reference to the modes of existence which originally inspired them. Even paragraph-material, if it discusses *how to become a Christian,* is closer to the intention of both Kierkegaard and New Testament Christianity than homiletical lustre which simply generates an aura of plausibility around accounts of *what Christianity is.*

Kierkegaard regarded it as the misfortune of his century that it was an "objective age," preoccupied with "what" questions. The corollary of objectivity is forgetfulness of self. That corollary can seem benign if it is believed that not all that is forgotten is gone. Western thinking has sponsored this soporific, tutoring men that they exist continuously, notwithstanding their lapses of self-aware-ness. Kierkegaard took a graver view. Self-forgetfulness, he believed, is the preface to the *loss* of the self. No great cry of alarm goes up among us over that. But take the world away from man and leave only his self—that is grand larceny. Six thousand years of human history, astrology, and veterinary sciences loom as more important than the self. Man has exteriorized himself into his world as a model exteriorizes herself into the clothes she displays. Remove the shoe and there is no foot, the brassiere and there is no breast. What does it matter? Put the clothes back on and guarantee your ongoing life. What does it matter if a man lose a soul, so long as he gains a world?

Contrary to the conventional canons of an objective age, a life of objectivity is a being in error. Loss of the self is a fundamental perversion of reality, not simply because of the loss of the self, but because forgetfulness of self is also a direct route to forgetfulness of God. Being objective in one's approach to the world has as its consequence not the loss of the self only, but the loss of God. Kierkegaard, therefore, is not to be seen as a "catcher in the rye," an artist who holds himself responsible for blocking humanity's fatal fall over the precipice of self-forgetfulness. He is a theologian, responsible for averting the death of God in the world. As a theologian it is his genius to have discerned that God's life is in some important way inseparable from man's consciousness of himself. Why, then, is he so preoccupied with attacks on Christendom, where God has no more ordained advocate? Because the defenders of Christianity are those most apt to betray it. The existence of Christianity is tied to the realization that "subjectivity is truth." As Kierkegaard has said, "This principle . . . in its maximum is Christianity."[3] Kierkegaard believes that since the New Testament epoch, Christendom has been converting Christianity into objectivity. But if "subjectivity is truth," the quickest way to falsify the truth of God is Christendom's way, treating God as the object of belief. The essence of Christianity is in the question about *how* one becomes a Christian. Christian faith is not a teaching about God but a mode of existence. New Testament teaching is not a doctrine which one subsequently applies in existence. It is a doctrine which is nothing if not in existence and when treated in any other way than an existential way withers away in consumption. What that means, how the very truth of God hinges upon the existence of man, is the point of Kierkegaard on which present day Christians have not yet clearly enough focused. I will therefore attempt to make it clearer by isolating several of the major facets of this claim.

(1) *Objectivity and subjectivity are two ways of being in the world.* Failure to distinguish these clearly is the source of confusion everywhere. Failure to realize their essentially different structure is the source of comic attempts to answer questions in a medium in which the questions have not arisen.

Objectivity grasps truth in such a way that the self remains outside what it grasps. Being an observer, the self shrinks almost to the status of a ghost. Subjectivity, on the other hand, includes the self in what it grasps. That does not mean it grasps only a spirit, a ghost. It grasps a world, but it is the kind of world being called in philosophy today a *Lebenswelt*, a world of life, a world inhabited by selves. Objectivity is thought pointed away from one's self, "thought without a thinker,"[4] where the person is irrelevant to his thought.[5] Subjectivity is existence where "thought (which points away from itself) is a foreign medium,"[6] and truth is appropriated inwardly, that is, where the self is embraced in the truth which it grasps.

Objectivity thinks in the realm of possibility. Contemplation is its method. It begins not with what exists, but with what is possible. "What really happened" takes a back seat to "What could happen." Subjectivity is understandably, then, the realm of decision which cannot endlessly contemplate because the conditions of existence, which it experiences at least in its own selfhood, press upon it as reality toward which one must adopt an attitude. Neither objectivity nor subjectivity are ever finished, but the ways in which each is never finished differ conspicuously. Objectivity is never finished because it never exhausts all the possibilities. It is always only an approximation. Subjectivity is never finished because becoming is precisely the truth. To have a final result in subjectivity would be a contradiction in terms. Objectivity is endless, as a natural science which, like the ant, collects experimental data interminably, always revising "its conclusions," is endless, or even as art, which constantly cancels the past in order to let the creative possibilities hitherto unanticipated emerge, is endless. On the other hand, subjectivity is endless as love is endless. In love results are irrelevant, because the essence of the reality is in the process, in the mode of appropriation.

Some things are true in subjectivity, therefore, which are not true in objectivity.[7] But "Christendom transposes everything" into the sphere of objectivity,[8] treating it as a "what" rather than a "how," an abstract possibility rather than a concrete process, thinking it without the thinker, without including the subject. That mode of appropriation is the mode Pilate chose when he washed his hands in the presence of Christ: sanitary detachment from the truth. That is the way Christendom loses God. For a God who is chosen apart from the self is less than absolute.[9] Faith in God is not a choice between God and oneself. Faith in God is an act of choosing God in choosing oneself absolutely.[10] Appropriating the truth of God is rather like the situation of a warrior in mid-battle, an arrow lodged in his chest (to transpose an analogy of Kierkegaard). One must not extract that arrow or the warrior will not live to see the victory. The truth of God is a reality to be suffered in passionate inwardness. That is its reality. To withdraw the truth from the realm of subjectivity is to place it in a realm in which it is no longer true. When the self moves from objectivity to subjectivity it does not change places. It changes.[11] That the self should be lost is the minor consequence. That the self should miss the end of the battle is the crucial loss.

(2) Kierkegaard's ironies, which so delight his reader and sting one into self-awareness, are built upon *the comic incommensurability of the objective and subjective modes of relation.* When examples of this incommensurability are sighted, the reader should undergo the sensation of a soldier at night in No Man's Land for whom a sudden flare overhead has for the first time exposed his position. Let me paraphrase some of his choicer illustrations:

There was the man who disseminated the doctrine that no man should have disciples. At least ten candidates applied to him for the privilege of preaching his doctrine.

It has been said that "all receiving consists in producing." The sentence came to be used in copy-books as a model for handwriting.

A certain professor devoted his whole life to explaining all of existence. Along the way he forgot his own name.

How shall an artist satisfy his desire to depict Mars wearing his invisible armor?

Doctor Hartaspring regarded it as a miracle that he was converted to Hegel's philosophy which does not believe in miracles.

In a commendably infinite passion and with limitless concern Don Quixote pursued a fixed idea of a very finite sort, a fixation which was really of no real concern to anyone.

A seeker after truth enters into an objective inquiry through which the faith becomes more and more plausible. Just when he is ready to believe, he finds belief no longer possible.

Overheard: someone explaining an "unutterable joy."

After the wedding in which they pledge their love, the young bride believed she easily understood why her husband chose her. Can it be said she any longer loves him?

One has been known to claim that he is familiar with every possibility in the erotic realm, yet he is not in love.

When God was crucified, some sat down to contemplate the event objectively. At the very same time, the veil of the temple was being rent in twain and the dead were being raised from their graves.

In a Holberg play a medical doctor killed his patient through administering a certain medicine. But it is almost certain that the medicine cured the disease.

A character in a play threatened to blow up the whole world—with a syllogism.

Is it not possible to leave a question unanswered for so long that you begin to feel you have answered it? To tell a lie for so long that you begin to sense its truth? To remain in debt for so long that you feel debt-free?

A philosopher named Zeno, a sceptic, one day went out of his way to avoid a mad dog.

People today may be fearful of existence because it is so God-forsaken, which is why they gather *en masse* in order to feel "they amount to something."

An innkeeper, who sells beer for a penny less than he paid for it, was asked how he could keep solvent on that basis. He replied, "It's the large number that does it."

Christians have been known to treat the Kingdom of Heaven so much as if it were one of the earthly kingdoms that they may be expected to consult their geography text books for information about it.

Medieval monasticism was so infinitely concerned with the absolute that it pursued it in its own little corners of the world.

Speculative philosophers usually complete their comprehensive systems on paper.

For the view that one must hate father and mother, historians seek a basis in the facts of the past.

Consider: a preacher of repentance concerned about what people think of him.[12]

Comic incommensurability does not communicate truth, but it does create a clearing or a focus in which the truth can at last come to light. Kierkegaard's comic depiction of existence, notwithstanding its dramatic, even emotive language, is analytically rigorous. One must learn to distinguish between the approximation-process of objectivity and the infinite interestedness of subjectivity, for in one of these two structures it is not possible for God to exist. Objective certainty and subjective passion are as unlike as proof and faith, and God is real for only one of them. The infinite God is real only in infinite decision, so that methods of relating to the world which participate in an approximation-process foreclose upon the advent of God. The determination of the self to place its faith on an objective basis directs the human spirit outward, beyond itself. Faith in God, however, precisely involves the relationship of the subject, the involvement of the spirit.

(3) *The decision of faith is a decision for subjectivity* in which the comic incommensurability between objectivity and subjectivity is overcome. The one conviction of Kierkegaard most likely to be known today is the view that faith is "objective uncertainty." That is generally taken to mean that a man of faith can believe almost anything so long as he has enough energy of will: no objective tests

for the validity of faith are relevant. If that were the truth, it would be too trivial to assert. The belief in leprechauns in watches commands no objective certainty, yet that quality of belief is scarcely what our Lord had in mind when he anticipated that the Son of Man would find faith on the earth when He comes. (Luke 18:8)

Faith is the "decisive expression for subjectivity"[13] and "the highest passion in the sphere of human subjectivity."[14] As such, faith is not a correlate of doubt. Doubt is an expression for thought insofar as thought deals with possibility. Possibility is no correlate of faith, because faith is a determinant of subjectivity, and subjectivity is a passion for reality, as opposed to possibility. Faith *is* a correlate of despair, however, because despair is an expression for the whole of the personality, as faith is.[15] To say that faith is a decision for subjectivity, then, is to say that faith involves the question of reality-as-a-whole, that is, reality inclusive of the self. Faith is a totalizing act which includes the self in the whole of the reality embraced, standing over against the detotalizing act characteristic of the objective, cognitive process. Objective truth is reality minus one, minus the self, hence reality "detotalized" (to borrow an expression of the French philosophers René Le Senne and Jean-Paul Sartre).

Objective certainty is alien to faith because it initiates a process of knowledge which never gets further than an approximation of truth. When linked to an infinite passion, it manifests comic incommensurability. One who desires to know if he is among the elect will never know, because he is asking the question in a medium other than the medium in which he is seeking the answer. His question, raised in subjectivity, seeks its answer in objectivity, and that is comic. If one holds the pearl of great price in his hand while giving his all for it, he has no faith, for he has not ventured himself. Faith is not the grasping of objects but the appropriation of a reality inclusive of oneself. Faith does not possess: it is a mode of acquisition.[16] One who understands that can understand why it was necessary for Christ to go away before the Disciples could follow Him. "Taken away from the eye of sensual imagination . . . it may appear in earnestness of the decision whether (a man) will follow Him."[17]

Can one any longer ask "what" faith is, then? It is only profitable to ask "what" if one has an inkling in advance that the answer cannot be given in terms of thought or possibility or abstraction. For the "what" of faith is "that it is the 'how' of faith." The objectivity of faith is located exclusively in its subjectivity.[18] Faith is "the fact that God has existed."[19] How easy it would be to swallow up that formulation in the sphere of objectivity, as traditional theology has tended to do. But Kierkegaard knows "God does not exist."[20] Are believers, then, caught in a position where by a sheer act of will they affirm something for which there is no basis? If "God does not exist" yet faith affirms that "God has existed," are we caught in Tertullian's *credo quia absurdum*? In William James's "Will to Believe"? Is faith a "blind leap"?

"God does not exist; he is eternal." To be and to exist are not the same. Being has its reality in itself and even in the possibility of thought, but for Kierkegaard nothing is real and concrete in thought which has not been mediated by existence, that is, by the realm of subjectivity, which is the realm in which acts of thought embrace the thinker himself. Faith being a decision for subjectivity does not affirm that God is, but that God exists. Indeed, faith does not *affirm* the eternal God; faith *exists* the eternal God. More felicitously, God only exists in faith, that is, for an existing man.[21] Faith, therefore, is "not an act of will,"[22] although "faith, surely, implies an act of will."[23] For faith is the mode in which the God who "is" becomes the God who "exists." Faith is "the eternal power *in man.*"[24] To say that "faith is *the fact* that God has existed" need not be taken as permission for faith to slide off in the direction of objectivity, thanks to Kierkegaard's pre-Heideggerian penchant for philology. "Fact" derived from *factum* is "a word which etymologically implies that I have an active part to play."[25]

By identifying faith with subjectivity, Kierkegaard does not reduce God to an epiphenomenon of the human spirit. Faith as the mode in which God exists answers to what he calls "the decisive criterion of faith," namely, that "a believer is one who is infinitely interested in another's reality."[26] Faith is the appearance of God in existence, in subjectivity. By this formulation Kierkegaard has anticipated phenomenological philosophy where the only reality man knows is reality as it "appears" for the human consciousness. Consciousness is never a consciousness of itself, however. It is a structure of intentionality which points beyond itself, always directed to a reality other than itself. The realities it knows are correlates of its intentions and not fictions of its wishes. These realities appear in existence not as possibilities, as abstractions, as objects of cognition, but as realities, as concretions, and as objects of personal inclination. As Kierkegaard says in a very phenomenological way, "The only reality to which an existing individual may have a relation that is more than cognitive is his *own* reality, the fact that he exists." Faith is existential knowledge of God because it is God's way of being present in existence, the eternal's way of being contemporaneous. Faith is "the Christian teaching in the New Testament that the eternal happiness of the individual is decided in time."[27]

(4) *Paradox is the occasion for faith.* As such, it is "the characteristic mark of Christianity."[28] Not as logical contradiction, not as the perpetuation of doctrinal absurdities, not as permission to affirm in faith just any kind of irrationality, but as the occasion for faith it is Christianity's characteristic mark. Paradox achieves this exalted status by virtue of its effective barricades against objectivity as the route for seekers after faith. Intensifying subjectivity as the sole locus for faith, paradox provides the very condition for the possibility of faith.

What is the paradox, that it can do all this? Formally speaking paradox is the juxtaposition of heterogeneous realities at a definite place and in the same moment. The Christian paradox, fulfilling this formal requirement, has a specific *content.* Temporal existence and eternal truth coalesce in the historical time and place named Jesus of Nazareth. He, therefore, is the paradigm of faith, because to follow Him is to have an *historical* point of departure for one's *eternal* happiness. Nowhere in all of Kierkegaard's thinking does he seem more traditional than here. The paradox of the faith appears to be expressed in the Chalcedonian formula, asserting two natures in the one person of Christ. "God has been born," he says.[29] "The Deity, the Eternal, came into being at a definite moment in time as an individual man."[30] But if the Chalcedonian formula becomes the occasion for speculation, transforming the God-Man into a "speculative unity of God and Man *sub specie aeterni,* manifested, that is to say, in the nullipresent medium of pure being," then it is to be rejected. The paradox belongs to subjectivity and not to objectivity. It is a rebuke to abstract thought in order to appeal to concrete existence, where faith occurs. Hence, the emphasis in Kierkegaard's Christology, as in theology today, is more along the

lines of Lessing's formulation than of Chalcedon, adopting historical rather than ontological categories, existential rather than speculative categories: "The God-Man is the Unity of God and an
individual man in an actual historical situation."[31] When Christianity
announces the presence of God in Jesus of Nazareth, it offends anyone who relates himself to the world objectively. That is the intention of the paradox: to discourage efforts at appropriation which
omit one's own existence from the reality appropriated. The corollary of this intention is that paradox inflames subjectivity, stimu-
lates self-awareness. "Paradox and passion are a mutual fit."[32] The
Christian faith is the realization that God *exists*. Paradox is the agent
through which the eternal becomes an *existential* reality. The eternal, coalescing with that individual, Jesus of Nazareth, and existing
in Him is contemporary with us. His eternal being exists in us so
that it is as true to say that man provides the basis for God's existence as it is to say that God provides the basis for man's existence.
The symmetry is what the Christian faith affirms in the paradox
of the Incarnation and in the extension of that paradox through
preaching.

It is wrong that Kierkegaard's emphasis on paradox has been
discounted as an irrationalism. Undeniably he has asserted that the
paradox "requires faith against the understanding."[33] However,
the meaning of that provocative assertion should now be clear.
Paradox is no possibility for the understanding, so that the mode
of relation to the world which looks for possibilities, that is, the
objective mode, is repulsed by paradox. That simply means that
paradox places man in the proper position for faith, the position of
subjectivity, where the reality of the Eternal God can be existed.
By elevating paradox as the specifying element in the Christian
faith, Kierkegaard believed he was fulfilling the vocation of "making room for God to come."

In fulfilling this task by way of his doctrine of paradox,
Kierkegaard is the forerunner of contemporary demythologizing.
Paradox is an explicit attack upon mythological and paganizing
tendencies in Christendom. Myth treats eternal truth as if it were
directly recognizable. But "direct recognition is paganism."[34] The
paradoxical, incommensurate reality of faith is an attack on all
direct recognition and on all claims for commensurability. "An
eternal historical fact is a play on words, and it amounts to trans-

forming the historical fact into a myth."[35] That is to say, the eternal, if made *commensurable* with an historical fact, is treated mythologically. Paradox affirms the incommensurability, asserting the eternal and the historical as external to one another, so that the historical *is* not the eternal but the occasion for the presence of the eternal. Paradox does not override contradictions; it unites them.[36] In so doing, it denies any possibility for "direct recognition" of God in history, which is the hallmark of mythology and paganism, and thus puts faith "in its right place."[37]

(5) *The expression for this paradoxical faith is a form of Christian worldliness.* In denying us God as a direct object, Christian faith gives us the world. By refusing to allow our infinite passions to be satisfied in worldly processes, which always only approximate, the whole world of relativity is given a new character of finality. These apparent paradoxes are not really paradoxical at all, but only humorous. They are the divine comedy which one experiences as the redemptive meaning in life, through the paradox of faith. They carry us beyond the sting of comic incongruity in the world.

Through the paradox of faith God exists in man, yet the man of faith looks no different from anyone else. If he tries to look different, chances are he will force his life out of inwardness and subjectivity, which is the world in which he exists his meanings, into the public world of thought, abstraction, possibility. But that is the way to drive faith out of the world.

In the inwardness of subjectivity one's passion for the infinite is gratified by the God-relation. What is the consequence of this for Kierkegaard? Some Protestant equivalent of monasticism? Some retreat from the world? Some spiritualizing of existence? Oddly, the consequence for Kierkegaard is the opposite of monasticism. It is a new accentuation of temporal existence, the creation of a new kind of world. The object of a Christian's love is not now God but the world. "To make God the object of love is sickly religiosity."[38] The implication of faith is not preoccupation with the absolute but, in faithful relationship to the absolute, preoccupation with the relativities of the world. Monks were comic, then, to express their absolute faith by removing it to a corner of the world. A husband would be comic to express his eternal love for his wife by setting aside a little time each week for her. Christians would be comic to express the passion of their faith in church on Sunday, forgetting that their living rooms are also embraced by the world. Faith is meant to overcome comic incongruity and not to reassert it. "The task is therefore to exercise myself in the relationship to the absolute *telos* so as always to have it with me, while remaining in the relativities of life."[39] The religious individual does better to visit the local park than to enter a cloister, because "it is the humblest expression of his God-relationship to admit his humanity, and because it is human to enjoy oneself."[40] Through the movements of faith one does not lose the finite, then, "but gains it every inch."[41] That is why it can be said of the Christian that "he belongs entirely to the world."[42] His faith has translated him out of the world of unreality, of abstraction, of objectivity and ideality, which is not a world one lives, into the real world where one can grasp existence as a whole. "By faith I make renunciation of nothing, on the contrary, by faith I acquire everything."[43] Faith the size of a mustard seed is a very worldly reality because it is the kind of reality that removes mountains. It is true that the rich young ruler was asked to give up his worldly goods. The irony in the incident is that he felt he could not afford to give up the world, yet, if he had taken the movement of faith, "he would have gotten every penny back,"[44] as Abraham got Isaac back when he acted in faith. "He who when he has the world is as one who does not have it, then he has the world, otherwise the world has him."[45] Like a grand commentary on Galatians 4, Kierkegaard culminates his theology of faith on a note increasingly compelling in contemporary thought: the man of faith is "the heir apparent to the finite."[46]

Our own objective age, an age of calculated worldliness, is also the age of the loss of the self, the death of the gods, and the consequent volatilizing of the world. Kierkegaard has shown us how, through subjectivity, not simply to find ourselves, but how thereby to let God exist, and, as a consequence of that, to receive back the world we otherwise evaporate by our direct gaze upon it.

EIGHT

Holiness and the Maturity of Faith —John Wesley's Theology

Preaching and not theology was the main concern of John Wesley. That is why he was not a theologian in the systematic sense. Lord Shaftesbury had established for the eighteenth century that "the most ingenious way of becoming foolish is by a system,"[1] and Wesley declined to be that kind of fool for theology's sake. The "first principle of a Methodist" was "wholly and solely" the foolishness of preaching.[2] Not that there were no other ministries besides preaching. On the one side, Wesley regarded the sacrament of the Lord's Supper as "more powerful" than preaching.[3] For that reason, if forced to choose, he would have preferred the service of the Church of England with its sacramental life to the service of a Methodist society with its kerygmatic edification.[4] On the other side, instruction and discipline were regarded by Wesley as more durable than preaching, so that without them preaching merely prepared lambs for the world's slaughter.[5]

Notwithstanding these limits to preaching, however, at the rise of the Methodist movement a single virtue was made of twin necessities: Methodists were licensed only to preach, and the sacramental community almost everywhere refused its pulpit to Methodist preachers. In virtue of this, "field preaching" or "preaching abroad" became the Methodist mode. Preaching, definable not in relation to the pulpit but in relation to the people, was "speaking before a congregation,"[6] wherever assembled. Even if all that went on before the congregation was the reading of the Scriptures by a layman,[7] that was preaching. Out of "this strange way of preaching"[8] the Methodist movement was born.

One of the responsibilities of a theologian within the communion which Wesley's preaching inspired is to illuminate the doctrinal character of that influence. This responsibility also involves an evaluation of the respects in which Wesley's influence continues to support the Methodist communion meaningfully, both in its own corporate life and in its contacts with other Christians and with the world. Wesley's preaching constitutes almost the entire frame of reference for such a theological investigation. He preached on an average of three times daily over a period of some sixty years and left a deposit of some 141 printed sermons. Actually, the numerical output was not overly impressive, considering his preoccupation with preaching. During his lifetime he prepared no more different sermons than a parish minister is expected to preach in the course of a two-year ministry. That is why his sermons, continuously refined in being preached repeatedly and under the most diverse conditions, and finally subjected to studious scrutiny for publication, constitute so solid a base for the discernment of his theological patterns. Occasionally his *Journals*, incomparably barren alongside his sermons, and his *Letters* illuminate his preaching with theological insight. His *Notes on the New Testament* are an additional key of great value in revealing the exegetical decisions underlying his homilies. The hymns then rhapsodized the faith which the sermons communicate more chastely. Nor ought one overlook *The Christian Library*, a twenty-five volume selection of theologically discerning writings, assembled and published by Wesley for the instruction of Methodist preachers, which can be assumed to have been the writings most likely to have influenced Wesley's own theological formation or to have corroborated his developing point of view.

Does this frame of reference in the Wesley literature reveal any significantly distinctive Wesleyan motif in theology? Wesley himself specified two, and subsequent Methodism has been alternately arrogant and ashamed in being associated with them.

The more apparently vapid and embarrassing of the two claims has been that Methodists "think and let think."[9] In Wesley's judgment Methodism was the only religious group that did not base affiliation upon some precise doctrinal formulation or mode of worship. Hence, in its relation to the churches, erroneous opinions could be tolerated[10] and heretics could be defended.[11] In its attempted rapprochement with the churches, the ecumenical rule for fellowship was change of heart, not change of doctrine.[12] Wherever Wesley put Christian experience above doctrine, however, the doctrine at issue had for him the status of "opinion," in contrast with what he variously called the "essentials" or "fundamentals."[13] The "dogmatic attitude" was what he opposed.[14] The dogmatic attitude, like opinion, was definable as an adamant clinging to doctrines which had no bearing upon the vital experience of the Christian with God and his neighbor.

What is often made to seem like a contest between doctrine and experience in Wesley, in which experience always wins, is really a contest between experientially irrelevant doctrine and doctrine which inspires experience. Everyone knows that Wesley, like his times, was in reaction against so-called lifeless orthodoxy in the church and against the equally arid rationalism of the Age of Enlightenment. What is not so often realized is that his reiteration of the language of human sentiment—"heart," "conscience," "life," "feeling," and "experience"—was not a simple assertion of romanticism in the face of an advancing spirit of geometry and its physicalistic handmaiden, natural science. These evidently sentimental terms are definable within the carefully disciplined human sciences, such as are now associated with those who seem to have influenced Wesley's method the most: John Locke, the father of the modern consciousness in Britain[15]; his pupil, Lord Shaftesbury[16]; Francis Hutcheson, Shaftesbury's interpreter; and those who first specifically applied these humanistic gains to theological method, the German pietists Johann Albrecht Bengel and Friedrich Christoph Oetinger. In the new human sciences of the eighteenth century aesthetic categories replaced natural science categories as principles of interpretation. Shaftesbury likened "nature" to a work of art, and Bengel likened scripture to a work of art. Therefore, saying in that framework, "If thy heart is right, give me thy hand," was not a waiving of intellectual or doctrinal responsibility in the interest of the new spirit of toleration. Doctrinal responsibility was by that slogan squarely placed in the context of the human sciences where authentic thinking involved the experience of the conscience, or cognitive wholeness, the point at which divine and human concerns overlap in mobilizing life significantly. When it is seen how Wesley elaborated this insight about Christian experience, it will become evident that it is no invention of the eighteenth century but a principle confidently presupposed in the Biblical faith itself.

The second claim to Wesleyan distinctiveness is the one on which Methodism has lingered the longest but with the greatest consternation to others: scriptural holiness, or Christian perfection, "the peculiar doctrine committed to our trust."[17] The Methodist people did not originate this view. They simply believed they were raised up by God to expect what the Church of England daily requested when it prayed: "Cleanse the thoughts of our hearts by the inspiration of Thy Holy Spirit that we may perfectly love Thee and worthily magnify Thy Holy name." An expectation so central to the main tradition of Christianity ought not be allowed to be boxed off by the epithet "enthusiasm," as the established churches tended to do. Nor is a view which so closely associates "heart" and "experience" with the human sciences, where the wholeness of life and its meaning is at issue, so easily dislodged by the criticism that Methodism has converted the Gospel into a "new law," into moralism, as the churches and sects oriented to the continental Reformation tended to charge.

In short, the theology of John Wesley, notwithstanding its irregular medium in sermons, exegetical notes, autobiographical anecdotes, and hymns, sponsors a somewhat rigorous point of view with classical roots. The major themes of this point of view have no distinctiveness in the history of the Christian faith other than by the way in which they stabilize and unify major Christian emphases, emphases that have often been allowed to decline and fall into oblivion. Against the background of these consistently applied major emphases the distinctive themes—the religion of the heart and scriptural holiness—simply sharpen the focus of what has from the beginning been essential Christianity. When these themes have been reassessed today, they may provide rallying points for Christendom and some promise for the integrity of Christianity's life in the future.

That prognosis is based on the realization that the self-understanding of the modern world, notwithstanding the Protestant Reformation, has not yet affected the formulation of the Christian faith sufficiently. Christians continued to believe like medieval men long after the Reformation, and long after revolutionary modern thinkers, like Locke and Shaftesbury, had pointed the way to new understandings of reality. Wesley, like most of the rest of his time, moved ahead theologically under the inertia of tradition. No case can be made which denies that. My purpose here is simply to suggest respects in which, however slight, Wesley seized upon the possibilities, available to Christendom almost for the first time in his day, which emancipate faith from the drag of cultural anachronism.

Therefore in the first part of this discussion what appear to be three of the major but rather traditional themes in Wesley's theology will be presented. In the second part, these will come to a head in the distinctive Wesleyan emphases on heart, religion, and holiness, merged in what will be called "the hermeneutics of holiness."

I. MAJOR THEMES IN WESLEY'S THEOLOGY

A. Faith is Instrumental to Works

In the Protestant tradition one who is accustomed to supposing that the end of Christianity is faith might be a bit shaken to find that for Wesley faith is only instrumental. Works are given the primacy. On behalf of that conviction he was constantly at war with "antinomianism," allegedly deficient in works. Because of it, he was constantly being branded a papist, allegedly putting works before faith. The "first principle" of Christianity was summarized for him in the four-word formula "by grace through faith"[18] and the "cornerstone" of Christianity was identified as "justification by faith,"[19] but "the gospel leaven" was "faith working by love—, inward and outward holiness."[20]

The place of works in Wesley's system is made to seem ambiguous because of the way the meaning of the word "faith" jumps about in his allusions to it. In Wesley, faith has two major components. First of all, it is a form of "evidence." This most rudimentary kind of faith derives from the familiar account in the Epistle to the Hebrews, "the evidence of things not seen" (11:1).

It is not distinctively Christian faith, for it is purely procedural, having no relation to the particular Christian object of faith which is Christ. It is not, therefore, what can be called "justifying faith."

"Evidence" is the faith which will one day be swallowed up in sight.[21] Sight comes to faith when the criteria of the Scriptures reveal to faith its true object. Up to that time, to walk by faith is simply to "reach beyond the perceptive world."[22] Faith at this first level is an "inner sense for the invisible" analogous to the five outer senses. As such, the spiritual ear is the most strategic of the senses, but the spiritual eye and even the spiritual "palate" are not extraneous. One not only may hear God's word. He may also "taste and see" it.

The inclusion of the "palate" among these inner senses is an important clue to the extra-Biblical backgrounds of this emphasis in Wesley. The Scottish philosopher Francis Hutcheson, in applying the principles of Shaftesbury's aesthetics, adopted "taste" as a major interpretive canon, likening "the sense of beauty" to "fine taste." John Locke, first of the British empiricists, had already laid a basis for this view when he defended the position that God cannot be said to stamp his truths on the human mind, for he has furnished the mind with faculties which have the power to sense and reflect upon God's truths for themselves. Shaftesbury developed the understanding of this formal power of the human consciousness in his notion of "common sense," or *sensus communis*. The German pietist, Oetinger, son-in-law of the Bengel who inspired Wesley's *Notes on the New Testament*, was the first to translate Shaftesbury's *sensus communis* into the word "heart."[23] To appreciate the *esprit de finesse* in Wesley's use of the word "evidence," one should realize that the word "heart," the "inner sense," functions not in support of but in resistance to the mathematical sense of the Enlightenment, branded by Oetinger as the geometric mode (*mos geometricus*), and called by Pascal in the century before him "the spirit of geometry."

To appreciate the casually non-theological role of faith at this level in the eighteenth century, it is enough to know that when Wesley said this faith "presupposes nothing in us,"[24] he did not mean the senses are not ours. He meant that we experience these senses in a mode of deficiency, as the eyes sense darkness and the palate thirst. Faith supplies the defect of the physical senses "by a new set of senses in the soul."[25] Faith as evidence is itself a sense in the mode of vacuity, in the mode of reaching out for what is not possessed because it is invisible. In that regard, the spiritual senses are "nothing in us." Hence, Wesley can say that faith is not the evidence *of something*. "Faith alone, is that evidence,"[26] not in its possessing but precisely in its reaching out for and receiving what it does not possess. Abraham is "the pioneer of faith" only in that dimension of lack, where Abraham does not discern Christ as the correlate of his inner sense. Wesley never invokes the text "before Abraham was, I am," for Christological purposes. Furthermore, it should be remembered that when Wesley says of this faith that it will one day give way to sight, he is speaking from the standpoint of the inner senses which will only be satisfied by "seeing" what is "invisible" to physical senses. His principal illustration of this kind of spiritual sight is taken from Hezekiah's treatment of the bronze serpent. "*Looking* unto Jesus, the author and finisher of our faith," is a kind of "looking" which the Israelites were expected to perform in the presence of "the brazen serpent." What that "looking" sees is not a bronze serpent but the promise of God.[27]

Beyond faith as evidence is the second level called "confidence." Faith as confidence is defined by Wesley in the terms of the Articles of Religion of the Church of England. It is "a *sure trust* which a man hath, that Christ saved him, and died for him."[28] The remarkable thing about this definition is that while it is centered upon trust, which generally connotes a subjective energy, for Wesley it is faith in its most objective form. "Evidence," which connotes an objective correlate, is actually just the opposite: faith in a subjective form.[29] Yet, faith as confidence is referred to as "the faith which is *in* us."[30] Is that not subjectivism undisguised? "Evidence," while subjective, was a mode of reaching out for some reality still unappropriated. Confidence is the remedy for the blindness of evidence, for in it "God is seen."[31] Confidence is not, as evidence, a subjectivism, because in confidence, unlike evidence, faith gets its object. "Faith implies light; the light of God shining upon the soul. So far, therefore, as anyone loses this light, he for the first time loses his faith."[32] Light, and not luminous states of the soul, is crucial to faith as confidence. The essence of confidence is "seeing God."[33] But God is "seen" in the sense in which "the gospel dispensation" makes it possible to see God, in the sense that

Christ is Immanuel—God with us.[34] Faith in this sense was not given to Abraham.[35] One who moves, as the Apostle Paul designates, "from faith to faith," is one who moves from "evidence" to "confidence," from faith as the form of servanthood and pedagogy to faith as a form of sonship, from faith in general to faith in particular, "by a gradual series of still clearer and clearer promises."[36]

Faith even in this higher form, however, is not the goal of the Christian life. There is a higher form of Christian existence than the life of faith and that is the life of works, which is "faith working by love." Faith did not exist before the foundation of the world, but love did—in God, and in the angels.[37] How transitory, then, is faith by the standards of love. Faith is only the condition of or the means to works. To say, therefore, that Christ is the pioneer of faith is not to say that faith is the end of Christ's mission. Of faith it can be said that Christ "begins it in us, carries it on, and perfects it."[38] But Wesley sides repeatedly with Paul and James in their proposed extensions of Christian existence beyond faith: "Though I have all faith and have not love, I am nothing." (Paul) "By works was faith made perfect." (James) Faith is instrumental to love and "the temporary means which God has ordained to promote the end of love."[39]

This sense of the conditional and instrumental character of faith is what alarmed the Reformation-oriented churches against Wesley's preaching missions. Wesley reveals that he himself was once scrupulous about using the word "condition" with reference to faith until he discovered that "none of the reformers objected to it." It is "an innocent word."[40] What made it innocent for Wesley was the way he used it. Some criticized him for talking more about the faithfulness of man than about the faithfulness of God."[41] By his use of the term "condition," however, Wesley clearly indicates that faith is "the *only* instrument of salvation," thereby ruling out works as conditions for salvation.[42] Faith is a "downright robber," intolerable to a religious man who by his own riches expects to pass through the needle's eye into the Kingdom of God. To believe that only faith can avail for salvation seems more unreasonable to the "religious" man than even the doctrine of transubstantiation.[43] Faith being the condition of works, works can never thereafter be the condition of faith. "Faith has one energy in operation; works another; and the energy and operation of faith are before works, and *together with* them. Works do not give life to faith, but faith begets works and then is perfected by them."[44]

There may be such a thing as "naked faith," but Satan is responsible for peddling that picture of faith.[45] He is the one who sows the tares of "faith without works" among the good seed of the Gospel.[46] For to be "saved by faith" involves holiness, and faith without works is not holy.[47] Works are necessary to salvation, for without love one cannot enter into the kingdom.[48] Therefore, while Wesley refuses to concede that the works of the faithful in any way augment Christ's saving efficacy,[49] he also declines to say that behavior does not add in the least.[50] Where faith, hope, and love abide, the greatest of these will be love.

The terminological key which locks the door against works-righteousness for Wesley is his distinction between "meritorious" and "rewardable" works. Works which perfect faith are not meritorious, but they are rewardable.[51] The mistake of the antinomians and of the antiperfectionists alike is accounted for by the absence of this distinction.[52] Wesley himself failed to make that distinction prior to his Aldersgate experience, during which time he erred by seeking merit in his works. That was because, as he says, he was then living "under law."[53] But in the "new science of spiritual respiration," "the soul continually received by faith is continually rendered back by love."[54] Therefore, to say "Christ has done all" would not be "false," but it would be "ambiguous."[55] Wesley is aware of the Pauline *summa*, "the just shall live by faith" (Romans 1:17), but he is also aware that this particular slogan of the Reformation is concluded from the Old Testament report of an incident in which, when the Chaldeans attacked Jerusalem, those Israelites whose lives were saved were those who both believed in God and acted according to their beliefs.[56] When Wesley affirms reward for works he is doing so in order not to make works meritorious, but also in order to underscore man's responsibility to his faith. God, he believed, will one day reward men "in proportion to their fidelity and diligency."[57] That Wesley thinks of a day of reward is nothing to underscore, for it was a very conventional belief for his time. Even John Locke regarded it as revealed truth. Pointing to the rewardable character of works, however, is simply Wesley's way of saying to his congregations that while works are "not the cause" they are "the fruit of their acceptance with God."[58]

B. The Gospel Embraces the Law

To stem "practical antinomianism," Wesley refused to concede any "contrariety between law and gospel."[59] "Practical antinomianism" characterizes men "under grace" who indulge themselves more than they did "under law."[60] For Wesley, one is not "saved" by grace through faith unless he is performing the works of love. The "marrow" of antinomianism is its assumption that "faith supercedes holiness."[61] The Gospel, which is the good news of our salvation, embraces the law insofar as the law guides man in the fulfillment of love through works. That law, far from being antithetical to the Gospel, is called by Wesley the "evangelical law."[62]

What, then, could the Apostle Paul have meant in calling Christ "the end of the law"? Does not the preaching of the Gospel involve liberty from law as from sin and death? The only law to which the Gospel puts an end is what Wesley calls "the covenant of works." This law was based on a covenant with Adam, who was man in the image of God, and it was ordained by God for man's life.[63] Sin crippled man's capacity to live by law, as the Apostle Paul discovered, who experienced that law of life as an instrument of death. Originally "coeval with man's nature"[64] and written on man's heart, subsequent to man's fall it loses the capacity to bring life. That is why the new covenant in Christ, the covenant of righteousness, puts an end to the old covenant with Adam. The covenant of righteousness, already prefigured in Abraham,[65] does not require anything but belief. Explicit in Christ, the new covenant requires only "to believe in the Lord Jesus Christ," which belief is simply a prescription of the conditions needed for regaining the image of God. The very purpose of the righteousness of Christ is "that the righteousness of the law may be fulfilled in us."[66] Christ's righteousness supercedes the righteousness of the law; thus Christ puts an end to the law as a means of procuring righteousness.[67]

Two other kinds of law exist alongside this "covenant of works." Does Christ in any sense put an end to them? One is the ceremonial law of Old Testament times. Christ puts an end to that, and we experience the supplanting of ceremonial law as "one branch of the liberty where with Christ hath made us free."[68] The other is the law of Moses, the moral law. That law is not ended by Christ in respect of its right to man's obedience and observance. Only its condemnation and curse is ended in the Gospel. After Christ that law is still enforced, but it has no power to condemn. Ceremonial law was brought to an end in order "to bring a better righteousness," "the image of God in the inmost soul."[69] The moral law was written on the hearts. "Every part of this law must remain in force upon all mankind and in all ages."[70] Thus, in addressing the Corinthians Paul judged that laws governing the use of meat offered to idols as well as the laws in the Mosaic code governing the use of meat "are all indifferent, and have their use, though it is only for a time. . . . but the case is quite otherwise with fornication. This is not indifferent, but at all times evil."[71]

In drawing the law into the Gospel in this way Wesley is participating in the traditional Protestant classification of the uses of the law. To my knowledge he explicitly invokes the categories of "use" only once.[72] When he does, they do not resemble the customary outline of the three uses, but they do throw light on Wesley's use of the law. The law is used, according to Wesley, (1) to convict of sin, (2) to bring sinners to Christ, and (3) to "keep alive and prepare the believer for larger communion with God."

With respect to law in its third use, law is embraced in Gospel. Far from being ended by the Gospel, the law is brought to life by the Gospel as a law of kindness.[73] When Christ says he is "come to fulfill the law," he does not mean that by his perfect obedience to the law he has delivered others from the necessity of obeying it. He means that he has established it "in its fullness, in spite of all the glosses of men."[74] The Ten Commandments were a "complete rule of life and manners."[75] The commands of Christ in the Sermon on the Mount brought them back to light.[76] As such, they are "a copy of the eternal mind."[77] Legalism was the reduction of the commands of God by human glosses. For instance, the law of the tithe was "legalistic," for it specified the giving of one-tenth, or one-third, or one-half. The "evangelical law" restores the moral clarity of the Mosaic law in removing this legal calculation and concluding that one must give "all."[78] To be a "preacher of the law" in that sense ought not be a "term of reproach."[79] It is rather the conversion of the law into an "evangelical principle of action."[80]

The difference between the law as irksome and condemnatory and the law as an instrument of grace is "the new birth" for which Christ's ministry prepares. The preaching of the law on the lips of Christ is the preaching not of command which burdens, but of permission and promise. "Thou shalt love the Lord thy God" heard as a command is quite a different kind of reality when heard as permission or promise.[81] As a promise, it is Gospel. As a command, it is a curse. The commandments of Christ "are not grievous," because in him all the commands of the law are "proposed by way of promise." "Every command in holy Writ is only a covered promise" and Christ removes that veil from the law.[82] As one is accustomed to saying traditionally, "He gives what he commands." He turns the commands into a "privilege."[83] Because of Christ, "the moral law itself, though it could never pass away, yet stood on a different foundation from what it did before."[84] Christ "turns all the commands into promises" in order that we might "walk in holiness all the days of our life."[85] According to Wesley's translation of the New Testament, what Jesus says in his Sermon on the Mount in summarizing God's command is not "be ye therefore perfect" but "ye shall be perfect." Commenting on the passage he says, "How wise and gracious is this, to sum up, as it were seal, all His commandments with a promise. . . . He knew how ready our unbelief would be to cry out, This is impossible! and therefore stakes upon it all the power, truth, and faithfulness of Him to whom all things are possible."[86] In the light of this understanding of the use of the law, one can easily judge why Wesley would react to a certain antinomian with sarcasm. When the antinomian proclaimed freedom from "sin, hell, death and law," Wesley retorted stiffly, "You put the law in goodly company."[87]

C. Perfection is Possible within History

Methodists who flinch at the suggestion that they are expected to go on to perfection in this life generally invent their own connotations for the word "perfection" and therefore rule it out as inachievable. The third use of the law is intended as a rule by which

Christians can structure a life implicit in receiving grace through faith. "The gospel does not promise justification to those who continue in sin," Wesley said, commenting on Galatians 2:18. What is the alternative to continuing in sin? "Go on to perfection." (Hebrews 6:1) For, "without holiness no man shall see the Lord." Christian sight is not a matter of clear ideas but of what a man does. Holiness entails "explaining and enforcing the commands of Christ briefly comprised in the Sermon on the Mount."[88]

Does not holiness turn the Christian faith into a new law, inspiring the wretchedness of unfulfillment? The life of holiness is not so much the life of fulfillment as it is the life of progress in works of love. Holiness is not to be identified with what is "perfected" but with "perfection." One is an end. The other is a process. The perfect man is not the man who is "ready for reward" or "ready to receive the prize." The perfect man is one who is simply "fit for the race," that is, "strong in faith" as opposed to one who is not perfect, the "weak in faith."[89] Now, while it is true that faith does not begin in works because it is at the base of works, it is also true that the life of holiness, which is unabashedly the life of good works, increases faith. Works are the perfection of faith in the sense that the vigor of faith is excited by its works and increased "as the natural heat of the body" from exercise increases the body's activity.[90] It is in this sense that Wesley can consider the law as a source of nourishment, as if it were food to the believer, sustaining and increasing his spiritual strength.[91]

Christian perfection is a gift of God, being grounded in grace by faith, that is, being prepared for by God's presence in Jesus Christ. It is "the most glorious gift which God ever gave to the children of men upon earth."[92] As a gift of God it is easier to comprehend than as an expectation of man. "What is then the perfection of which man is capable while he dwells in a corruptible body?" Wesley's answer to that question is in the double command, the common term in which, as Paul pointed out, is "love." The double command, turned into a promise by God's gift in Christ, holds out the hope that in history man may love both God and his neighbor. "These contain the whole of Christian perfection."[93] For, to put it as Paul has done in Galatians, perfection is "love, joy, peace, longsuffering, gentleness, goodness, fidelity, meekness, temperance." Christian perfection is all these "knit together in one, to be united together in the soul of a believer."[94] In his sermon "On Perfection" from which these descriptions of perfection are drawn, one is told that even "if we should not attain it, the very expectation of this deliverance gives us present comfort."[95] Is this a reservation which compromises the claim to perfection as realizable in history? Not if one remembers that for Wesley perfection is a process and not a goal. When it comes to being "saved" by perfection, Wesley clearly believes it is by "hope" that we are saved.[96]

The "beauty of holiness," then, does not answer to a set of moral norms. Even the Mosaic law was not considered by Wesley to be a code of morals, although it was called "the moral law." Morality for the eighteenth century was not a legal concept but a personal concept having to do with a man's total way of life. It was closer to an aesthetic than to a legal notion. Life "under law" for Wesley as for Paul did not refer to a life in conformity to moral standards but a life burdened with the lovelessness and anxiety which personal unfulfillment brought. Correlatively, life under grace, in holiness, was not a condition of conformity where one was successfully fulfilling moral principles. Life under grace was a life in love where the most benevolent simplicity was introduced into all one's affairs. Holiness, therefore, in Wesley's doctrine of Christian perfection, is a life of truth where truth is understood to be beauty and not ideas. It is a life of energy where energy is the expression of beauty, a beauty which is neither innate (Descartes) nor derived from experience (Locke), but which more closely resembles what "belongs to the substance of the spirit" (Shaftesbury). It is, in short, a life of simplicity, characterized as "faith, humility, willingness to be taught, and freedom from all evil reasonings."[97]

II. DISTINCTIVE THEMES IN WESLEY'S THEOLOGY

Up to this point the discussion has concentrated on themes in Wesley which, however novel they may seem in the context of today's church or however peculiar they may have seemed to those who heard Wesley preach, were regarded by Wesley either as standard in the Christian tradition or as revivals of scriptural religion. From this point on the discussion will seem increasingly bizarre, because it is an effort to see how Wesley, in sharpening the focus of his major themes, has contributed suggestions which have yet fully to seize the mind of the church. These distinctive elements classify as a hermeneutics, and they are distinctive primarily for the way in which they emerge from the Wesleyan emphasis on holiness.

Hermeneutics is the science of interpretation, especially the interpretation of texts, and in the case of the theologian, particularly the text of the Bible, but involving a theory of language and of understanding. In his Preface to the *Notes on the New Testament* Wesley is most conscious of hermeneutics in his program. It is there he associates himself with Bengel's methods, discusses the sense in which human words communicate God's word, and cites Luther as Bengel had to the effect that the proper study of theology is "a grammar of the language of the Holy Spirit."[98]

The suggestions about to be proposed here will not seem so forced if one recalls how the concept of hermeneutics shifted in the very epoch in which Wesley thought and preached. With the rise of the historical consciousness which followed upon the dawn of experimental science, the concept of the science was qualified to include methodologies more congenial and distinctive to human studies, such as history, law, religion, and art. Within this development John Locke gave hermeneutics an impulse when he attempted to interpret Paul's letters on the basis of the apostle's own use of language. Inspired by Locke's effort, a Dutch Remonstrant, Wetstein, developed what Wilhelm Dilthey has called "the seed of subsequent grammatico-historical method" in his *de Interpretatione N.T.*[99] At the same time, with the development of pietism in Germany, interpretation was no longer considered complete with simply determining the meaning of a text. Application of the meaning was expected. In this epoch the view of hermeneutics as the science of the interpretation of a text thus underwent a transformation. Thereafter to interpret meant to read the text in such a way that the reader's own existence was given meaning.

In Bengel's *Gnomon*, which appeared in English in 1742, the preface expressed his principles of interpretation. Among them was the new view of *applicatio*. "I have not thought it necessary," he said, "to subjoin *Practical application, 'usus,'* as they are termed, to each chapter; for he who submits himself to the constraining influence of Divine Love in the search after Divine Truth, imbibes from the Divine Words, when he has once perceived their meaning, all things profitable for salvation as without labour, and without stimulus."[100] In England in the early part of the seventeenth century *applicatio* was already held to be one facet of the procedure for preparing oneself to hear the word of God with understanding. In the treatise of Robert Bolton, "Concerning the Word of God," which Wesley included in his *Christian Library*, Bolton comments: "No plaster can do the patient good, unless it be applied; no meat be able to do us good, be it dressed ever so curiously, unless it be eaten and digested." This is not the startling item in Bolton's discussion, however. I refer rather to the three classes of rules given for "hearing": rules governing what to do before hearing, after hearing, and "in hearing." The startling thing is that *applicatio* is included not under the rules for what to do after hearing but for what to do "in hearing." Application in hermeneutics is not something one does after he has understood. It is inseparable from the process of understanding.[101]

Now Wesley was a supernaturalist in a very traditional sense. The fact is reflected nowhere so convincingly as in his understanding of the work of the Holy Spirit in the communication of the word. Only the Holy Spirit can teach, he said. "We can do nothing."[102] "I spoke," he said of his encounter with an "unconcerned" congregation. "But it is only the voice of the Son of God which is able to wake the dead."[103] In the letter of the Scripture when read there is "no inherent power. . . . the whole power is of God."[104] God can even give understanding where there is no understanding.[105] On many occasions after preaching, Wesley reports that he washed his hands of the whole affair and absolved himself of all further responsibility for the souls of his auditors. "God answers for himself," he would say; "I am clear of their blood."[106] On one occasion, however, he began to say the same thing, then changed his course. "I am clear," he said, then interrupted himself: "No— let God judge."[107] Or, earlier, "God answered for himself to all *candid* hearers."[108]

Such moments of tentativeness toward his customary supernaturalist attitude about preaching may be evidence of his own explicit hermeneutical understanding. "Though it is God only changeth hearts," he said, "He generally doeth it by man."[109] When Wesley appeals to "the right of private judgment,"[110] he is not merely conditioned by the age of toleration. He is participating in the rise of the hermeneutical method in which human understanding and the divine word are brought into correspondence. "Concern" is thereafter said to precede "enlightenment."[111] Importance to man is thereafter held to be important.[112] Not just any kind of importance, such as importance motivated by "curiosity," would be adequate for proper understanding, although one is led to believe that an understanding begun in curiosity is more sensible than an understanding which does not even have curiosity to stimulate "the desire to know."[113]

Attention to Wesley's reflections on the attitudes of the congregations to which he has preached, as recorded in his *Journals*, would reveal a man aware of the hermeneutical implications of his responsibility. At the outset of his career he despaired of preaching to the American Indians because he found in them no desire for instruction. After Aldersgate the Holy Spirit seemed a more powerful and autonomous agent in the communication of God's message. For many years Wesley's view of how the Holy Spirit works was illustrated by the device of breaking open the Bible for a passage which would speak to the situation at hand. Two things are notable in the eventual disappearance from Wesley's *Journals* of any account of that practice. First, on one occasion he failed repeatedly to break the Bible open to a suitable text, so he cast lots instead.[114] Second, and dating almost from that lot-casting incident with its tacit exposé of his bibliomancy, Wesley began to find scriptural solutions being suggested to him from within his own interrogative situations.

To illustrate these two methods: On the day before his Aldersgate experience he records, "I opened my Testament on these words . . . 'Thou art not far from the kingdom of God'."[115] Contrast this incident: Late in his career, on the day of a shocking death by drowning, Wesley reports that the sermon preached on that occasion was from the text, "Be ye likewise ready; for ye know not the hour when the Son of Man cometh." He comments that he believes the text was "suited to the occasion."[116] Illustrations of both these procedures abound in Wesley's *Journals*, although the former preponderates in his early writings and the latter in the later writings.

As hermeneutics, one should judge the latter strategy to be method-ologically sounder, notwithstanding the crudity involved, than the former, notwithstanding its edifying content. In any case, it be-came a matter of policy with Wesley that preaching, which includes the interpretation of the text, was related for its effectiveness to the situation in which the hearer existed. "What hold can you have upon a people who neither know books, nor men; neither them-selves, nor the Bible; neither natural nor spiritual things?"[117] All hear the preaching. Some hear it in vain. When the word sent does not return empty, when the hearing ear and the understanding heart are found to be in some rapport, interpretation has occurred. Some sermons, like Italian opera, lack the capacity to awaken the soul.[118] Why did Wesley find the Scottish people the "best hearers"?[119] Why, when speaking to Dissenters, did he expect very little good to result?[120] Why were the laboring men regarded as "the most susceptible" to the Gospel and "the rich" the least?[121] Why do some scriptures "commend themselves to our conscience before others"?[122] Why are those who mourn "the absence of God" called blessed?[123] Because hearing without understanding is as futile as "eating without digesting."[124] Because "no man can be justified and not know it!"[125] Because the foundation of religion "stands on the nature of God and the nature of man, together with their mutual relations.... for it begins in a man's knowing himself.... it finishes all, by restoring the due relations between God and man."[126]

A. Holiness Augments the Hermeneutical Circle

What Wesley calls "concern," "desire," "importance to man," "mourning," and the like are known to current hermeneutics as a form of pre-understanding for the Gospel and participate in a "hermeneutical circle." Such pre-understanding is the ground in man on which the word of God, when it falls, grows up, even though it is no credit to the ground that the seed grows. The rela-tion between man's pre-understanding and God's word is a circle because the circuit of understanding is never complete where either functions in independence of the other. Pre-understanding (*Vor-verständnis*) was not unknown to Wesley. Probably it was known to him, technically, in German before it was in English, even though, as has been said, the Englishmen Locke and Shaftesbury gave the notion its earliest philosophical development. It was Oetinger, however, who gave to the experience of "presentiment" and "taste" the German translation *Vorempfindungen*.[127]

Wesley expressed the hermeneutical function of pre-sentiment or pre-understanding in two forms. One was in his general definition of faith as "evidence," a *sensus communis* in man of a spiritual sort which yearns for something invisible that it cannot itself supply. The other was in his use of the law as a schoolmaster to Christ, traditionally referred to as the *usus theologicus*. A living faith, Wesley believed, must be preceded by a sense of sin.[128] The chronology of pre-understanding seems actually quite irrelevant to Wesley's case, for it is as conceivable that one believe in Christ first as it is that one be convinced of sin first, so long as the sense of need and the sense of gratification for the need correspond.[129] The strategy of preaching the law as a preparation for the Gospel is based on the assumption that one ought not to offer Christ to sinners. Not that they do not deserve him but that they cannot discern him. Only one in a thousand is apt to be awakened by the Gospel, so that to preach the Gospel to sinners does not serve a properly hermeneutical function.[130] The model for the proper procedure is Paul's sermon at Lystra where Christ is not even mentioned. The same was the case with Paul's witness before Felix. It is true that Paul and Silas speak of Christ to the jailor, but, as Wesley comments, "He was already convinced of sin."[131] "Prior to faith" the law is preached to render men poor in spirit, giving them a knowledge of themselves.[132] When pardon is granted, the law continues to be preached as a rule for believers. There are not two laws but two uses of the one law. One who preaches Christ will necessarily preach the law because to preach Christ is "to preach all things that Christ hath spoken," which include his commands as well as his promises.[133] But God unites law and Gospel in the preaching of Jesus. Therefore in the preaching of the church, what God hath joined let not the preacher put asunder, "otherwise he cannot be said to preach the whole gospel."[134]

The hermeneutical circle, in which man's concerned questions are addressed by God's word, is strikingly illustrated in Wesley's view of conscience. Four distinct operations of the conscience, all hermeneutical in significance, come to play in Wesley's view.

First, conscience relates to pre-understanding. Here the *sensus communis* of Shaftesbury foreshadows Wesley's "conscience." In every man there is a "common humanity," Wesley affirmed.[135] In his account of Hutcheson's *Essay on the Passions* Wesley explains what this common humanity means. It embraces a *public sense*, which is sensitive to the misery of the fellow man, and a *moral sense*, which endorses benevolence and condemns cruelty both in others and in one's self. Both these senses were included by Hutcheson, following Shaftesbury, in the human conscience.[136] Conscience as an instrument of understanding is a form of pre-understanding insofar as it is a capacity for "knowing with another." That is, it presupposes a reality beyond itself. Its understanding (*scientia*) has a social (*con-*) character.[137]

Second, conscience relates to holiness. As has been pointed out, Oetinger had translated Shaftesbury's *sensus communis* as "heart," and Wesley in that tradition made the heart the central agent of holiness. Holiness is loving God and neighbor "with the whole heart," that is, with "all the united powers of the soul in their utmost vigor."[138] When "our heart condemns us," what is meant, said Wesley, is "our own conscience."[139]

Third, conscience relates to language. "Knowing with another," which is how Wesley defines *con-scientia*, takes place for the Christian in correlation with the written word of God.[140] Conscience is man's "agreement" with God's word. It can be said to function when it is "duly enlightened by the word and spirit of God, and comparing all our thoughts, words, and works with that word, pronounce that they agree therewith."[141] The law condemns the conscience. But the conscience finds the word of Christ "agreeable."

Fourth, conscience relates to witness, when that witness or confession (ὁμολογία) is the agreement (ὁμο-) of God's word with man's word (hence, ὁμολογία, or *con-scientia*). "Whoever shall confess me," said Jesus, "shall acknowledge me publicly." One whose conscience will be "void of offence" must be oriented outward, as would be expected of the theology of "faith that worketh by love." For conscience pertains to "the outward life," simultaneously directed "toward God and man."[142] The content of that outward confession will be obedience to the commandments of God and faithfulness to his whole doctrine.[143] When Wesley comments on Romans 10:9 concerning confession with the mouth and belief in the heart, he interprets "with the heart" to mean "not the under-standing alone." While this interpretation does include understand-ing in the connotation of "heart," it also tends to diminish the con-notation, raising doubt as to whether what I am calling attention to in Wesley's view of conscience is consistently appealed to by him. While I would not claim so, it is nevertheless important to observe that in his *Notes* on Revelation 2:23, "hearts" is equated with "thoughts."[144]

The really curious element in Wesley's position, however, is not the fairly standard view of the hermeneutical circle. The start-ling thing is how his understanding of the Christian faith as a life of holiness seems to call for an augmentation of the pre-understand-ing supplied by the law in its *usus theologicus* with another form of pre-understanding suitable to the Christian in his life of "faith working by love." It is as if the circular strategy of hermeneutics were pushed by Wesley into a cyclical strategy. The pre-under-standing of man before faith, which the preaching of the law is designed to clarify, operates at a quite different level of understand-ing from the pre-understanding of the Christian man. Actually, a spiraling transcendence is what is meant by hermeneutical circle, for questions which are open to answers, as the circle proposes, stand to be transformed by the answers. I specify cyclical rather than circular here to accentuate this factor in the hermeneutical circle for Wesley in which attention is being called more to the answer than to the question. A man who is grasped by God's grace is asking about what he must do to go on to perfection. He is, as Wesley describes him, "groaning for full redemption,"[145] desiring to "endure to the end,"[146] "agonizing to be altogether Christian,"[147] "now more ashamed of (his) best duties than before of (his) worst sins,"[148] "zealous to attain the whole mind of Christ."[149] In sum, unlike the pre-faith pre-understanding, the holiness pre-understand-ing is the dimension of expectation which keeps believers from growing cold. Its role as pre-understanding for the newer and higher stage of the Christian life is reinforced by Wesley in his refusal to concede that perfection is only realizable at death, beyond history. "I say an hourly expectation; for to expect it at death, or sometime hence, is much the same as not expecting it at all."[150]

The man who lives "under law" lives under a sense of con-demnation and has the pre-understanding appropriate to that mode of existence. The man who lives "under grace" is "going on to perfection" and has the pre-understanding appropriate to that mode. The former is characterized more by concerns oriented to fear and frustration, the latter to concerns oriented to love and exhilaration. Wesley cites John Locke as asking, "What moves desire?" Locke's answer is twofold in much the same sense in which Wesley's hermeneutical pre-understanding is twofold. Desire is moved both by "uneasiness" and by "happiness." These two *Vorempfindungen* correspond almost precisely to Wesley's existence "under law" and "existence under grace" or to his uses of the law as *usus theologicus* and *tertius usus*.[151]

To the heart whose pre-understanding has been elevated from "uneasiness" to "happiness" our Lord must speak a second time.[152] The content of his speech will be the same as before: the Gospel with its law. But this time the law will sound different. Even though it is the same law,[153] the preacher's use of it will be different, because the hearer's pre-understanding will be different. The manner of preaching the law to "those pressing on to the mark," holding up the love of Christ, will surely differ from the manner of preaching to the "careless."[154] One need never preach to the accepted the terrors of God, such as the law before faith inspires. "Love is then the strongest of all motives, . . . always drawing, rather than driving."[155]

B. Holiness is a Type of Demythologizing

A science of hermeneutics is not exhausted in the exercise of interpreting human existence in the light of a text. Also provided in hermeneutics is a critical procedure for evaluating a text. No one is surprised to see Wesley making the customary orthodox statements about the inspiration of the text and its authority for faith. To find him setting up a basis upon which the text can be criticized, notwithstanding its authority, is less usual, however.

What basis can a man find for criticizing God's word? Surely nothing outside God's word will qualify. However, if the word of God is essentially and fundamentally concerned with "holiness," then anything in the text which deviates from that concern is subject to judgment. The text is allowed to judge itself. What is being alluded to here are not the more patent canons of interpretation which Wesley learned from Bengel. It is true, as he said, that one must let a text derive its meaning from its context, and it is true that if texts seem to contradict each other, one must be patient in determining whether the larger context helps to resolve that contradiction. What is being contended for by Wesley beyond that is that not every statement in the Bible has the same status for faith.

References to faith in the New Testament, for instance, need not all be harmonized, for not all the forms of faith referred to are equally valid. The Gospel talks of a faith that removes mountains. (Matthew 17:20) Hankering for that faith is openly criticized by Wesley, not because he has some kind of modernized soft-pedaling of what is possible with God, but because he has discerned the New Testament faith to be the "faith which worketh by love." That faith is the "saving" faith. The faith which removes mountains has been demonstrated by devils. "It is only a supernatural persuasion given a man, that God will work thus by him at that hour. Now, 'though I have all' this faith, so as to remove mountains, yet, if I have not the 'faith which worketh by love,' I am nothing."[156]

One can refer to this sort of practice as demythologizing, without too great a risk of *vaticinium ex eventu*, because demythologizing is a form of hermeneutic in which the text is criticized by the text in order to let the kerygmatic concern of the text manifest itself to human understanding. As in present day demythologizing, Wesley's critique takes the form of reinterpretation rather than annihilation of the passages which are, on the surface, deficient in scriptural holiness. To cite another similarity, the deficient passages are usually those which rely excessively on the world view presuppositions of the first century. As has been acknowledged several times, notwithstanding his avowed adoption of the Copernican world view and his avid pursuit of an experimental knowledge of nature, Wesley seems to be completely at home in the first-century world view. That fact makes it all the clearer that his few efforts to reinterpret are not based on some apologetic passion to appeal to a scientific age or to retreat in the face of advancing science, although he has said that Methodism desires to be as "free from superstition as from heresy."[157] He is mainly eager to let the Biblical message become important to human concerns without Biblical impediments. That classifies as hermeneutics rather than apologetics. In a sermon on a text in Mark 9:38, 39 having to do with "casting out devils," he affirms that "every minister of Christ does cast them out." How? By bringing sinners to repentance, which is both an inward and outward change in man. "This is, in a sound sense, to cast out devils." And how does repentance come about? "This change was wrought by his hearing this man preach."[158]

In another sermon, "The Signs of the Times," the customary messianic signs are listed: the deaf hear, the lame walk, and lepers are cleansed. Now Wesley is one who repeatedly insists that the text be allowed to manifest its "plain meaning." Plain meaning is a prohibition against indulging in imaginative play with the text[159] and encouragement to remain faithful to the childlike simplicity and openness of the text.[160] One might even hazard calling attention to Wesley's use of the word "historical" as a synonym or, at least, rhetorical parallel for "plain." In his note on "the foolishness of preaching" he comments, "*we* go on to *preach*, in a plain and historical, not rhetorical or philosophical, manner."[161] It is surely no accident that John Locke had used the identical parallelism in the prior century, "the historical, plain method," and that Voltaire, the first historian in the modern sense, expressed approval.

To return to the sermon on "The Signs of the Times," how does Wesley illustrate his historical method, his method of plain interpretation? The deaf who hear are those who were deaf to the outward and inward call of God. The lame who walk are now running the race that is set before them. The lepers who are healed are those inflicted with "the deadly leprosy of sin."[162]

In his sermon "On the Trinity" he raised the question about the mystery of the incarnation, about how the word was made flesh. He concludes that "there is no mystery in it." The mystery does not inhere in the "how," the "manner" of the incarnation. "I know nothing about it; I believe nothing about it; it is no more the object of my faith, than it is of my understanding. . . . I believe just so much as God has revealed, and no more."[163]

In his treatise "A Farther Appeal to Men of Reason and Religion," Wesley emphasizes that the miracles alleged to have occurred in the apostolic age are no longer required of the church to perform. They were "outward miracles." The church is called to perform the "inward miracle."[164] The very desire for miracle is the sign not of piety but of infidelity.[165] Miracles can be wrought in support of falsehood, so ambiguous are they; whereas "the proper topics of scripture and reason" are sufficient without miracle, but "miracles without these are not."[166]

In the same treatise the prospect of salvation from heaven and hell is raised, only to be countered by the assertion that the Christian salvation is concerned with the present restoration of the soul to health. "Holiness . . . is the thing itself."[167] "Myself am hell," he later said,[168] and holiness delivers one from himself. Earlier in the same series he bypassed another question about the future in order to focus upon the present. "I will not now shock the easiness of your temper by talking about a future state; but suffer me to ask you a question about present things. Are you now happy?"[169]

C. Holiness Secularizes the World

The hermeneutics of holiness is a method of interpretation which relates to the Biblical text in such a way that the text interprets the reader, effecting a significant change in his situation. Just because the language of holiness sounds like the language of piety and religiousness does not mean that holiness needs to support a species of otherworldliness. In practice it has tended to do just that. Wesley himself is unblushing in his otherworldliness. But otherworldliness was the language of almost all churchmen in the eighteenth century. That is why it is illuminating to see the extent to which, when the Bible is allowed to express its intention, the result for the world is transforming. The world is brought to maturity. From the faith of a servant the believers are elevated to the faith of a son.[170] Sonship in the New Testament faith involves responsibility for God's world.

One who understands existence in the light of scriptural holiness anticipates "this strange sight; a Christian world." The time will come, said Wesley, when "Christianity will prevail over all and cover the earth."[171] Wesley's several and violent repudiations of Constantinian Christianity[172] are ample evidence that he had nothing like that kind of acculturation in mind. In fact, the Caesaropapism of the Church of England in which he capitulated makes him Christianly naive in respect of the worldly involvements of the Christian movement. That fact is borne out by his failure in all his discussion of the uses of the law to embrace or even refer to the *usus politicus*. Chiliasm would be closer to his intention, rejoicing in the sign of "God's arising to maintain his own cause, and set up his kingdom over the earth."[173] Possibly he even dreamed of some kind of utopian world brought about by widespread change of men's hearts. He showed he was capable of that naiveté, for instance, when he deplored the need for prisons in Christendom.[174]

Actually, the extent to which Wesley saw that the holiness interpretation of the Bible called for a new worldliness is so negligible that it is hazardous even to attempt such a case on his behalf. The major mistake in his view of holiness was in requiring what could never be carried off either empirically or exegetically. He assumed that a man who loved God and his neighbor with his whole heart, which is the central definition of holiness, would and could show it in a way that would distinguish him from other men. Ever since that position was expressed it has been under attack for its built-in, self-inconsistent temptation to pride. The more formidable objection, one would think, would be its sheer misapprehension of the Christian view.

Prior to faith the Wesleyan preacher used the law as a schoolmaster to Christ, that is, as a means of quickening a pre-understanding for the Gospel. The result was the raising of the question, "Why can't I do what I ought?" For those in faith, his hermeneutical circle was spiraled into a secondary level where a new question was raised: "What do ye more than others?" By Wesley's own account this message was branded "a damnable doctrine,"[175] presumably because it violated the Protestant principle of justification by faith alone, which it did not, as has been shown. Nor was it damnable for requiring Christians to exteriorize what is in the first place an interior reality, although that view has merit. It is damnable because it has miscalculated the extent to which human history, both within and without the Christian cause, has arrived at the capacity to assume responsibility for the world, loving one's neighbor and manifesting fruits indistinguishable from the fruits of the spirit. In requiring the Christian to do what distinguishes him from the world, Wesley put himself in the graceless position of depreciating the very world which was assuming its responsibility without explicit faith. As long as Wesley was working with acknowledged drunks, thieves, and adulterers, holiness on his terms had an appeal. With responsible citizens he tended to invent distinctions in order to fortify his case. One cannot be a true friend, he claimed, if he is false to God.[176] When he visited the Netherlands for the first time, he seemed perplexed to discover that "inexpressible innocence" among Dutch girls was virtually a national trait.[177] Occasionally in his contacts with Christian congregations he would confess to his diary that he preferred an "honest heathen" to a Christian. Then he would repent, adding that while it is true that the "honest heathen" would condemn gluttony and drunkenness, would he condemn "a regular, reputable kind of sensuality, an elegant epicurism?"[178]

The least attractive aspect of the Wesleyan view is the way in which he persistently depreciates the world. When he is tempted to admire the poise and success of a British statesman, he interrupts his reverie to say, "What is a Lord but a sinner born to die?"[179] In a moment in which he seems thoroughly to relish the beauty of the Irish landscape, he checks himself by saying, "The eye is not satisfied with seeing till it see God."[180] Toward his seventieth year he turns his cynicism upon his "oldest acquaintance": "He is the greatest genius in little things, that ever fell under my notice. . . . I really believe, were he seriously to set about it, he could invent the best mousetrap that ever was in the world."[181] When young people fall in love, he insinuates that the Holy Spirit has left them.[182] When he witnesses the talents of a blind artisan, he retorts, "What is he better for all this if without God in the world?"[183] Strolling through a temple garden with its oriental images, he murmers, "Images of devils! . . . Nudities!"[184] Beholding the benevolence between people on every hand, he responds, "Benevolence has no virtue except it proceed from the love of God!"[185] He applauds the story of the parent who explains to his child his fondness toward him by saying, "It is God that makes me love you."[186] Observing the King of England donning his robes for an appearance in the House of Lords, he asks himself, "Is this all the world can give even to a King? . . . an huge heap of borrowed hair, with a few plates of gold and glittering stones upon his head! Alas, what a bauble is human greatness! And even this will not endure."[187] It is true that Wesley's main text for this attitude was, "What doth it profit a man if he gain the whole world and lose his own soul?" But it is also true that his uncompromising line, "Let nothing satisfy thee but the power of godliness," with its corollary "Canst thou hope to dig happiness out of the earth?"[188] played into the hands of such an unrelieved cynicism that it no longer seemed odd to him why a man should prefer death to life in the world.[189]

Consistency in this position made Wesley reluctant to concede any joy in life apart from holiness. His own joylessness is uninspiring. He could rarely enjoy the company of friends because of his compulsion to go out and preach.[190] He was uncomfortable in the presence of genteel people because he had only one subject of conversation.[191] When placed next to the mayor at a municipal gathering, he could only punish himself with the injunction that he must not desire honor but fear it.[192] "I am to be a wanderer upon the earth," he believed.[193]

At the outset of his ministry Wesley ruled out joy as a fruit of faith in the face of the obvious Biblical inclusion of it.[194] Later he hesitantly endorsed it,[195] although "the noisy joy of the people in the streets did not agree with me," he admitted.[196] In his developed position he finally regarded joy—or happiness—as "a criterion of the love of God."[197] "He who is unhappy is not a Christian," he ultimately said.[198] How then shall one account for the evident good fun in the world around one, notwithstanding its apparent indifference to Christian faith? They are only "merry," Wesley explained, introducing one of his fine terminological distinctions. Christians are "happy."[199]

There might be some possibility of explaining this joylessness in the world from the aesthetic of Shaftesbury, which surely influenced Wesley if only indirectly. Shaftesbury held the position that art was not a process of enjoyment but a process of formation and creativity. Unfortunately, however, there is too much evidence in Wesley to show that creativity in the world was not for him the alternative to joy. The deprivations of his world were not an invitation to forming it anew but reminders of a world to come.[200] "The sole end of life" was to prepare for eternity, to "know, and love, and enjoy, and serve his great Creator to all eternity."[201] One could observe that this statement was made when Wesley was aged eighty-five, therefore pardonably otherworldly. Wesley himself records an accusation against his view. It was said that he sponsored a religion which cannot be preached without interrupting "the common duties of life."[202] That, indeed, was the ground for major attacks upon Wesley's field preaching. Laborers were attracted away from their work by his meetings, at a time when the national safety may have depended on the productivity of its labor force. In one account Wesley is censorious toward a "gentleman" who dispersed the people at one of his meetings by telling them to "get home and mind their business," which he meant quite commercially.[203] Wesley unwittingly testifies against himself on another preaching occasion in describing his victory over this kind of worldliness: "There was no buying or selling until I concluded."[204]

In the face of this evident and conventional otherworldliness, what is striking in Wesley are the scattered signs of a kind of Christian worldliness. His intention is not really otherworldliness but attack upon the corruption of the world as it is. Worldliness is defined by him as "loving the world," where that love competes with the love of God.[205] There is no final question about the usefulness of the world but only about how, when one seeks the ultimate source of his happiness there, the world becomes an idol.[206] By nature—sinful nature, that is—man loves the world and worships the creature.[207] That is why the big question at the last judgment will be, "How did you *use* your worldly goods?"[208] It is fairly clear that this kind of worldliness, which idolizes the world, weakens the chances for a holiness which is oriented to the love of God and not to the love of the world.[209] The question being raised here is the same question Wesley himself once raised: "Would not one who was . . . sanctified be incapable of worldly business?" The answer Wesley gave: "He would be far more capable of it than ever, as going through all without distraction." Question: "Would he be capable of marriage?" Answer: "Why should he not?"[210]

Which is to say, the problem is the same, and so is the solution: when you buy, you will hold what you possess as if not possessing, when you marry, as if not married. Christian worldliness removes the distraction of idolatry and thus liberates a man to assume responsibility for the world. Without that liberation, one could turn the world into an idol to which he felt responsible, thus losing his capacity to be responsible for it. For Wesley the ὡς μὴ of I Corinthians 7 means we are "only stewards, not proprietors." The interpretation is not based on the implicit Judaistic apocalyptic of the Pauline passage on the perishability of the world by contrast to the eternity, the durability of God.[211]

How, then, can you tell a business man who is a Christian from one who is not; a married man who is a Christian from one who is not? After undergoing this dialectic, it is no longer so easy for Wesley to rebuke and discipline his religious societies, as was the Methodist practice. He once admitted that he was unable to distinguish the good from the bad in his societies without the help of informers.[212] He provided long descriptions of the empirical, observable traits of those who live under the covenant of works and those who live under the covenant of grace, but the lists were almost indistinguishable.[213] Noting this, he agreed that the difference was not to be found in the visibility but in the God-relation, in "the whole soul now sensible to God."[214]

Odd how on his voyage to America Wesley made so much about the freedom of the Moravians from fear of storms at sea but had nothing to say for the sailors who "believed they were in no danger."[215] In his American ministry Wesley was impressed with the integrity, though not with the industry, of the Indians. This raised with him the question, "What has Christianity that the Indians haven't?" He mainly concluded, "the answer to unemployment!"[216] But he made during his lifetime many more theologically illumined concessions to worldliness. On attending a drama of Terence, he observed appreciatively, "Oh how do these heathens shame us!"[217] On hearing of the plundering of the colonies by the British, he observed that the heathen are more just.[218] "Who shall convert the English into honest heathen!" was more than once his cry.[219] After continuous doubt over the likelihood of the genteel or rich entering the kingdom, Wesley finally conceded that it was "possible with God to raise a lady and a saint in one person."[220] He once quoted a business man as saying, "In pursuit of my business I have as full communion with God as if I was kneeling alone at the altar."[221] In his celebrated sermon on "The Use of Money" he acknowledged that "the children of this world are wiser in their generation than the children of light" (Luke 16:8), and extracted from this lesson "that first and great rule of Christian wisdom, with respect to money, 'Gain all you can'."[222]

Why then did Wesley feel it necessary to contend against Hutcheson when the Scottish philosopher advanced the view that God is not the necessary foundation of human virtue, in fact, that no virtue at all is involved if one does his works for reward?[223] Wesley answered, because "it is a plausible way of thrusting God out of the world he has made. They can do business without him."[224]

But why is that really Wesley's final answer? Is it not rather the case that the virtue of the "honest heathen," his capacity to assume responsibility for the world, is a kind of secular fulfillment of the promise that "the meek shall inherit the earth?"[225] Why is not "the honest heathen's" evident capacity to subdue the earth without reference to the supernatural devices of more superstitious religions, and more superstitious times in Christian history, a new pre-understanding for the gospel of holiness? Not that life now conforms in all details to Wesley's description of what "the Christian world" will be when "scriptural Christianity" has filled the land,[226] and not that the new task of Christianity is to announce and identify that Christian world, but that the works of love as they are being done in the world inside and outside of the church are not to be depreciated as alien to the Christian intention, even though they are not avowedly oriented to the Christian God, but rather to be recruited for discipleship under God.

The question raised by the pre-understanding of a holiness that is mature enough to embrace worldliness is then no longer, "What do we more than others?" It is simply, "How long can we love our neighbors without bringing that love under subjection to the love of God?" Responsibility for the world can easily become responsibility to the world, for to "love the world" is, as Wesley said, "an almost insuperable temptation." Or, to say it in the way he did, more rigorously, "From Atheism there is an easy transition to idolatry; from the worship of no god to the worship of false gods."[227] Holiness, without disparaging the world, is committed to orienting the world to God in order not to turn the world into the very idol, exclusive devotion to which obstructs the sense of responsibility for it.

In this understanding the pre-understanding of the law as *usus theologicus* would give way and the hermeneutical circle would be restored at the new level to which it had spiraled through holiness. A man to whom responsibility for the world comes naturally is as immune to the condemnation of the law as Wesley found the wife of William Penn to be.[228] Why any longer classify the responsible man of the world with the Pharisee who had "the form of religion but not its power"? The case of the Pharisee had to do with his efforts to justify himself in the eyes of God by ceremonial and moral practices which had lost their capacity to mediate God's power.

The modern man, already in Wesley's time, is no longer religious in form. In his newfound secular freedom he can be responsible for the world without exploiting the world on behalf of his own salvation. One ought not, therefore, expect to succeed in subjecting modern man to the dialectic of a law which is contrived to produce repentance, if the religious dynamics of the law have been eliminated.

Wesley's holiness pre-understanding, "What do ye more than others?", when stripped of its futile implications of empirical comparison, would sound like this: "How shall we assume responsibility for the world without turning it into a new object of devotion?" and the Gospel answer would be, "Ye shall be perfect!", which is to say, "Love the Lord thy God with all thy heart, and thy neighbor," meaning, the new law of life which is a word of promise and permission: "Receive the world from God!"

NINE

Jesus of Nazareth
and the Word of Faith

The appearance of Jesus of Nazareth in human history has radically called in question the form which man's existence tends to take in the world. Everything in the apostolic testimony to his life and work, from his humblest acts to his climactic resurrection, witnesses to a single theme: God has chosen Jesus of Nazareth as the one in whom he calls the world to obedience. By virtue of that call the new age has come, the age in which men may live in the world with reference to God and not with reference to the world. Sin, death, the devil, and all other threats of meaninglessness which the world poses are overcome by the dramatic obedience of Jesus who endures death to claim the world for God.

Why God would do this is a mystery. Why God would join his purpose for mankind with Jesus of Nazareth is a secret which the Christian faith continues to conceal successfully under the vocabulary of love. How Christians believe that this is what Jesus is about, however, is no mystery. Jesus is there, as any datum of history is there, bidding to animate existence with the meaning intended in his occurrence. A man may possess Christ's eventfulness as he possesses any datum of history, through the witness of a faithful community. There is one important respect, however, in which the history of Jesus differs from all other events. Jesus of Nazareth is the one in whom God has chosen to call history to obedience to himself. Therefore, ultimate meaning can now be found in history there. How a man can bring himself to think such a thing and even to live where he thinks is the story of how one becomes a Christian. Becoming a Christian is a possibility existing somewhere between the irreducible mystery of God's selective love and the aggressive unmasking of the enigmas which parade in history in the absence of that mystery.

I

The history of Jesus of Nazareth reveals that Jesus conducts the struggle for his vocation at three levels. First, as the one in whom God is calling the world to obedience, he eats and drinks with publicans and sinners, washes the feet of the disciples, and at last empties himself in death on the cross. These events interpret each other. They mean that Jesus chose to obey God's call to act on God's behalf. On God's behalf he extended mercy to sinners. Apart from that reconciling act, life in the world has promised nothing for sinners but a drama of flight from the infernal flatness of "the wrath to come."

Second, Jesus stands against all organized attempts to thwart the continued disclosure of God's call to obedience. How is it Jesus acts with mercy towards sinners yet with severity toward the religious? The answer lies in his single-mindedness. To preach himself as the one in whom God is calling the world to obedience requires him at one and the same time to embrace the sinner with mercy and to annihilate with judgment all calculated resistance to the coming of this new age.

Third, Jesus decides what warrant there is for a carpenter and rabbi to act for God. The parable of the pearl of great price, the reading of Isaiah 61 in the synagogue with his own epilogue of self-identification, the temptations in the wilderness, the confession of Peter at Caesarea Philippi, the hesitation in the Garden of Gethsemane and eventual resoluteness concerning death—all interpret each other. That is to say, Jesus had no built-in certainty about his vocation. Spiritual things being spiritually discerned, his vocation occurred in freedom, without coercion by the evident. Albert Camus has said, "Between history and the eternal I have chosen history because I like certainties." That is one way to resolve the ambiguity of vocation. Jesus, however, surrendered certainty in the world for the uncertain pearl of obedience to God's call. Christians have sometimes believed that the resurrection is God's vindication of Jesus' vocation, as if the church now possessed a certainty not permitted to Jesus himself. However, one who takes up the ministry which the resurrected Jesus has made the ministry of the church does so at the peril of affectation bordering on the histrionic if he does so without passing through to personal history of temptation, Gethsemane, and cross. It is now possible to understand as a Christian that the resurrection is for the church what the cross was for Jesus—the risk of faith, the confidence that God is exalted in Christ's obedience to his mission to call the world to obedience. The reason faith is a risk is not that, unlike nature, it is unverifiable, but that in faith *all* forms of worldly security are surrendered in exchange for the righteousness of God. The Christian dies with Christ—yielding up his own claims—in order to rise with Christ in the new life of righteousness which is based upon trust in God alone. The parable of the pearl of great price was Jesus' rationale to his disciples for adopting the call of God as the basis of his mission. The same parable becomes the church's rationale for making Jesus of Nazareth the Lord of our history, the beginning of the new age.

The status of Jesus in history does not suffer from the fact that he knows himself as the Christ only in the risk of faith, or that we know him as the Christ only in trust. It is to be expected that an event which terminates the old and inaugurates the new would have no appeal outside the framework which its very occurrence creates. Initiatory events are impenetrable to customary human tests. The reason for that is not to be found in the fact that the human wits are weak or even aberrant. Such events resist examination because they are the source of the very capacity to know them. "God was in Christ reconciling the world unto himself." The meaning of that *credo* is that in Jesus of Nazareth "the old has passed away" and "the new has come." It is an affirmation of faith, however, precisely because one who stands in the old has no basis for evaluating the new. "The old" is not simply a condition of chronological lag. "The old," as Calvin said, are "the things that have not been formed anew by the spirit of God." The Christ event is God's call to adopt obedience to him as the form of one's existence. Where that call is not heard, there is oldness, which cannot hear. Where it is heard, there is the eternal youthfulness of the new age, expressing itself in a vigor which it confesses to receive from beyond itself.

That is not to say there is no oldness in the new age. It may be there, as Karl Barth has said, to remind us that the new has *made* it old. In any case, since Jesus' time, oldness is defined from the vantage point of the new age of his appearing. Christians are not preoccupied, therefore, with the problem of how to know such an initiatory event, but with the mystery of how the new age arrives when they are faithful in their witness to what Jesus is about. The event of Jesus of Nazareth is a *creatio ex nihilo*. This structure is not without parallels in pre-Christian history. God created the world out of nothing. He led Israel out of the nothingness of Egypt and created life in Canaan out of life in the desert. Just as he constituted Jesus of Nazareth as the Christ *ex virgine*, so through the same Jesus he created the new age of freedom in obedience to God out of the old age of bondage to the world. The appearance of Jesus of Nazareth is not a genetic consequence of what has gone before but an event *de novo*, a new beginning for God's authority over life.

The Biblical view of time is of enormous importance for an appreciation of the cruciality of Jesus of Nazareth in founding the new age. Time is a neutral reality which derives its character from what qualifies it. Small children sense this. Let a child ask his mother, "What time is it?" The mother may answer, "Eight o'clock." Or she may say, "Bedtime!" The response to the former will be vacant; to the latter, restive. Clock and calendar qualify time in the most innocuous way. But to know what time is *for*, to know, for instance, that there is a time for marrying, and a time for dying, is to know that moments of time derive their substance not from calibration but from celebration, from meanings which qualify moments, as salt qualifies a dish (Gogarten).

A Christian is a man whose time is qualified by the advent of Jesus of Nazareth who acts on God's behalf and by that act calls the world to obedience to God. To say the world is called to obedience to God is to say man is invoked to give the God-relation and not the world-relation priority as the source of his time. Therefore, there is more pathos than comedy in the Milles sculpture unveiled in Kansas City several years ago. A little angel is insinuated into a very terrestrial scene, and on his wrist there is a watch. But as the Japanese theologian Kumano is fond of saying, there are no watches in heaven. Presumably in heaven the presence of God is the sole qualification of time. On earth we violate the soleness of God by compromises with the compositeness of chronological time. The new age, which is on earth, is nevertheless the age in which the savor of the God-relation is given preeminence. When Jesus says to the thief on the cross, *"This day* shalt thou be with me in paradise," he is not specifying a chronometric interval. "This day" indicates "the day of the Lord," the eschatological measure, the interval in which the call of God in Christ becomes the basis for life in the world. That is the time of the new age of which Jesus of Nazareth, by acting among us on God's behalf, is the source.

II

In Christendom today Mary is popularly called "mother of God." World Council Protestants officially confess "Jesus is God." Under such conditions it is not easy to recall that Jesus was provocative in his day because he was a man. When he said to publicans and sinners, "Your sins are forgiven," his spectators marvelled. "We have seen strange things (*paradoxa*) today!" (Luke 5:26) This man did what was expected only of God. Stubborn preoccupation with Jesus' thoroughly terrestrial antecedents, which is Ebionism, at first tended to neutralize the paradox. " 'Is not this the carpenter's son? . . . Where then did this man get all this?' . . . And he did not do mighty works there, because of their unbelief." (Matt. 13:55-58) Somewhat later the suggestion that Jesus was actually God threatened to erode the paradox in the opposite direction. One thinks of Ignatius and of gnostic docetism.

The church, however, has officially avoided calling Jesus either God or man. Christians who enjoy their oneness with the whole church may therefore confess their faith without taking either line, without either Ebionism or docetism. They may identify Jesus according to the standard formula of Chalcedon which says he is "truly God and truly man, without separation or confusion." This foliation of ecclesiastical metaphysics in fifth-century Christendom has its root in the consternation of first-century Palestinians. They knew Jesus as a man, yet he affected them with a kind of godliness.

Jesus' evident humanity mystified his observers because the intention of his existence was not evidently human. While his humanity was fully as human as anyone else's, it was so with quite a different significance. In Jesus' case, the humanity subsisted by virtue of God's word. That means Jesus had his *raison d'etre* in his vocation as word of God. Early Protestant theologians chose to document this truth with one verse in particular: "There is one God, and there is one mediator between God and men, *the man Christ Jesus.*" (1 Tim. 2:5) This passage meant to them that the personality of "the man Christ Jesus" is not comprehensible in itself (*anhypostasia*) but in the word of God which he mediates (*enhypostasia*). To behold Jesus, therefore, is not to understand him as a man, nor as a God, nor even as a man in the presence of God. To behold Jesus is to understand oneself as a man in the presence of God. The theology of the Gospel of John is the most familiar exposition of that theme. Jesus is the word of God become flesh. To discern him is to discern God. To hear him is to hear God. He and the father are one in an auditory moment.

The "more historical" theology of the synoptic gospels expresses the same meaning. The synoptics are called "more historical" than the Fourth Gospel because it is now fairly well established that the self-understanding of Jesus which is recorded there originated with Jesus and not in the post-resurrection faith of his followers. *He* is the father of the prodigal son, and *he* is the sower of the seed. *He* is the light which his hearers must realize cannot remain under a bushel, for he is the light of the world, the light that must light every man who comes into the world. *He* is also the seed (cf. John 12:24) that sprouts and grows, one knows not how. He is the importunate widow whose undeviating petition brings God's kingdom into the present. Through this testimony to himself, Jesus made it known that he had the authority to speak and act for God. When he spoke, sinners were forgiven and God's rule began to germinate. Because of him men may now "sleep and rise night and day" (Mark 4:27) with no more care than the lilies of the field and the birds of the air. That, then, is the evangelical scandal. Not the metaphysical scandal of how one person can be in two natures, but the historical scandal of how a carpenter can substitute for God. When Jesus spoke of himself he said the things that pertain to God. The scandal is obverted when one emphasizes Jesus' role as substitute for man in the presence of God. In the "more historical" faith of the New Testament he is mainly substitute for God in the presence of man.

This singular event is known to theology today as a "speech event." The formulation reflects the primitive Christian understanding of Jesus as a word-become-flesh event as well as Jesus' understanding of himself as a verily-I-say-unto-you event. By "speech event" is not meant a verbal pointing to some otherwise dumb objective occurrence nor even an event from which words can be abstracted as surrogates for the event. A speech event is a mode of existence inherently verbal. As an event it radiates its own interpretation because in that existence acts and words fuse in such a way as to precipitate and constitute meaningful events. Hence, Jesus believed the rule of God would arrive because he announces it. When he announces it, it arrives. When it arrives, its essence is that Jesus is "Lord," that is, the speech which brings the rule of God to pass.

A speech event is a form of history which is true in virtue of human participation in it. That is, it is an event in which a man is addressed and which therefore remains incomplete without the human reply, as questions are incomplete without answers or an invocation without a response. One exists in such an event more truly if his relation to it is expressed as denial than if he were affirming it from the outside, from a position of neutrality. As the New Testament message everywhere seems to say, speech events require one's yea to be yea and one's nay to be nay. In this case coldness is closer to the truth than lukewarmness. One who calls Jesus "Lord" simply does not know him if he is not acting upon his commands. Here is a truth that those who obey shall know and a word that is fulfilled in one's *hearing*. (Luke 4:21) The communication of Jesus by the Holy Spirit will occur in the faithful as his conception did in the Virgin, through the ear.

Because Jesus is a speech event, the logic by which one thinks about him is very precise. When Jesus speaks on God's behalf he employs forms of speech not easily assimilated to nondialogical logics. For Jesus' most distinctive cases are vocative and his moods imperative. "O Jerusalem!" "O men of little faith!" "Follow me!" "Do this and ye shall live!" Every response to the address of the word of God is structured by the vocative implication: "O Lord,

Son of David!" "A Son of God!" The delicacy of a vocative logic is precisely in its acoustical similarity to mere ejaculation. Unlike the vocative case, ejaculation has no status in the declension or inflection of a language. "O Lord!" may be a burst of profanity, an ambiguous articulation of dismay, a simple squeal of delight. In these instances it is not vocative but, as one says today, "emotive." While emotive noises are profoundly significant existentially, they are not particularly informative theologically. Before one too precipitously downgrades the cognitive value of emotional speech, of course, one should reckon with the likelihood that the earliest verbal form of the name of Yahweh was the simple interjection, "Yah!" Addressing God was externally indistinguishable from an emotional explosion. However, the logical difference between ejaculatory and vocative speech is enormous. Ejaculation gropes for a reality which may exist only at the level of diffuse emotion. Yet, by the use of the same sounds, vocative expression is cleanly denotative. Emanating from deep within one's life, it is nevertheless a movement outward toward another reality whose invocation is bringing man out of nothing into existence.

Such confessions as "O Word of God" have the appropriate verbal muscularity to mark this juncture between God's aggressive love for man and man's faithful response. The point of juncture is named Jesus of Nazareth, the word in whom God is calling the world into existence. When vocative address-and-response are coupled together in the act of mutual fidelity precipitated in and by this man, one has a speech event. It is the very structure of the reality which theologians examine under the heading of Christology. As seventeenth-century Protestant theologians were careful to indicate, the puzzling alliance of divine and human in this event is not a *unio essentialis* and it is not a *unio naturalis*. But what remains when ontological and natural categories are put aside? There is still the historical category, the *unio personalis*, the *unio verbalis*, the dialogical coalescence of two vocative words, the truly divine command and the truly human response, without separation or confusion. That is to say that in Jesus of Nazareth the word is believed to have occurred in which all the promises of God find their "Yes." (2 Cor. 1:19b, 20)

If Jesus is a speech event, what makes him different from just any believer? To others, God's word is simply given (ἐδόθη). In

Jesus, God's word occurs (ἐγένετο). That slippery canonical distinction has a firm structure, for Jesus is not simply another illustration of faith. He is the basis of faith: its pioneer and perfecter. Of no other can it be said that he is the God-substitute, the word that was God and has become flesh, the word in whom God is calling the new age into existence.

Is not speech the least durable of all historical realities, hence least likely to bear weight? I would say there is no history which is not a speech event, for historical events are distinguishable from other events by their capacity to survive, that is, by their capacity to interpret themselves. As for the *power* of the self-interpreting event, one need only recall that God created the world through the medium of speech. In Jesus of Nazareth he proposes to recreate the world by that same medium. It is misleading to interpret the power of that creative and recreative word in the natural categories of "law" and "force." The meaning of Christ as word inheres in the more significant Biblical categories of "light" and "freedom."

How is it possible to love a speech event? In love two independent realities set aside their independence and conjoin at the point of a word. There is no copulation deserving of the name "love" that is not set within the clear focus which the word creates. One does not love a speech event, therefore, because speech is the matrix of love, the mattress, so to speak, the underlying basis for the event of love. A lover always gives his word to the beloved, and the beloved lives in that word. It is said of a certain French philosopher that although he is not handsome, he has a beautiful voice which makes women peculiarly susceptible to him. One need not blush to insinuate a parallel to Jesus' relation to his bride, the church. *My* flock know my voice, he said. According to the Book of the Revelation the church can even be said to *exist* in the mouth of the Lord, so that our Lord could say to his church in Laodicea, because you are lukewarm "I will spew you out of my mouth."

How does a speech event suffer, die, and rise again? Jesus is not eventful in the sense that he is a boneless meaning, an idea in air, a *flatus vocie*. Nor is he eventful because he is immersed in corruptible flesh. Yet, neither is he some composite of these two, a mixture of meaning and mortality. Jesus is fully historical in his death and resurrection because that eventfulness, that human response of obedience unto death in the special vocation of God, is itself the word which presses upon our existence with such a gravity of grace and truth as to bring our life to an end in its old form and give it a new beginning. Protestants rightly acknowledge the intrinsically verbal character of this passion history when they insist it is the presence of the word in the Lord's Supper that makes a sacrament of the "body" and "blood." The Lord is indeed "clad in a robe dipped in blood." But "the name by which he is called is the Word of God." (Rev. 19:13)

III

When one chooses Jesus of Nazareth as the beginning of his history, he undergoes an ascent from the old age to the new. This transition is experienced as freedom. The experience is roughly analogous to what occurs when a traveler transfers from a bus to a jet, or when the son of a blacksmith succeeds as a wood-carver. World history has its parallel when an epoch like the middle ages gives way to a new spirit and the modern age arises. The philosophical experience of movement from the theoretical reason to the practical reason was called "freedom" by Immanuel Kant and in that sense it was a secular parallel to what Christians have meant by transcendence from the old age to the new. The movement in which synagogues became churches and classical dearth was assuaged by "the bread of life" is the Christian meaning of freedom. Obviously, therefore, when Christians talk about freedom they are not talking about just any ability to choose (*velle*). They are witnessing to a new context which places choice on a radically different level of possibility (*posse*).

Contemporary intellectuals like Nicolas Berdyaev and Ortega y Gasset make a significant point when they say the Greeks did not know history because they did not know freedom. What is customarily meant by that is that the Greeks knew free choice (*proairesis*), which is the selection among alternate ways of doing what one must necessarily do. But they did not know freedom of the spirit (*eleutheros*). Freedom of the spirit is the ability to say yes or no to a destiny and thus to make a choice which sets the whole course of one's life, one's very history. Freedom in that sense is not a psychological state but an event, a decision which is at the same time a way of life. Such decisions are the very possibility of history. Therefore, as is being said, one who does not know freedom does not know history.

The distinctive dimension of Christian freedom, however, is not the freedom with which one chooses, not even when that choice is a destiny-determining choice. Christian freedom is the freedom one experiences when the entire volitional facility of the human spirit is mobilized at the new and unanticipated level of the history invoked by Jesus of Nazareth. The new age initiated in Jesus has to do mainly with the issue of human freedom because it sets up the conditions which force upon the past the very possibility of a new authenticity.

Let me test the sense of the Christian meaning of freedom through a series of illustrations. The Japanese daughter of a Samurai was once sent to a mission school where she was given a plot of ground a yard square with which to do entirely as she chose. It was called a "do as you please" garden. She planted it according to her own design and afterward exclaimed it was the first time in her life she had known what it meant to be free. Christian freedom is like that, to be sure, but it is more.

Radhakrishnan, the Indian philosopher and statesman, has likened freedom to being dealt a hand of cards and being allowed to play out the game, but strictly within the limits of the cards in hand. Christian freedom also includes this sense of a certain latitude within prescribed limits.

Pascal's analogy of the wager comes even closer to what Christians mean by freedom. It recapitulates the others but adds still another element. The coin is tossed. One is free to do as he pleases with his decision. But he can only choose "heads" or "tails"; he must play out the game within those limits. What is added by Pascal, however, is urgency. One *must* call out before the coin has fallen. That is to say, man is not free not to choose. He is not free to filibuster with destiny beyond the deadline for authentic resolution. The Roumanian playwright Ionesco has recently called our attention to a new metaphor for freedom emerging from the space age. In outer space one has a sense of weightlessness which he experiences as a sense of infinite possibility. Nothing holds him down. Yet there is no place from which to brace oneself, from which to launch this sense of infinite possibility. That is the terrifying burden of human freedom. Is there no springboard, no point of purchase, no clearing or focus within which to set in motion what man feels to be the power of his freedom?

Choice, limitation, urgency, and burdensomeness—that is the progressive movement toward a realistic Christian view of freedom. But what of liberation, which is the promise implicit in the new age? The main ingredient in the Christian view of freedom is left untouched by implications in the foregoing analogies, however right and important they may be. For Christian freedom is not so much concerned with psychology, with the residual potentialities of the human spirit. Christian freedom is a reality primarily historical, an attribute of life in the new age. If the human spirit occupies the old age, and the "old" by definition has not "been formed anew by the spirit of God," nothing of final authenticity is possible to it. For that matter, how do you appeal to freedom of choice in a man who does not even know his name, who is dying of thirst, who sees only his light dying, who is seeking determinedly and listening but is greeted in his universe only by an "immaculate silence" (Samuel Beckett), whose thoughts about existence resemble more the transcription of his fever chart than a work on ethics or logic! Actually, the Christian faith does not simply call upon the capacities of man. Christianity is a redemptive faith which in some sense confers what it requires, such as the focus of understanding which makes choice possible. Freedom is therefore in some sense a gift before it is a task.

One final analogy, then. A young Irish couple was reported to have come to the very brink of marital disaster while failing to agree on the name of their expected son. He wanted the son named "Patrick" after the grandfather; she wanted the baby named "Noel" because his birth was about to occur at Christmas time. Consider the effect on the problem of choice when the doctor announced, "They're twins." Or, even better for the analogy to Christian freedom, if the doctor could have added, "And they're both girls!" Christian freedom closely parallels this sense of a shift in the whole context of choice. When God inaugurates the new age he puts all prior history in question. But he does so by mercifully setting up the framework for a wholly new basis for life, an entirely new history. The introduction of new possibility by the movement from one level of life to another, from the old to the new age, is what the Christian experiences as freedom.

What, then, is the content of Christian freedom? In what form does the transition to the new age express itself in Christians? What is the significance for human behavior in this "freedom wherewith Christ hath made us free?" Four realms predominate in which deliverance from the old age is specifiable.

First, there is *freedom from the world*. In Biblical faith "world" has two connotations. There is the neutral world which provides the stage upon which our lives are acted out, and there is the *hostile* world which is life in a stage of siege against God. Life in the old age draws its inspiration from the world, sets up the world as an object of devotion, hence obscures the world's neutrality by surrendering to it. The world unwittingly becomes man's captor. The freedom of the Christian man is liberation from such bondage and the restoration to man of the world as a stage for the expression of stewardship toward God. To say it as Gogarten does, the Creator has given us the world as the locus of our responsibility to him. But we have worshipped the creature rather than the Creator, perverting our responsibility *for* the world into responsibility *to* the world. The effect of the advent of Jesus is to restore to us the proper relationship by reintroducing obedience to God as the new possibility for life in the world. In the new age, we must be in the world while not of it. We must live in the world "as if not" in the world. We must buy the things of the world "as if not" possessing them and have our wives "as if not" having them.

This paradox of Christian existence is inherent in the transition from the old age to the new. In the world we "surrender to Christ and for the rest be uncommitted" (Herbert Butterfield). We must live in the world "as in a house sold for the breaking-up" (Albert Schweitzer). "He who when he has the world is as one who does not have it, then he has the world, otherwise the world has him" (Søren Kierkegaard). Freedom is the meaning of being a new creature. With it the oldness of bondage to the world has passed away.

Does not this promise crack with incredulity? Behind the confident mask of the minister who says it, is there not some pallor of skepticism? What woman would marry a man who loves her "as if not"? What business man can survive who holds his piece of the world "as if not"?

Yet, one who does not see its cogency may have settled for what the young minister in de Vries' *Mackerel Plaza* calls a "woolly mamma bear *Reader's Digest* optimism." A wrong orientation to the world can be ruinous in any relation. It is possible to lose one's soul even within such elevated relations as human love. Can one love another in any other way than "as if not" in a world in which there is only one God? To confuse human love with acts of worship is not simply romantic; it is demonic. Alternatives to the freedom of Christian love border on vampire acts which tend to bankrupt love by draughts upon it which disregard transcendent claims. Not even the institution of marriage was meant to bear such strains. The *Tristan and Isolde* myth relates this problem. "Two lovers destined solely for each other are already dead: they die of ennui, of the slow agony of a love that feeds on itself" (Simone de Beauvoir). That is why marriage is a rite of the church in which one openly acknowledges that he receives his love "as if not," that is, before God. Marriage is a relation of absolute fidelity because one receives his partner before God, not because one gives himself wholly to another. The same structure which makes of human love a marriage makes of business a vocation. Life in the world is a stewardship for those who live in the new age of obedience to God in Christ. That obedience lifts us out of the age of exclusive investment in the world where lives inevitably depreciate. The Spanish philosopher Unamuno knew of a farmer who died without the final blessing of the church because the priest could not pry open his hand to pour the sacramental oil in his palm. He was clenching three dirty yellow coins. The pathos of the incident is not that the farmer missed the blessing of the church but that he had probably lived as he died, holding so tightly to the world that he was "turned away from the eternal."

A second aspect of Christian freedom in the new age is *freedom from the law*. The structure of a Christian's relation to law is similar to the structure of his relation to the world. Law like love and work becomes demonic when nothing is allowed to transcend it. Moses knew as Kierkegaard did that the law he received was subject to "teleological suspension." Therefore he veiled his face to hide the embarrassment of handing down something which could be superseded. Paul saw clearly what was only dimly implicit in Moses' receiving the law from God. He saw that "Christ is the end (*telos*) of the law." For Paul that meant "all things are lawful."

Does the freedom of the Christian man really border so closely upon license? Actually, license is not the conclusion to be drawn from freedom from the law. The peculiar feature of the law in the old age was the fact that its lack of finality and its oppressiveness were tied up together. Therefore when Christ becomes the law's end, teleologically suspending it by the inauguration of the new age, it is not license he introduces. It is freedom from the oppressiveness of requirements which had no inherent finality, hence no genuine ability to confer authenticity.

The oppressive thing about the law was the way it took ethical decisions out of man's hands. The law served as a custodian to man, as children have nurses when too young to be trusted to their own decisions. Now, however, since the coming of Jesus and the inauguration of the new age, man is no longer a child but a mature son to whom God restores proprietorship over the world. "All things are yours" and "everything is lawful," because the conduct of life has been restored more nearly to the basis God intended before sin and law slipped in. For the mature son who lives in the new age the law is reducible to one word, "love." What that means in any specific instance is left to the son to decide. That apparent license is actually freedom for mature responsibility.

Another oppressive thing about the law was the way it tricked man into adopting a device he could not carry off. If one could keep the law, he believed he could make himself righteous, or, as Paul said, "before the law blameless." The pre-Christian man delighted in the law as an opportunity to gain acceptance from God. His delight "before the law," however, turned to a burdening sense of the curse of the law, for the consciousness of a God who would base acceptance upon acceptability turned first to dread, then to hate. It was in the context of such subliminal discontent that Jesus ate with publicans and sinners and surrendered at last to the cross, acting on God's behalf. That action of reconciliation with sinners ended the law as a system for self-vindication. In the new age God does not propose probity as the precondition of piety. Precisely because that is so, the liberation in God's gracious act through Christ sets men free from the secret dread which stifles creative acts of love.

Some ministers confess to feeling nauseous when they enter their pulpits to preach. Analysis frequently discloses they are sickened by the disjunction between their profession as preachers and their performance as persons. The pathos in their lives is not this weekly discomfort, however, nor even the interior friction which produces it. The pathos is that in their eagerness to please the eternal, they have actually turned away. Settling for life on the basis of blamelessness before the law, they have not allowed their lives to be formed by the spirit of God. They have not chosen themselves in the new age of freedom from the law. If during Jesus' lifetime one had wished to find him, one would surely have asked where the publicans and sinners gathered. Is it not strange, then, that the man who stands in the pulpit of the church would wish to deprive his people of so authentic an index to Jesus' whereabouts by disassociating himself from sinners? Donatism, which made communication of the Gospel contingent upon purity in its spokesmen, was heretical for early Christianity because it tended to minimize God's authority in the church. In these more Protestant times Donatism is heretical because it upstages the Gospel by the law. Luther was consistent with the Gospel when he counselled Melanchthon to "sin bravely," knowing he could "believe firmly." God receives sinners, even when they are found among those who have His authority to receive sinners. Kierkegaard was faithful to his Reformation heritage when he coached ministers on how to speak God's word to sinners. They are not to project their voices as if they are dramatizing *God's* speech. That would be sheer "histrionic mummery" (William Cowper). They are to speak as if they are themselves *hearing* God's speech. Mastery of that technique would soon put an end to the "phony" sound some detect in the voice of the church.

A third realization of freedom in the new age is the *freedom from sin*. The concept of sin in the Biblical faith represents a significant contrast to non-Biblical points of view. Sin in the Bible is primarily a religious and not a moral concept. Every instance of sin is reducible to a single dynamic: rebellion against God. Even in the system of legalism where sins are morally specifiable, the root sin is known to be the disobedience to God implicit in the violation.

In the new age which Christ's appearing has inaugurated, however, the content of sin undergoes an important revision. Sin is no longer simply rebellion against God, but rebellion against the particular form in which God has chosen to call men to obedience. Disobedience to God is now defined as refusal to accept Jesus of

Nazareth as the source of one's history. In the old age there was only one sin: rebellion against God. All sins were exemplifications of that basic infidelity. In the new age there is only one sin: anachronism. One who lives after the appearance of the new age by the framework and standards of the old age is not living "up to date." Confidence in circumcision, sacred festivals, and laws which no longer have authority is a breach of faith in the new age God has wrought in Jesus of Nazareth. Hereafter, "that which is not of faith is sin." Sin is to turn one's history into mere pastness.

One sign that contemporary theology has understood the hamartiological seriousness of anachronism is its widespread rejection of natural theology. Theologians who orient their thinking fundamentally to God's special act of revelation in Jesus of Nazareth do so not because God cannot be known in any other way. Even the confessing church of Germany in its Barthian-inspired Barmen declaration of 1934 allowed some sense in which God could be known in nature by reason. But to understand God at the level of his natural disclosures in an age when God has called man to obedience in Jesus of Nazareth is like navigating by the stars long after the discovery of the compass (John Donne). It can be done, but it is anachronistic; and anachronism participates in rebellion, stiff-neckedness, ingratitude, and the many other evidences of slowness to trust.

A Christian is one who by definition is free from the sin of anachronism because he has adopted God's call in Christ as the form of his existence. The apostle Paul's counsel to the Corinthian church illustrates the sense of this freedom. A Christian ought not eat meat which has been offered to idols if it causes his brother to renew his confidence in an out-moded way of life. But sooner or later his brother ought to be made to realize that the mature Christian is one who should be able to eat meat with equanimity. It is anachronistic to travel by raft in the age of the airplane. But it is an innocent thing so long as one does not invest his hope for travel in the raft. The modern man would get a bit nervous to see Polynesians basing their commerce on a fleet of rafts. But he is completely able to assimilate "Kon Tiki."

There may be a clue in this historical understanding of sin for resolving the old question of how free from sin a Christian really is. The Johannine literature is the chief source of the quandary primarily because of its more genetic concept of redemption. The Christian there is one who is "born again" and one is customarily either born or not born. There is no middle ground, unless in fact there is such a thing as "*being* born." The language of birth does not appear in Pauline literature, however, at least not with reference to the Christian experience. Historical categories predominate there. Hence it is unwarranted to assume that "a new creation" in Christ is a man with a "new nature." He is a man with a new history. A new creature is one who participates in the new age of Christ by virtue of which the old has passed away. It is in that sense that "no one who abides in him sins" (1 John 3:6), for to abide in Christ is to transcend anachronism, adopting the conditions of the new age as the form of one's life.

Of course, "if we say we have no sin we deceive ourselves." That is to say, the old age does persist in the new. Some exurbanites after many years in the country still gauge "bucolic distances by New York City blocks" (J. D. Salinger). A cleavage in histories is not as distinct as a cleavage in natures. Two histories may run together; two natures can be counted off in sequence. But "if we walk in the light as he is in the light the blood of Jesus Christ cleanses us from all sin." That means the Christian's freedom from sin is the continual spiritual renewal of being lifted up into the new age by adopting Christ as the form of his existence.

Finally, *freedom from death* is promised in the new age. That would surely be freedom in its least equivocal sense, for any freedom which was finally cut across by death would be a hopeless sort. A man could submit his freedom to spatial limits and even to intermittent deadlines without violation of the sense of authenticity in freedom. But if a man must die at last, where is the *freedom*? If one's space is ultimately reducible to nothing and if one's time is ultimately running out, all talk of freedom is a hoax, like "fishing in a bathtub knowing nothing will come of it" (Camus). Sartre is right, therefore, to reject Heidegger's definition of a man as a being-toward-death. For it is impossible to be fully a man where the whole enterprise called humanity is terminated in death. Not that Sartre denies all men are mortal. It is simply that for him mortality is not what defines a man. For Sartre, freedom-notwithstanding-mortality is what defines a man. So he asserts his freedom in deliberate disregard of death. Yet, while his existentialism may be more defiant than Heidegger's, it is scarcely more free as long as the threat of death is not removed.

Freedom from mortality, however, does define the Christian man. The ultimate choice is the decision which the new age precipitates. To make Christ the source of one's history implies the beginning of a being-toward-life and thus a final vindication of all one's freedoms. Now freedom from death is the most extravagant aspect of a Christian's consciousness in the new age. The clue to it has come with the resurrection of Jesus, which is the sign of the new age. The logic of it is that death is the wage of sin, so that with freedom from sin there follows freedom from death. Death is "the last enemy" only in a chronological sense. Its power over life is overcome when Jesus acts on behalf of God in reconciling sinners. Jesus' own resurrection is already implicit in his atoning deeds. Therefore, he could say, "I am the life; he that believeth in me hath eternal life already." Man's victory over death is likewise implicit in his participation in the new age which Christ's deeds precipitate.

A retired minister once stood by me at the memorial service of a colleague. He told me how he had just been reading something I had written on the crisis of death. He suggested that what I said there was more important to him than to me. He said this on the assumption that, being older, he is closer to death than I am. He was wrong. If death is in the future, he could be right, of course, for actuarially speaking death is more imminent for him than for me. Yet, death as a fact can be experienced by neither of us, while death as a possibility is as near to me as it is to him. According to the Christian faith, however, death is in the old age, and the old age is past now that Jesus has acted in history on God's behalf to reconcile sinners. Therefore, in Christ death is no longer an important concern for either of us.

In the light of the promise that the new age is freedom from death, the polemics which abound in current theological literature on the question of the resurrection of the dead and the immortality of the soul tend to misfire. Our hope for freedom from death does not involve a decision as to whether there is an imperishable soul in man or whether man will in the end be resurrected from some total death. Our hope hinges upon whether we can trust the promise God has given in Jesus of Nazareth whose own resurrection was the first fruit of the new age. Promises can only be trusted, of course, not verified. As we have seen, we are involved in the same risk of faith in participating in the fruits of the new age as Jesus was in accepting the role as its pioneer and perfecter. If the Apostle Paul made the point that we will only really verify the resurrection of Jesus when *we* are resurrected, for if we shall rise it will be *because* he arose, that was his way of turning our attention away from the future to the present.

Meanwhile, we face our death as we live our life—trusting that God will be then as he is now, "all in all." When Sartre pursues a freedom-notwithstanding-death he bodies forth in his philosophy a resonant defiance equalled only by Dylan Thomas when he sings, "Death shall have no dominion!" It is mankind's brave "no" in the face of the apparent silence of the universe about the ultimate hopes of man. But Christians believe God has spoken in Jesus of Nazareth and that the apostles have heard what he has said. He has said, "Death shall have no dominion." He has said it not in defiance, however, but as a promise—a promise filled with the logic of his atoning risk of faith.

The promise of freedom from death is not meant to drain off our attention from life. Just the opposite. It is meant to set us free to assume our responsibilities toward life. As Bonhoeffer has said in his discussion of the "idolization of death," one who believes death will have dominion over life is apt to live in one of two positions. Either he throws life away, believing justifiably that what dies in the end is ultimately worthless at any point; or he holds on to life convulsively, trying to squeeze an eternity out of the instants bequeathed to him, like actors who must vindicate a whole career in one play. The new age settles the matter of our death, however, and gives our lives a context conducive to responsibility. In that sense, theological statements about life after death do not point to life after death; they point to this life and application to its causes which deliverance from preoccupation with death grants us.

A seminary student gave me an instance of a display of such responsibility in the life of one of his parishioners. The elderly gentleman was having his first airplane ride in a small craft over the Pocono mountains when the engine failed and it appeared that he was going to crash. Later he confessed to his pastor how strange it seemed to him that upon facing death he entertained no questions about the eternal destiny of his soul. He asked himself only one question: "Have I paid up my insurance premiums?" That man went down to his house justified, for he knew the responsible freedom of living by the promises of the new age.

The contemporary theologian most influential in my delineation of this view of worldly faith has been Friedrich Gogarten. While details in my presentation vary from him, the main lines are instructed by his view. Let me summarize it as it is stated in his recent volume, *The Reality of Faith*.[1]

What is the nature of the reality in which Christians participate when they have faith? How does this reality differ from the reality of the world in general, or from sheer human invention? Gogarten's answer is that the Christian faith involves a relation to the man Jesus Christ, who experiences the nothingness of the world. Acting in complete obedience toward God, Christ takes the nothingness of the world upon himself and thus introduces into history a new kind of reality, the reality of freedom from bondage to the world. The freedom *from* the world and *for* God is the reality of faith.

The Christian understanding of faith as freedom is held by Gogarten to be the source of modern man's self-consciousness. In the modern world man for the first time can assume responsibility for the world because he knows he is not in bondage to it. This rejection of the world as a basis for one's self-understanding ought not be confused with Gnosticism's dualistic repudiation of the world. For when God makes man his son and heir, he gives man the world as an inheritance. The very responsibility for the inheritance supplies man with the conditions for his freedom as a son. Forfeiture of this responsibility, however, is not an innocent thing. It results in worship of the world rather than worship of the creator, and worship of the world turns the nothingness of the world into a fate, a law which enslaves man. To say Christ frees us from the law is to say he frees us from the religious worship of the world.

The Reformation expressed this position in its doctrine of justification by faith. God did not require men to perform the works of the law in order to justify themselves. Man was justified by the very freedom in Christ by which God sets him free from the world and its laws. Modern science is a twin phenomenon with the Reformation because it defines man's relation to the world in similar terms. In both modern science and Reformation Christianity man is responsible *for* the world, not *to* it. By liberating man from the worship of the world, Protestant Christianity effected a kind of demythologizing of the world, called secularization, setting science free for unrestricted experimentation with the world.

Subjectivism emerged at the point at which modern science confused its freedom from the world with lordship over it. Subjectivism is a world view which binds modern science as a fate in the same way the law bound the pre-Christian man, for it bases man's independence from the world upon man himself, making man the source of meaning for all reality.

Faith, on the other hand, is the reality which has the task of liberating man from just such bondage to the world. In the preaching of Jesus, man is summoned to a new existence of freedom for God. In the preaching of Paul, Christ is proposed as the one in whom bondage to the nothingness of the world is overcome in such a way as to restore man's freedom for God. For Luther, this word of preaching creates faith as man's obedient existence, a condition of reality prior to all man's acts. Luther's strictures against free will can be regarded as his warning that a man is not free to liberate himself on the basis of his own acts. Even his acts of right belief presuppose Christ's act of granting man selfhood in freedom for God.

The discussion with subjectivism, which is the main focus of Gogarten's volume *The Reality of Faith*, must be carried on at the source, at the point where man has chosen to worship the creature rather than the creator. While it is the legitimate task of modern man to assume responsibility for the world, it should be understood that this responsibility is the very form in which modern man is now encountering the law. The responsibility for the world burdens man as a fate when man lacks the freedom for God from whence that responsibility originally arises. Modern man is right to feel responsible for the world. The preaching of the church makes it possible for man to remain free for that responsibility by receiving it from God.

IV

Preaching is the grammar of assent to the new age of freedom. When the church interprets the apostolic faith in Jesus of Nazareth as the source of the new age, it is engaged in preaching.

"Preaching," therefore, is not a term which can be limited to what the minister does from the pulpit. Every mode of Christian interpretation is embraced by the term. Nor is preaching simply the setting up of propositions for intellectual assent. Preaching creates the very possibility of the transition from the old age to the new. In continuity with the living word of Jesus, it is a sign that we are now in the new age and that because of Jesus the situation in the world has radically changed. (2 Corinthians 4:13, 14) When Mary saw the empty tomb, she believed in the resurrection, not because of the empty tomb but because of the interpretation the angels supplied. As Luther has said, "the angels are the best preachers" for they do not allow us to seek the living among the dead. In commenting on the Emmaus road experience, Cyril of Alexandria observed that Christ's encounter there illustrates that all the evidence for the resurrection was insufficient for belief. The eyes of the two travelers were closed until "the word had entered stirring up their hearts unto faith."

Preaching, therefore, is a form of Christian historiography. Preaching is the hermeneutical mode by which God's presence in Jesus of Nazareth, always potentially past, is kept up to date. The function of preaching is so to exegete the history of Christianity that it will be destroyed in respect of its pastness in order to bring the present time under the Lordship of Christ and into his new age. Acting on behalf of God, Jesus has called the world to the decision by which it enters into the new age of freedom. The preacher is the one who is vested with the responsibility of renewing that call. He is therefore not a reporter of past events but a herald who announces the intention of God in Christ in such a way as to precipitate the new age among us. Proclamation (*kerygma*) is not the message simply, nor even the act of preaching. Proclamation includes the call to life in the new age which comes as a claim upon the hearer. One might proclaim, "Jesus really existed." That would not be preaching, for there is in it no call to decision. One can respond to such assertions with sceptical filibuster. One can say, "I doubt it!" or one can question, "Is it true?" Such responses are fair evidence that preaching has not occurred. On the other hand, one might proclaim, "Be ye reconciled to God!", to which there are only two possible responses: "I will" or "I won't." That would be preaching. Of course, one could announce, "Jesus is Lord" and be met with incredulity. But the intention in the statement is preaching, for the announcement of the Lordship of Jesus intends the response of obedience in which Jesus actually becomes Lord.

The propositions of preaching, then, are neither true nor false. They are the occasions for the authentic life of meaningful participation in the new age. When John the Baptist announces, "The Kingdom of Heaven is at hand, Repent!", he is not commending repentance as a precondition of the coming of the Kingdom. He is proclaiming the coming of the Kingdom as the very possibility of repentance. Some Christians think that when the apostle declares, "Believe on the Lord Jesus Christ and thou shalt be saved," he is erecting right belief as the hurdle to salvation. Actually, he is sweeping the hearer up into the new age. Kierkegaard saw this truth in the preaching of Jesus. Unlike Socrates and other great teachers, Jesus supplied the conditions for the understanding of what he preached. Likewise, the apostle Paul communicated the faith with the consciousness that the words he spoke had been given him by his Lord, so that when he proclaimed the word he was at the same time effecting life in the new age.

If these things are true about preaching, the preacher can have the same sense of the holy when the word of God is in his mouth as the priest has when the body and blood of our Lord are in his hands. The coming of the new age of freedom in Christ is in some sense contingent upon his faithful exegesis of the apostolic witness to Jesus' witness about himself. As Gerhard Ebeling has said provocatively, without preaching the Bible is not history. The apostolic record alone is like X-ray plates without a doctor to tell you what they mean. Like an exposed negative, the text needs development. It is only when the Bible is preached that it is the Gospel, for only through the *hearing* of the word is faith evoked, and one does not hear without a preacher. Marcel Proust once observed that great events have no influence externally. What he meant was that influence is a function of interpretation. Copernicus, for instance, made the staggering discovery that the world revolves around the sun. The event made no impact upon history, however, until Giordano Bruno elucidated its implications in an interpretation. Significantly, it was Bruno and not Copernicus who died a martyr.

Jesus ate with publicans and sinners. That fact made no impact until Jesus preached himself as the one who had come to act on God's behalf. Only in the light of his interpretations did the understanding of his mission begin to seep through to his followers. These statements about his acts, remembered by his followers after his death, gave them the capacity to organize his eventfulness into a meaningful story. And, significantly, it was his words about his deeds and not his deeds alone that led to his eventual crucifixion. Finally, Jesus rose from the dead. The event had no impact until allegedly the angels, Jesus himself, and the apostles began to interpret what they had seen and heard. Again, it was their interpretations and not their acts which incriminated the apostles and led to their *imitatio Christi*.

Some truths never suffer from want of a witness. (I draw upon an analogy which Karl Jaspers suggests.) These are scientific truths which will sooner or later be found out by everyone without a witness. Therefore, Galileo was excusable in refusing to martyr himself for the truth that the world revolves around the sun. That truth would not be diminished even by renunciation of it. On the other hand, Bruno, who added to Galileo's facts his interpretation of its meaning, died rather than renounce his interpretation. He knew he was involved in a kind of truth which would suffer in the absence of a witness. Christian truth is of that character. I would not say that the truth of Jesus of Nazareth as the source of the new age stands or falls with our witness to it. I would only say that the possibility which our time has of living in the freedom of the new age stands or falls by our witness.

TEN

Christianity and the Finality of Faith

The Christian Gospel is a proclamation which strikes the ear of the world with the force of a hint. Some "get it"; some do not. To those who do, it is "the power of God unto salvation." To those who do not, it can seem a scandal and an offense. The scandal and offense of Christianity is that a bare hint in history should become the occasion for something the whole course of history taken together cannot provide. That is the sense of ultimacy which a Christian experiences when he hears about Jesus of Nazareth as the word of God. If the Gospel scandalizes and offends when it is preached, however, the ministers of God can know they have failed in their proclamation. For the purpose of the Gospel is reconciliation with God and not offense. The purpose of the hint is the illumination of human experience with ultimate significance. When the act of proclamation gives way to acts of examination into its truth value, it is a clear sign that the proclamation has failed. Not that such an examination is ruled out, or even unprofitable; but only that to be examined does not fulfill the intention in the proclamation.

Christianity can never be more than a hint in history. Its subject is the eternal God, but its mode of communication is history, and in history nothing is evidently eternal. Christianity need never be more than a hint, because where its proclamation is heard, it creates the possibility of an ultimately meaningful life. That meaning reorganizes man's whole experience at a new level of significance. The New Testament calls it the New Age—the body of Christ, eternal life. In this respect the hint has the revelatory power of a clue. It does not say everything there is to say. It simply supplies what is lacking to make the story of our life complete. Christianity *ought* never be more than a hint, because anything stronger conveys a falsely expanded, hence misleading impression of the eternal's verifiability under conditions of history.

I

The first Christians who caught and communicated the faith could scarcely have anticipated its consequences for the very structure of history as we experience it today. "History as we know it now began with Christ," Uncle Kolia says in *Doctor Zhivago*, "and . . . Christ's Gospel is its foundation." What that means is not so favorable to the Christian cause as it may sound. The hint about the availability of ultimate meaning to history has made mankind restless with an existence which pursues its ends without such hints. It has given rise not only to obedience to God, which was its purpose. It has also set off such protean human efforts to achieve ultimacy within history as states like Soviet Russia project. In that sense it is true to say that Communism is a Christian heresy and that the Marxian philosophy of history is a secularized Christian eschatology. On the other hand, by suggesting the historical reality of ultimate gratifications, the Christian proclamation has sponsored deep-seated historical despair, the fear that such gratifications have not seemed forthcoming. Although the American historian Herbert J. Muller deplores it, he is correct to observe that "the absolutist tradition of Christendom leads men to assume that if we don't have absolute standards we can't have any standards, and that if we are not standing on the Rock of Ages we are standing on nothing."[1] Existential nihilism is the result. To say as it does that nothing is ultimately possible in history identifies existentialism as a secular offspring of the Christian line.

Where history has been given the sense of absoluteness in life, the very structure of historical existence is changed. It is the intention of the Christian proclamation that mankind should receive its life from beyond itself, which is a life by grace. That would be to have a history in an ultimately meaningful sense. The failure of the world to get that hint from the Christian faith expresses itself in either revolt or resignation. The man in revolt denies there are such gratifications as Christians speak of and sets up rival absolutes. The resigned man settles for life at some less than absolute level, taking minor gratifications from the perishing moments of a history that is ultimately destined to die.

Like Archibald MacLeish's J.B., who fails to catch the hint in God's silence, the nihilist resolves to rebuild his life upon a perishing humanity.

> Blow on the coal of the heart.
> The candles in churches are out.
> The lights have gone out in the sky.
> Blow on the coal of the heart
> And we'll see by and by . . . .[2]

Like Albert Camus' restless, Biblical-type heroes, he satisfies his taste for ultimacy in a form of "mysticism with the world." Some fevered prisoners of the world have been known to see the face of the Holy Mother of God on the walls of their cells. Camus' nihilist sees only the face of Marie, his mistress. In history one can learn to settle for minor gratifications. But in a time that has heard there are ultimate gratifications, such a settlement turns every intercourse with the world into what Camus seems willing to call an experience of being "taken in adultery." Nihilistic forgiveness for inadequate adjustments to life inheres in the heroism with which one goes about them. The hero knows that although life is ultimately meaningless, this does not mean one may not salvage meanings.

Revolt and resignation are kindred efforts to cope with the history to which Christian proclamation has given rise, the history in which it has been revealed that there is an absolute meaning in life. The significant thing about the new religious situation in the world today, then, is not that Christendom is now becoming a mission field for non-Christian religions. That fact is a mere accident of history. The world is now small enough and the economic strength of non-western religions large enough to facilitate such reciprocal missions. Nor is the significant thing that the religions with which Christendom is now being confronted are themselves "post-Christian," meeting Christianity with positions already accommodated to Christianity. The really significant thing about the mission to America today is that for the first time in its history Christianity is encountering the non-Christian religions in the framework of a history which Christianity itself has formed. It is a history in which the failure to drink expresses itself as revolt and resignation. The effect of the encounter between the religions within that framework should, therefore, be markedly different from the effect the encounter has had upon the soil of non-Christian cultures. It is no longer simply the paramountcy of Christianity as a religion which is being placed in question. The very desirability of any ultimacy within history is now being challenged.

The eagerness with which non-Christian missions have come to America is rooted in the very characteristic which has made it so difficult for Christianity to succeed on non-Christian soil. Christianity in the past has been blocked in its mission because of the apparent satisfaction of non-Christian cultures with less than ultimacy in history. Now Christians are being made the object of a mission by these very religions which have made their peace with historical meaninglessness. Their chief success will, therefore, be among the rebellious and resigned who experience the structure of Christendom without having appropriated its substance.

Islam, for instance, affirms the existence of the absolute God but denies he is really present in history. Therefore the Christian doctrine of the Incarnation of God in Christ is the chief target of its apologists. Christians can make Jesus Christ the source and the form of their existence, the beginning of their new age, because God is believed to be present in him. Jesus Christ then becomes the focus for both the understanding of God and the understanding of man. On the other hand, Mohammed for Islam is the final prophet, the miraculous author of the final book, in the light of whose finality Jesus is only a penultimate figure. It is understandable by that canon that the transcendent reality of God is needed by Islam to account for both Jesus and Mohammed, but that nothing in history—neither Jesus nor Mohammed—can be said to account for the reality of God.[3]

The only historical finality known to Islam is the chronological finality by which the prophet is believed to say the last word for God. The finality which Christianity sees in history is an attribute of the presence of the fullness of the Godhead bodily in Jesus of Nazareth. Islam is said to combine the absolute monotheism of Judaism with the universalism of Christianity. That is a misleading part truth. For that combination overlooks the real genius of the New Testament faith, which is its particularism. In the New Testament a single event is endowed with finality by virtue of the presence of God in history. The possibility of an ultimately meaningful history is formed by that event. The absence from Islam of this sort of particularism could well account for the fact that so syncretistic and universalistic a "religion" as Bahai had its source in Islam.

Vedanta affirms the reality of ultimate truth but denies that it can be embodied anywhere in history. Its chief missionary target, therefore, is the exclusiveness found in self-conscious Christianity. The quasi-religious metapsychology of C. G. Jung has much in common with the Vedanta mission to the western world. As Jung has said in *Modern Man in Search of a Soul*,[4] "To the psychologist there is nothing more stupid than the standpoint of the missionary who pronounces the gods of the 'poor heathen' to be illusions." The statement by itself would be applauded by current Christian mission circles. What it intends to convey, however, ought not be classified as missionary etiquette but as theology. For Vedanta the statement would imply that the ultimate is too deep and still to enter the concrete and transitory life of history. That witness should leave a dearth in history from which man would wish to flee as from a desert.

For psychology, according to Jung, the statement means that "anything that acts for us is real, irrespective of the name we give it." Sigmund Freud, therefore, could not have meant the same as Jung when he wrote on religion as *The Future of an Illusion*. Freud anticipated a day when religious ideas would wither away because their usefulness as emotional props had been superseded by psychological stability. Jung, on the other hand, anticipates a day when the universality of historico-religious symbols will be achieved by a movement toward trans-historical archetypal symbols. Vedanta's mission shares that goal. When it comes about it will be seen that the contest between Christianity and "heathenism," between enlightenment and superstition was avoidable. All religious symbols are believed to participate in some non-historical realm of common human validities. Individual histories are therefore translatable beyond individuality into that collective humanity through a *participation mystique.*[5]

Christians find, on the other hand, that the naming of God is not a matter of indifference. "The God and father of our Lord Jesus Christ" is a God who makes himself known. That is the ultimacy in which Christians are involved. Furthermore, the God whom Jesus names makes himself known not beyond or beneath our individual histories, but within them. That indicates the *historical* ultimacy of the Christian's archetype. Historical mediation is of the essence of a faith in which it is believed that God is present in history. All history is thought to derive its hope from the event in which God is named. That is why Christians hold so stubbornly to their vocation to witness that the ultimate hope of history is tied up with "the name that is above every name." The indissolubility of the Christian witness, however, ought not be looked upon as an axis of exclusion. It is really only the access to the possibility of a finally meaningful history.

Ramakrishna, the modern Hindu saint and foremost inspiration of the Vedanta mission, took as a motto for his movement *Siva-Seva,* God and service. There are also expressions of responsibility toward the world among Hindus in India today, such as the "Land Gift" movement of the venerable Venoba Bhave. But the Vedanta position does not support this practical concern for history in principle. Contrariwise, while Christians default in their responsibility toward the world in practice, their faith does support historical responsibility in principle.

Zen Buddhism, like modern existentialism, abandons all hope in an historical absolute. Unlike existentialism, however, it can do so without agony. All the methods by which Zen justifies its life in history are characterized by abstraction and aesthetic detachment. In this sense, the "beat Zen" of Allen Ginsberg and Jack Kerouac is closer to existentialism (and Christianity) than the rather "square Zen" of the former Episcopal priest Alan Watts. Ginsberg must

> live
> in the physical world
> moment to moment
> I must write down
> every recurring thought—
> stop every beating second.[6]

Watts himself leans toward the more orthodox Zen. He prefers *Haiku*, the seventeen-syllable Japanese poetic form originated by the seventeenth-century Zen poet Basho. To cite one instance he selects,

> The sea darkens;
> The voices of the wild ducks
> Are faintly white.[7]

According to the Japanese theologian Kazoh Kitamori, the aesthetic, observer attitude preeminently heralded in Japanese culture by Basho is the chief hindrance to the Christian mission in Japan. Because it has become the spiritual element in which the Japanese people live, it is the greatest enemy of Japan's evangelization. *Haiku* and Zen are filled with "the pathos of *things*" (in Japanese, *monono aware*). In an existence in which ultimate meaning is anticipated, aesthetic pathos is an anaesthetic which kills the pathos of the person, the pathos which appears when the ultimate possibility in history seems unrealized. In Japan the aesthetic, detached way of life is called *iki*. Christians who live an involved life are felt to be rude and uncouth by comparison. That rudeness is known as *yabo*. As Kitamori says, *iki* people will have nothing to do with Christianity because of its *yabo-ness*.[8]

There are some structural respects in which Zen and Christianity seem a good deal alike. These are usually the respects in which Christianity has a kinship to existentialism. Martin Heidegger is said to have commented after reading a piece by the Zen philosopher D. T. Suzuki, "This is what I have been trying to say in all my writings." The point of similarity referred to is the Zen, Christian, and existential way of grasping the truth inwardly. Each of these emphases knows that the truth can only be communicated in hints, indirectly. Zen actually has a discipline, the *koan*, contrived to make the grasping of truth in objective categories impossible. According to an American novelist who has flirted with the eastern faiths, J. D. Salinger, "Logic" was in the apple Adam ate. "What you have to do is vomit it up if you want to see things as they are."[9] In his more sedate way Joachim Wach has observed that this passion for inwardness is found nowhere in western culture except in some modern philosophy "and in Methodism!"

A Methodist or an existentialist could say as the twelfth-century Zen monk Doken did, "When you are hungry or thirst, my eating of food or drinking does not fill your stomach. You must drink and eat yourself." Or, "borrowed plumage never grows." But it is not true for Christianity as it is for Zen that existence in the truth is an attribute of one's realization of oneself. Zen believes that man must find his salvation within himself or nowhere; therefore the hints in all its communication are contrived to block alliances beyond oneself. Zen's aesthetic detachment from the world serves as an opiate which quiets the surmise that on such a basis nothing will have the last word. It is no accident that many of Salinger's heroes confront the perils of their historical existence by dozing off. The device borders closely on what Vedanta knows as nirvana, Zen as satori, and psychotherapy as neurotic sleep. The Christian Gospel, on the other hand, speaks to the world in such a way as to evoke a nexus of faith with Jesus Christ, who is the Eternal God's way of being present in history. That presence provides a basis for responsible awareness in history.

In its proclamation of God's presence in Christ, the Christian Gospel has disturbed the world with a restlessness which has often been written off as western *yabo-ness*. The motivation of the non-Christian mission to America, therefore, is quite unlike the motivation of Christian missions to non-Christian lands. Christians go to non-Christians to proclaim that history can be ultimately meaningful because of Christ. When non-Christians fail to take the hint, possibly it is because it has not occurred to them to require history to be ultimately meaningful. The non-Christian history never remains quite the same, however, for having been exposed to the suggestion. That fact is evidenced precisely in the non-Christian missions to America. These missions come with the avowed purpose of persuading Christians to abandon the disquieting expectation of ultimacy in history. Salinger's "Teddy" exposes their concern. Teddy is an American boy who believes that in a previous incarnation he was a holy man of India. Due to some misdemeanor in his previous life he was punished, as he believes, by being reincarnated in an American body. For, as he says, "It's very hard to meditate and live a spiritual life in America." A mission to a "Christian" land is a non-Christian culture's alternative to and first line of defense against the Christian mission and against its psychologically perilous by-products, infiltrating the world in the form of Americanism and western rudeness.

The non-Christian mission will be stubbornly resisted within a Christianly structured history, because of the penchant for the absolute which Christianity has developed here. It will be as stubbornly resisted here as Christianity is in the more relativistic and detached non-Christian cultures. But it may also be more enthusiastically received than Christians would care to concede. The grounds of that enthusiasm cannot be found in any detailed delineation of the comparative similarities and differences between the doctrinal systems of Christianity and the non-Christian religions. It may be found, however, in the fact that the difference is expressible in one name, Jesus Christ. That difference reduces the significance of the similarities to a merely academic level. Jesus Christ has a twofold meaning for the religious experience of mankind. He is God's call to the world to take history with absolute seriousness and he is God's sign in history that the invocation has His eternal benediction. Those who hear the invocation without the benediction are either fatigued by the prospect of realizing anything ultimate in history or inflamed by the desire to do so on their own terms.

The whole Gospel is not at hand, however, until it is known that in Christ God gives what he commands. That knowledge is the ground of repentance for the rebellious and the resigned alike. That is why there is a thirst on western soil for what these non-Christian faiths can offer. The thirst can be attributed to the reactions of revolt and resignation which the Christian proclamation has produced among us in the West. The non-Christian religions, which come appealing to the West to surrender the Christian claim to ultimacy, at the same time offer these dissident elements in Christendom an attractive alternative to Christian repentance. They offer it in the form of new possibilities for revolt and resignation, and with the blessing of organized religion. That sweet seduction will not be easy to resist.

II

What, then, is the content of the Christian message that its faith continues to be held out as a basis for the focus of man's life in the world? To what extent are its often arrogant and exclusive claims capable of appealing to a world in revolt against ultimacies and finalities? In what measure are the questions which men all over the world are now asking also the questions the New Testament is asking and answering? The pivotal message of the New Testament has traditionally been summarized in Christian theology under affirmations concerning the incarnation, crucifixion, and resurrection of Jesus of Nazareth. How do these large and frequently mythological meanings any longer embrace what is meaningful for men and fit the concerns of the world?

A. Crucifixion has become the church's way of referring to Jesus' death on the cross and the power of that death to effect reconciliation between God and men. What is there about the death of a man which can confer a sense of the forgiveness of God upon a person who feels estranged from God and unworthy in his life? I once saw a college girl hold a discussion group at bay for an entire evening with the repetition of a single question: "What is there about the death of a man that forgives sins?" No one has answered that question more astringently than Bishop Butler in the eighteenth century. He bluntly admitted that there is nothing about Christ's death which forgives sins. God simply "accepted" Christ's death as atonement for man's sins. That view, called the acceptilation theory of the atonement, cleared away a good deal of rubble in the church's thinking about the death of Christ, but it still did not come entirely clean. Jewish and pagan myths of sacrifice have been applied to Christ to make his death look like the sort of thing on the cosmic level that the slaying of a lamb would be under more parochial circumstances. But once these myths of atonement are penetrated for what they are, it comes clear that it was not Christ's death which atoned for sin at all, but his *obedience* unto death. The early church insisted on saying that "the Jews killed Christ," not to foster anti-Semitism, but to make it clear that God did not kill him as he seems to have expected Abraham to kill Isaac. This was no sacrificial death where Jesus was the victim of the sins of the human race. What, then, would it mean to say "God spared not his own son, but gave him up"? (Romans 8:32) It simply means, as Anselm said in the eleventh century, "God did not rescue him." But does not the Gospel say of Jesus that he "gave his life a ransom for many"? (Mark 10:45) It is a deep mystery in the history of Christendom how that text could have been made to bear such a heavy weight of meaning, as if God used Christ's death in a bargain with the captor of human souls, the devil, to set men free from the bondage of sin. In the first place, Origen, theologian of the third century, who is generally regarded as the author of that theory, believed Christ overcame the devil through the pedagogical power of his obedient life. In the second place, when the verse appears in the Gospel of Mark, it is not in the context of Christ's death, but in the context of the episode in which he washes the feet of the disciples. It is his *life* he gave as a ransom. His death is redemptive only in the sense that in his faithfulness to God in life he chose a course which eventually resulted in his death. He was, so to say, "obedient unto death, even the death of the cross." His death was in the line of duty, but it is his line of duty which "saves" us.

B. "Incarnation is therefore a word that looms more prominently in the understanding of Jesus' ministry of reconciliation than does crucifixion. For incarnation more evidently embraces the total life of Christ in its response to God's demands. The word specifies the content of Christ's obedience to God. What did Jesus do in his life which can be said to reconcile men to God?

1. He came not to die, but to preach. On God's behalf, through the word of his preaching, he called the world to repentance. When he spoke, God was heard as the meaning of the world's existence. The gospel picture of Jesus' ministry is most dramatic in this regard. Great crowds would gather on the hillside awaiting his appearance—the blind, the diseased, the lame, the socially oppressed. The situation always seemed to call for some momentous action. But Jesus would approach the crowd, walk among them, and *sit down*—scarcely a posture for action. Then, as the gospels say, "he openeth his mouth." Mere words? This purely verbal activity of Jesus led the Gospel of John in its prologue to characterize Jesus as "the word." Incarnation means he was the word of God made flesh, dwelling among men, full of grace and truth. The apostle Paul also noticed this preaching role in saying of him that faith, which is what he inaugurated, comes by hearing. In his commentary on this passage in Romans 10, Martin Luther called faith "an acoustical affair."

2. What did Christ's word accomplish when he preached? By his word men were called to obedience to God. That is the most general way it can be said. But what is implied in this call to obedience?

a. By his word, Christ brought God out of the future and made him present. As Albert Schweitzer has said, Jesus of Nazareth is the only instance of an apocalyptic figure who attempted to precipitate the rule of God by a word alone. Other apocalypticists exploited socio-political crises and cosmic catastrophes. Jesus simply preached. When he preached, God's promises were fulfilled in the hearing of the people. (Luke 4:21) Those who heard him, he said, had heard the father.

b. By his word, Christ ended man's search for God. Karl Marx understood that very well when he said of all the religions of the world Christianity is the sole religion to have only one incarnation of God. God being in Christ reveals he is nowhere else, and by that act puts an end to religiousness, to the quest for God. In his speaking, Christ is said to be God's word because he did what only God may do. He accepted sinners. He assumed responsibility for the world. He substituted for God. The enormity of his pretension brought him to the brink of blasphemy as far as men were concerned. But his place in God's design had a pre-existence in God's own will. His assumption of God's role in the world was believed by him to be God's own design, not his own pretension. The significance of the temptation stories in the New Testament may have to do with this. He acted for God, but did not overplay his role. He accepted God's design for him in such a way as not to offend God. When he said, "Thy sins be forgiven thee" or when by his wordless acts he gave acceptance, such as eating with publicans and sinners, sinners felt accepted by God.

c. By his word, Christ inaugurated the age of faith. Mainly his way of doing it was putting an end to the law. Living by law was a worldly way man had of attempting to gain security in God's eyes. By putting an end to law, Jesus opened up the possibility of a life based on trust in God alone. But did he not come to fulfill the law? Surely not by keeping it: he broke it notoriously, especially the laws having to do with Sabbath observance. But in his teaching he fulfilled the law by showing how it would look if carried to its limit, if not a jot or tittle were removed, if one realized what it really meant. Jesus fulfilled the law, so to speak, hermeneutically. "Thou shalt love thy neighbor." Easy enough. But what does it mean? "Enemies, too." Impossible! "Thou shalt not kill!" Not many are tempted in that direction, but what does it mean? "Anger to-

ward your brother is murder." Who then can be saved? "Thou
shalt not commit adultery!" Kinsey's report was surely an exaggeration: most men are moral. But what does it mean? "He that
looketh on a woman to lust hath committed adultery." Who then
can be saved? A man who lives by law is like a rich man. He can
no more enter the kingdom of God than a camel can get through
the eye of a needle. What hope is there for us? That somehow God
will get through the needle's eye to us. And, pray, how will God
accomplish that? Well, it is a kind of electronic affair. He does it
through his word alone. Faith is simply throwing oneself upon the
promise in God's words.

The word of God in Christ has the effect of turning the world
over to man as his responsibility. Before Christ, men lived by law,
in the security that every little detail of life had a prescribed way of
performing it to satisfy God, as children in a tightly run home
know just when and how to do their chores. As long as laws dominate life, no one matures. In terminating a life of law, while giving
man God's accepting love, and in reducing the content of obedience
to God to one word, "love," Jesus at one and the same time bound
us to God and set us free for the world. "All things are permitted."
That is, now you are responsible for God's world. Up to that time,
men were slaves, or children. In Jesus' word men become sons,
mature heirs of God, and if heirs, then responsible for the world
(Galatians 4: 1-7) A life of faith is a structure in which a man who
is responsible to God expresses that relationship in terms of responsibility for the world.

3. But what does all that say about Christ and his incarnation?
Does not the Christian doctrine of incarnation tell us in what respect Christ is both God and man, two natures in one person?
Indeed. When Christ, a completely human being, speaks, God's
word is heard as the meaning of our life. To treat Christ as God
is not only mythology; it misses the point of faith. Faith does not
make statements about Christ; it preaches Christ's preaching, and
in that preaching God is heard again. And what can it possibly mean
to "hear God's word"? It means to find one's world brought to
repentance, reoriented to the purposes of God.

But did not Jesus perform miracles? So did, and do, many
others. There is nothing distinctive or divine in that. The significant thing is that he performed miracles on the Sabbath in contra-

vention of the law. But was not Jesus said to have been born of a virgin? That claim is no distinction, considering the numbers of others of whom it has been said. Tertullian, third-century theologian, made the case that if Jesus introduced a unique age, it was suitable for him to have had a unique birth. But in the same century Origen pointed out that there was nothing so unique about a virgin birth, considering that even vultures have offsprings monosexually. But wasn't Jesus as son of God pre-existent from all eternity? That was also said of Saul, King of Israel. (I Samuel 9:1) What it means is that Jesus' role as Christ, as Messiah of God, was in the intention of God before it was in the consciousness of Jesus. But does not the prologue to the Gospel of John say that the word that was in Jesus was not only with God, but *was* God? English has no satisfactory way of rendering the careful Greek from which this claim is cited. *Kai theos en ho logos* reads "and the word was God." But "*theos*" without the article "the" is a predicative use meaning "Godlike," or God in the mode of his self-revelation. That, indeed, is the meaning of incarnation. Not that Jesus is God, but that in Jesus' speaking, God's speaking is heard. "He that hath heard me hath heard the father." That means that the significance of Jesus' incarnation is not that he is God and not that he is man, not even that he is a man in the presence of God, but that he is the man who presents God to us.

C. Whoever understands that is in a position to understand what is meant by the "resurrection" faith. The resurrection message is the proclamation of the new life of obedience to God made possible by Christ's life and death.

The poorest way to say it is to say it negatively, yet much dead wood must be cut away from the church's efforts to account for Christ's victorious advent. Negatively conceived, resurrection is not a miraculous proof of anything. Christ came to inaugurate faith. Why, then, should it be thought that a miraculous verification would be consistent with his purpose? Resurrection is not a divine certification or certainty of Christ's redemptive role, a certainty Christ himself did not possess during his own life. In faith, all forms of worldly security are surrendered in exchange for a life of trust in God alone. The Christian dies with Christ when he yields up all claims to security. He rises with Christ in the newness of a life of trust.

Nor is the resurrection of Jesus something that adds to Jesus' life. When the Gospel of John includes the story of the raising of Lazarus, it has Jesus say, prior to his death: "I *am* the resurrection." "Whoever hears my word and keeps it *hath* eternal life." Resurrection faith begins in Jesus' proclamation.

Even more importantly, Jesus' resurrection is not a way of overcoming the failure one might have imputed to his death. Easter sermons tend to harp on how after his death Jesus' disciples wandered off to their old jobs in discouragement. Only the resurrection pulled them back again. Understood in this way, the life of Jesus is looked upon as something that death could invalidate; the resurrection is turned into an abstraction which depends on nothing related to his life.

Actually, the resurrection faith is the understanding that Jesus' death was not a defeat, because it was the final mark of his faithfulness to his vocation under God. Judaistic mythology required a messiah to be delivered miraculously when death threatened. Christians who make resurrection a miraculous deliverance from death mythologize the Easter event. The Gospel of John attacks that trend when it depicts Jesus faced with the decision about death in the Garden of Gethsemane. "What shall I say," Jesus asks of himself in the presence of God. "Shall I ask to be delivered from death? No, rather I will let God be glorified precisely in my death." (John 12:27-28) When Mary allegedly reached out to touch Jesus in the garden after the resurrection, Jesus said, "Touch me not." "What shall I do then?" Mary replied. "Go to the disciples and tell them I go to my father. Henceforth, my father is your father." The resurrection is the knowledge that God is glorified, that is, brought to light in the death of Jesus. The father of Jesus is God. That message is not invented as an excuse for his death. It is already the message he came to proclaim in his life. Therefore, when Jesus allegedly walked with two men on the Emmaus Road after his resurrection, they did not recognize him until he began to interpret to them from the Scriptures, beginning as far back as Moses and the prophets, and including his own history. When the disciples gathered in the upper room at Pentecost, the Holy Spirit did not descend until they recollected not his death and resurrection, but all the things he had said and done. When the apostle Paul listed the witnesses to Jesus' resurrection, he placed himself among them, thereby reducing the status of the other witnesses to the status of his own: the full realization of the meaning of Jesus' messiahship as a mission which his death, far from destroying, sealed.

Positively, then, resurrection means the new age of faith, which is life made possible by Jesus' preaching of the advent of God's kingdom, a kingdom in which God reigns as father over sons who live by trust and with responsibility.

Resurrection is the faith that God is present in Jesus' words. That is what makes his words "eternal." Therefore, Jesus could say, "If any man keep my saying he shall never see death; he hath eternal life."

Resurrection is the faith that the meaning of obedience to God's word is love. Love escapes the erosive power of death, for love never ends. That is Paul's conclusion in his first letter to the Corinthians. Karl Barth and Rudolf Bultmann, seniors among the foremost contemporary Protestant theologians, have agreed that I Corinthians has a predominantly eschatological theme. Barth concludes so because of chapter 15, which deals with the resurrection of the dead. Bultmann concludes so because of chapter 13, which deals with love. I would conclude, with the pupils of Barth and Bultmann, that chapters 13 and 15 deal with the same question, for love alone is the deathless reality.

Resurrection is the faith that God and not death is in the future. But then, if it is God who is in our future, it is not our immortal soul that is in our future. That would not be ultimate enough to warrant a faith. And anyway, as the pastoral epistles make amply clear, "God alone hath immortality."

Resurrection is the faith that we are *with Christ*. But "being with Christ" ought not conjure up the image of an interpersonal relation of the sort one has in face-to-face contacts. To be with Christ is to be in the new age that his preaching and death made possible. To be with Christ is to exist in the place where we understand, as his message has made it possible for us to understand. We are with Christ in the presence of the church's preaching of Christ, in the same sense we are with Picasso in the seeing of his painting, or with Bach in the hearing of his cantata. Why should that be thought strange, when as the Protestant reformer Melanchthon said, "To know Christ is to know the *benefits* of his salvation"?

If, then, the resurrection life is a being in the world which

Christ's proclamation creates, and if the content of Christ's proclamation was in the way in which, on God's behalf, he turned the
world over to man as his responsibility, then the content of the
resurrection life is man's assumption of responsibility for the world
as a heritage from God. In the sixteenth century, the French essayist
Montaigne told of a man who left a legacy in which he gave to one
friend the care of his aging mother and to the other friend the
marrying-off of his daughter. Many who heard the last will read
believed it must have been a joke. But those upon whom these
legacies were conferred were quite content.

ELEVEN

Eschatology and the Horizon of Faith

The affirmation of the finality of Christ is at best a theological option. However, it is a dubious option. For truth is an attribute of its occurrence, and Christ's finality does not occur when Christ is being affirmed as final. The history of Christology is the graveyard for just such direct claims about Jesus of Nazareth, because direct claims have no essential capacity to evoke a living faith. Jesus was believed to be anointed by God for the fulfillment of a mission. Yet the history of theology has been the history of the adulation of his person, and grandiose claims for Christ have lacked an essential connection with "what really happened." The titles of Jesus express a quite different reality when considered as events of disclosure than when considered as predicates of Jesus' person.

The first important break with Christology as direct claim for Christ came in the Protestant Reformation, when theology replaced what had become honorific personal titles with titles which indicated what he really did, titles bearing upon his functions, his offices, generally called the offices of prophet, priest, and king. The second and even more decisive break with the history of Christology has occurred in modern times in the realization that the person of Jesus functioned within an entirely eschatological horizon. Because of that, it can now be seen that finality is not an attribute of Jesus of Nazareth himself, in his person, but of the eschaton whose imminence he signalizes. Finality as a Christological claim, then, is not a wholly salutary option. The finality of Christ in the horizon of eschatology, however, is not optional at all, but simply redundant.

The primacy of eschatology in Christian understanding has come to light quite recently as a consequence of modern man's ability to treat the sources of faith with historical seriousness. Biblical exegetes applying modern historiography have come to know the nature of the early faith better than the apostles knew it themselves, and differently than the dogmaticians, who until now have expanded upon and embroidered around the apparent historical gaps in the apostolic faith. Despite the great range of emphasis in current interpretations of eschatology, Jesus of Nazareth is unanimously regarded as an eschatological reality. The implication in that consensus is that it is unwise for the church to continue to build its faith upon claims for the person of Christ in himself.

Christology in the horizon of eschatology is nevertheless an important factor in eschatology. For one thing, a proper Christology has kept the church from allowing its eschatological message to become engulfed by apocalypticism. Apocalypticism is both a-historical and anthropocentric. It is a-historical because of the way it depreciates the world in the interests of an otherworldly future. Eschatology, on the other hand, ties the thought of God to the reality of history. Apocalypticism is anthropocentric, because apocalyptic "last things" visualize Christ as the judge of men according to human merits. The eschatology of the New Testament, however, is a fundamentally Christological reality, tutoring man in the expectation of what God has brought about in Christ, rather than of what pious men will deserve. Apocalypticism may well have been the dominant theology of the early church, and, as such, set Christology off on the wrong foot, making claims for Christ based on his alleged possibilities for the future, rather than on the achieved realities of his mission. The expectation of the kingdom of God in the preaching of Jesus, on the other hand, had the power to transform the world through the response of repentance. When his death and resurrection appeared to have terminated his preaching, direct claims for Christ were allowed to supplant his indirect, kerygmatic effect. When these claims were apocalyptic, they converted faith, which was a *bona fide* transformation of history, into an attitude of waiting. The person of Jesus illuminated by his achieved history, however, serves as an open rebuke to the a-historical and anthropocentric deviations of apocalypticism.

Christology is a significant aspect of eschatology for another reason. It now seems plausible, from an historical vantage point upon the early faith, that soteriology became the church's alternative to its ailing apocalyptic. Christological gains were made in the early ecumenical councils on the basis of soteriological alternatives to apocalypticism. In order to forgive sins, it was argued, Christ must have been more than a man, hence the direct claims for his deity. Eschatology, however, when seen as the horizon within which Christological statements are to be made, subordinates soteriology, with its emphasis on Jesus' role in the forgiveness of sins, to history, with its call for a change of orientation toward the world. Forgiveness of sins is a phenomenon known prior to and outside the Christian movement, hence not at all unique to it. When it is taken up into Christianity, it is simply instrumental to eschatology. If Jesus himself underwent no transition from sin to salvation, why should such a motif be thought so central to the faith which he inaugurates? If Jesus in his associations and in his preaching accepted sinners on God's behalf, why should it be thought necessary to floriate his chaste preaching into baroque myths of sacrifice based upon his cross? But forgiveness of sins is announced by Jesus in order to free men for the new age of responsibility for the world, as defined by the imminence of God and his kingdom. The history of theology has acknowledged the purely prefatory character of forgiveness wherever holiness and not forgiveness has been the distinctive mark of faith. To have turned Christ into a new agent of salvation, replete with the soteriological claims which Judaism had applied to its altars and Hellenism to its cults, was to have blunted the edge of his mission to make God's reign imminent through preaching.

Therefore, the finality of Christ from an eschatological point of view is the finality of the eschaton whose imminence he heralds. In the event of his inauguration of God's kingdom, *Christ fulfills the office of prophet.* He is prophet, but not because he points to some far off event in which God will yet manifest himself. He is prophet in such a way as to put an end to prophecy. In his word, all that God promises is realized. (Luke 4:21) The god of the future is brought into the present. Hope is grounded in faith. Standing with him in his word, men now have faith, which is the final mode both of their being with God and of their being in the world. *Christ* also *fulfills the office of priest.* He is priest, not primarily because he intercedes for us at the right hand of the father, but because he puts an end to the law, which is the occasion for sin because it tempts men to live without trust. Thus he strikes a blow at the institution of priesthood which exists for the mediation of forgiveness. Now that the eschaton has ended the age of law, men no longer need to exploit the world for religious purposes, using it as the arena for fulfillment of the law and thus for self-vindication. All such piety is terminated when Jesus of Nazareth on God's behalf accepts sinners notwithstanding the condemnation of the law. *Christ also fulfills the office of king.* Not that in so doing he reduces man to the status of servant, lordship being unique only to him. He rather redefines lordship in terms of servanthood. From now on it is the last who shall be first. Then he passes the royal status on to man, a status distinguished by the crown of thorns, hallmark of the eschaton. By his words and acts, then, in one event, Jesus united men with God in the purposes of his kingdom, overcoming their religious bondage to the world which the law enforced and setting them free for responsible stewardship in the world. Understood in that way, the definition of Christ in the Chalcedonian formula is essentially eschatological. The Chalcedonian formula, in calling Christ "truly man and truly God, without separation and without confusion," gives testimony to the finality of Christ because it means that God's destiny for man is immutably tied to what Jesus of Nazareth has done. Thus Christology is primarily eschatology and the finality of Christ is a truth occurring within the horizon of eschatology.

At least three large problems confront us in these generalizations. What do they mean? How can we believe them? Why do they signify finality?

I

Eschatology means that in some sense Christ is the "end of the world." But what is meant by "end" and by "world"? "End" does not connote a limitation in some spatial or temporal sense, but a determination. One does not "expect" an eschaton as one expects the end of a journey or the end of an affair. Eschaton is an end insofar as one lives under its influence. Nor does "end" connote a cessation, such as death imposes upon life, but a coming of fulfillment. The fulfillment involved, however, may not be simply by anticipation, as of some larger realization yet to come. Eschatology does not have to do with what will be the case when history has run its course, known now only in part. Eschatology is the knowledge that the sort of reality which comes to expression because of Christ is reality in its final form and that this reality is all-we-have-and-all-we-need. Paul, for instance, may not really be complaining when he says, "Now we see through a glass darkly," as if counseling the Corinthians to await some face-to-face encounter. He is inviting the church to the resolve of faith which is in itself the eschatological existence, an existence in which it is *better* to believe *not* having seen. Or, again, the words of John's Gospel on Jesus' lips, "until I come," are the words of primitive Christian apocalyptic. Therefore, they are not normative for faith, and are immediately challenged in the very next verse, which safely lodges the answer to the question of Christ's return in Christ's own secret will. (John 21:22, 23) Therefore, when Jesus says to his disciples in his farewell address, "yet a little while and I will come to you," he is not endorsing apocalypticism, because, in fact, he immediately advises them that the world will see him no more. For the New Testament faith, the judgment of the world is fulfilled in Christ. To know that Christ will be with us always is, therefore, to enter "a new history"[1] which will end all other histories and bring all other worlds under judgment by its finality.

When one says of eschatology that it designates the "end of the *world*," one means by "world" a fundamentally historical reality. For that reason, the early church's attitude toward apocalypticism was justifiably ambivalent. Apocalypticism was a development in late Judaism which visualized a universalism for God's relation to the world of a geographical and ethnic extensiveness unprecedented in earlier Hebrew thinking. God's apocalypse would be a revelation, not simply to Israel, but, so to say, to the "world." At the same time, the apocalypse was to occur through cosmographic manifestations which gave to "world" the connotation more of what we now know as nature, than as history. But when it comes to the world cosmologically conceived, eschatology is closer to the prophetic than to the apocalyptic tradition. While apocalypticism visualized a radically new world, it did so in terms more expressive of worlds of nature than of worlds of history. While prophetism visualized changes being made within the present world form, it expressed these changes in largely historical terms. When the New Testament does seem to be expressing its eschatology in the cosmological terms of apocalyptic, those expressions are usually in the service rather of the history of salvation. To take a single example, when the letter to the Ephesians holds up hope for the ultimate reconciliation of the "cosmos," it is clearly referring to the uniting of Jews and Gentiles in "one body," the church (2:11-22), an historical entity.

"World" in the New Testament, then, is not a quasi-scientific construct, a cosmographic arena upon which history plays out its game. World is a dominantly historical reality, a matrix of relationships within which one derives the meaning of one's own existence. World is not a space which preexists one's participation in it. It is the relationship which comes to fulfillment as one has his being in it. World is not the box one is in. World is the mode of one's being-in. Thus there is the scientific world, the sports world, the art world. Yet, like the horizon, a world is not the creature or the product of man but rather makes the discoverability of man a possibility. For "world" is the kind of reality which has a fundamental expressibility —in acts, gestures, and words. The end of the "world" to which eschatology refers is the end of the world which occurs when, through his symbolic action and his parabolic speech, Jesus of Nazareth exposes the life of man to the horizon of God's imminent kingdom, giving man a whole new mode of being-in.

Interpreters seem clear that eschatology does not involve a timeless truth. The reason usually given is that it is a truth which happens and therefore is eventful. That, however, is not the full story. Eschatology is a truth which occurs under the conditions of time, which is not mere eventfulness, but transience and finitude. Are not the expectations in finality and finitude incompatible? In apocalyptic, yes. In eschatology, no. The decision between eschatology and apocalyptic was made once and for all by Jesus of Nazareth in the Garden of Gethsemane in his final hours, when he refused to ask God to rescue him from death. That eschaton is the horizon which continues to bring man's very finitude to light as final. Eternal life is not deliverance from finitude but obedience to God even unto death and the realization that God can be glorified by an obedient death. (John 12:27, 28)

Those who understand the temporality of the eschaton do not always realize that they must also choose against its universality. Universality may be possible in a theology of grace where God's acts prevail despite their actualization in life. Or, universality may be possible in a cosmological theology where God's acts have relevance for things apart from mediation by men. But the eschatological world is a world of rapture over the joy of faith, and faith, unlike grace, is man's life qualified consciously by the presence of God in the person of Jesus of Nazareth. The joyful world of the eschaton is the world of a happiness which *knows* it is happy. As John Wesley once put it, "No man can be justified and not know it!"[2]

Under the parabolic proclamation of Jesus, the truth of the eschaton is an historical truth. That means that the truth does not inhere in the correspondence of propositions with the things they signify. Parabolic propositions are not words which signify things. The words are the things. Luther knew that when he understood that the justification which comes by faith alone is also by word alone. Wesley knew it when he referred to the redeeming blood of Christ as "a speaking blood."[3] Parabolic truth inheres in the events in which words bring to expression a new world, a new history, a newly qualified consciousness. If *such* events are final, as the term eschaton implies they are, they will have to be final, then, in a sense that includes neither infinite nor universal. And if such events are of the character of worlds, then they are worlds which live by words, worlds like creation itself, if, indeed, God created the world by his word. One could therefore say that Jesus of Nazareth has talked the world into the kingdom of God, or, more accurately, Jesus has talked the kingdom of heaven down to earth. Little wonder, then, that the Gospel of John has called him "the word," the apostle Paul has interpreted faith as an acoustical affair, and the synoptic gospels record that he said nothing to the people without a parable. (Mark 13:34)

II

How does one arrive at such a vast conclusion about the eschatological significance of Jesus of Nazareth? In the same way Jesus did—historically; therefore, in the same way one would ar-

rive at anything historical. Jesus of Nazareth, a fully historical being, was placed in a world. Worlds are invitations to decipher
meaning and to reshape the world by that newly deciphered meaning. Worlds are historical realities. A world is a structure of reality
in which tradition and interrogation interact in a circular way.
Questions interrogate events and events illuminate questions. In
the process of the historical world, meanings sedimented in historical events are stirred up by mankind's sentiment for meaning. "Are
you he who is to come?" "Whom do men say that I am?" The
circular dialogue between traditional meanings and the quest for
meaning is only terminated by a risk of judgment, such as, "thy
will be done!"

As historical beings, men stand within events which are conferring meaning. Jesus is no exception to this fundamentally historical structure. He is the one through whom it comes to evidence
that the God of the future has come into the present as the basis
for man's ongoing life. In his baptism, he is brought to light as the
Messiah and the kingdom of God dawns. (John 1:26, 31) His baptism, therefore, is the sacrament of eschatological history. In his
parables, he is speaking as one who is already standing within the
eschatological nearness of God. (Luke 4:21) Like a poet who always says more than he knows, Jesus in his parables brings to expression the movement of God's kingdom. His expression provides
the basis for his comprehension of himself and bursts like lightning
over the terrain of his whole time. He says, "The kingdom of God
. . . ," and the world is swept up into the kingdom. He says, "*I am*,"
and the world articulates back to him its newfound stance, "Thou
art!" In his preaching Jesus stands as the sign of the kingdom of
God that is upon him and in whose presence there is no neutrality.

But that was in his time. How does our time any longer sense
the imminence of God's kingdom? The answer is: we do it in the
same way Jesus did, except that now we do it within his horizon.
The story of his life is sedimented in the history into which we now
direct our sentiment for meaning. We make the risk of judgment
that he made, but on the basis of his judgment. To be a man of faith
is to live in remembrance of him. Our resolve will decide whether
his judgment will find its consummation in our history. Luther
alleged this to be Paul's meaning when he said in Galatians, "The
life I live is Christ." Christ is *mea forma*. That means that the eschaton comes in the speaking of Jesus and continues to come when

the church remembers Jesus in its speaking, that is, when the church enters into the horizon of understanding within which Jesus stood when he spoke.

In Richard Kim's novel *The Martyred*, the son of a Korean minister has revolted against his father's faith and has become a professor of history in the university. The father, I believe, is justifiably confident in his son's spiritual destiny, not because as a Presbyterian he is convinced that in the end God will unite all things in himself. Rather, as he said,

> If one is a good historian . . . he will invariably come to the large question of whether or not history must have an end one day . . . if he does that some day, then I shall have to admit that we are not so far apart from each other as it might appear.

Kim said that what the pastor had in mind was not "some sort of teleological question. . . . No, he said, it was an eschatological question."[4]

Christian faith is a fundamentally historical enterprise, not despite its eschatology, but because of it. Jesus of Nazareth brought a new horizon to bear upon history. Because the church reminds us of his word, his horizon still mobilizes us, so long, that is, as it answers to something in us, to our sentiment for meaning. We must not assume that we are being historical if we think of his words in detachment from our own concerns, any more than we are being historical if we attempt to conserve the laws of the land as they were at their inception. When Jesus said to Nicodemus, "Ye must be born again," he was not issuing a universal command. He was sensitizing Nicodemus' pre-understanding.[5] To acknowledge the importance of a pre-understanding is to concede that the meaning at stake in any relationship is something that will occur in one's own situation. We now bring that prior question to our faith as the faith has been traditioned by its history: Is there anything in the words of Jesus heard across these centuries by which we may be "born again," anything which promises us something we still really want? If there is not, then we shroud the church in the shawl of a sect, standing guard over claims we are able to venerate but which no longer give birth to a history for us, claims we can express in our will to rhetoric but which no longer quicken our imaginations. Theologians who are resisting this sectarian trend for the sake of a lively historical meaning ought not be written off as innovators whose passions (as Eusebius of Caesarea once warned) only lead to heresy. An irrevocable conviction which does not move the world is no fitting symbol for a faith whose lord defined his existence as mission.

Two such convictions especially thwart the birth of faith in our time. One is a futuristic eschatology which sees in the doctrine of the resurrrection of the dead "the absolute metaphor."[6] Other metaphors in Christian preaching are taken to be merely proleptic moments of that metaphor, such as Jesus' resurrection, and conceivably even the life-giving word of Jesus in his parabolic metaphors. The warrant for this view is that it is strong in the early church and can even be said to have been the dominant theology of the early church. Its objectionable feature is not simply that it becomes a species of eschatological verification for Christian faith, delaying the real engagement with the world to some far-off divine event. The real objection is to the way it depreciates the eschatological significance of Jesus' historical eventfulness. There is a theology implicit in the preaching of Jesus which conflicts with the allegedly dominant apocalyptic theology of the early church. The new quest for the historical Jesus has brought it more clearly to light than previously in the church. The meaning of that message is that the eschaton comes, not in the chronological last days of history, but in the speech of Jesus. Jesus' resurrection is a sign, as the Gospel of John makes clear. But it is a sign, not of his future conquests, but of the victory already achieved in his word, of which he says, "I have overcome the world." (John 16:33) Faith looks for nothing more. Apocalyptic theology awaited God in the distance. New Testament eschatology brought the distant God near. We ought not be allowed to forget that the characteristic literary form of early Christianity was not the apocalypse, but the Gospel.[7]

The other conviction which may thwart a candid arrival of faith is the doctrine of the Holy Spirit in so far as the Holy Spirit is said to be our continuity with Christ. An understanding of history and language has made that use of the doctrine superfluous as it was superfluous in certain sectors of the early church. The distinction made between human witness and the witness of the Holy Spirit is a distinction familiar, for instance, to the Acts of the Apostles, but not to the Gospel of John, not even to the synoptic gospels. Mark, for instance, has no narrative regarding the post-

Easter descent of the Spirit upon the disciples. For the Gospel of John, the paraclete who will relieve Jesus, as in the changing of the guard, is the word of preaching. Witness to the word is not a second reality alongside the witness of the spirit. Why is it not the case, then, that the word for us as for Jesus is the mode in which God makes himself present? Those who hear the preaching of the church hear Jesus, not because some independent action of the Holy Spirit makes him present, but because the word itself overcomes chronological distance. Those who hear Jesus hear the Father, not because the Holy Spirit intercedes, but because the human word itself has the power in history to substitute for God. The doctrine of the Holy Spirit in this relation becomes a mythological way of alluding to "the power of preaching in the church." The intention of the myth was utterly kerygmatic. It meant to conserve the valid and indispensable conviction that when the word is preached it is God's word that is heard, word in the dimension of eschatological disclosure. When that myth is conserved, however, it has the effect more often of weakening the church's historiographical responsibility in exegeting and traditioning the apostolic faith, and it fosters hopes for spiritual manifestations more powerful than the plain meanings conveyed in merely human words. "Holy Spirit" has been the church's way of saying "the presence of God." Since Christ, however, the presence of God is given in the word of Christ. It is true that in the first five centuries of Christendom the doctrine of the Holy Spirit, taken up into the formulation of the doctrine of the Trinity, was in effect a demythologizing of the polytheistic tendencies in the developing Christian doctrine of God. When the works of God in creation, revelation, and redemption began to splinter God three ways, to the jeopardy of monotheism, the church found a way of saying that Father, Son, and Holy Spirit are not three gods, but one God three times. It was also true, however, that the doctrine of the Holy Spirit in the early church was a rival to Jesus' eschatological message, even while being an alternative to apocalypticism.

III

What of finality, then, is really brought to light when the word of Christ is spoken into our situation today? What does it mean to say that the word spoken by Jesus of Nazareth and heard by us today *is* the eschaton? If an eschatological event is an event in which faith is made possible, what is that structure which makes it so final?

To say this event is *unique* would not exhaust the meaning of its finality. In history, all events are in some sense unique. To say it is *ultimate* would not be enough, either, because all events which occur through obedience to God are, in respect of their God-relation, ultimate. One question remains: What makes the Christ event *final*? What is there about Jesus of Nazareth that makes him absolutely important and valid for all the future? Why must salvation be bound up entirely with faith in him, so that the relation to him can be called the determination of the final destiny of men? Why is it legitimate to call him *alpha* and *omega* without any sense of doxological hyperbole? What can it mean to say that faith in God is so irrevocably dependent upon Jesus of Nazareth that the wisdom communicated in this event makes all other wisdom anachronistic and obsolete, so that subsequent to this event nothing can appear that will supersede it, indeed, so that man needs to look nowhere else for God and God needs to do nothing more, and so that Jesus can be said to have had the last word?

The *question* of the finality of Jesus is the question of what it means that he has spoken of God. The revelatory significance of Jesus' speech is not that he communicated information about God, but that he stood in an event in which men were once and for all enabled to let God be, even when they could not say what he is. The eschatological encounter with God is an encounter with a reality who allows himself to be brought out of the future into the present. But it is not an apocalyptic encounter, as with a child at hide-and-seek who, unfound, must at last show himself. Jesus speaks of God in such a way as to encounter men with God's hidden presence. Like a faithful Jew who would rather call upon the kingdom of heaven than upon the kingdom of God, he scarcely even uses the name of God. One could almost say of him what Montaigne once said of the apostle Paul: "Of all the cults St. Paul found in Athens, the most pardonable of all seemed to him the one dedicated to the 'unknown God'."[8] Jesus' name for God is *ho pempsas me*, "He that hath sent me." (John 1:33, 4:34, etc.) That is why Christology is so crucial to theology: the identity of God is somehow bound up with Jesus. And who, indeed, is Jesus? He is "son of God" whose office is eschatological, namely, to finish the Father's work. And what was the Father's work? To let himself be revealed as "Father." Henceforth, anyone who has seen Christ has seen the Father, anyone who has received Christ has received the Father. Anyone who has heard Christ has heard the Father. Christ and the Father are one in an event of speech. If Philip's request is any solid indication of the human pre-understanding, Jesus' revelation of the Father is final: "Show us the Father," Philip asked, "And it sufficeth us." When that revelation occurs, man's joy is said to be full, and no one can take it from him. (John 14:8; 15:11)

The *answer* to the question of the finality of Jesus is not primarily that God is now known to be Father, but the historical effect of that realization, namely, that men understand themselves as sons of God. The eschaton, therefore, derives its finality not so much from supernatural inference about the presence of the Almighty as from the status conferred on history by the knowledge of man's sonship and the consequent insinuations of maturity in history.

The work of the Father which Jesus finished was to make men sons of God, no longer slaves or even children, but sons, and if sons, then heirs. Unlike a slave or a child, a son is an heir to whom the Father turns over responsibility for what is his. In the word of Jesus of Nazareth men are brought to maturity in the world by receiving the world as an inheritance from God which henceforth remains their responsibility. (Galatians 4 and Romans 8) The time in which that act occurs is the fullness of time. Thereafter man is to govern himself as one mature and not as those who are unstable in all their ways. (James 1:4ff.) They are the mature, as contrasted with the babes. (Hebrews 15:13) In Christ men have been brought to completion. (Col. 2:10) Precisely in the word in which God is addressed as Father, Jesus takes sonship upon himself and on God's behalf confers sonship upon those who hear his word. By that performatory word he turns the world over to men as their responsibility, and the ground of the world's maturity is once for all established. To hear the word "Father" addressed to God is to participate in an event in which man's sonship comes to expression.

Becoming a son (John 3:1–8) is being born into an eschatological existence, being set within a whole new history. To know oneself as son of God is not to have *information* about oneself. That would turn theology into anthropology. To know oneself as son is to receive the gift of humanity, that is, to have permission to be a man, that is, to be free to be only a man. In this event in which the Fatherhood of God becomes the basis for man's sonship, history emerges in its eschatological form. There one is free—free from all requirement for realizing salvation through the world, free from the fear of finding devils in the world, free from the possibility of identifying God with any part of the world, free from the psychological need to hide one's moral fears and failures from the world, free from the superstitious ruse of using God to explain the wonders of the world, free from the fear of death because our life is lived toward God and not toward our own erosive future, free from any necessity to fill the future with conjectures based on our limited knowledge of the world, free from the temptation to derive our ultimate meaning from our limited tasks in the world, free from the problems which come from regarding the world as a riddle for men to solve, thus free from worldly care as are the birds of the air and the lilies of the field, free from what Aristotle called "the itch of desire," free like art, which does not always have to be for-the-sake-of-something, but can be simply what it is, "not bent on grabbing, because we know we inherit" (D. H. Lawrence).

Jesus is final, then, because in him the conditions for immaturity in history have been terminated and the conditions for maturity are now at hand. Now we know what creation is. Creation is the matrix of relationships in which, because there is a God who is known as Father, men do not belong to the world, but the world belongs to men. Creation is the historical structure of reality in which, because men receive the world from God, they can be responsible for it, not being responsible to it, not turning the creature into a creator and worshipping the creature, thus not forfeiting the grounds of responsibility for the creature.

Does it not seem in such an understanding of eschatology that God has abdicated and is even virtually dead, having nothing left to do? It is true that he has nothing left to do, except what he has already done, namely, to turn the world over to men, making them sons. But as Father, he remains the living ground for man's continuing sonship, thus for man's everlasting responsibility. When sons forfeit their inheritance, the Father does not reduce them again to servanthood; he reaffirms them in their sonship by giving the world back to them again, as the Father did the Prodigal. (Luke 15:11ff.) Therefore, we do not say with William Blake,

> Thou art a man, God is no more,
> Thy own humanity learn to adore.

The eschatological speech of Jesus remembered and renewed in the church liberates the creature from the self-preoccupation which perverts creaturehood into demonic bondage to the world. In Christ God delivers up his rule to men, but he continues to reign.

However, neither would we say in Thomas DeQuincey's rather eschatological terms (to use the paraphrase of J. Hillis Miller[9]), "In God's time all time is fulfilled, and the dreadful hemorrhage of time has stopped." Eschatology holds out no dilated hopes for man. It discloses the situation of man as it most really is. The eschaton is not that than which a greater cannot be thought, the dream of some humanly desirable utopia. The eschaton is that than which a greater need no longer be sought now that the revelation of the end is at hand. Expressed in the lordship of Christ and his crown of thorns, eschatology sees obedience unto death as the "red badge of courage" in which the mature son is the one who willingly sheds his own blood in imitation of the obedience of Christ, not asking for more. The sower sows the seed. The rest is up to the land. (Mark 4:3–9)

You may say to me, then, "you allege as Christian what any modern man can know without that faith." I do not wholly deny it. Modern man has learned to get along without God in all the important affairs of his life, assuming a fully historical existence which is an existence in which man holds himself responsible for the world. I could, of course, attempt to register as a matter of history that modern men have not, in fact, known responsibility for the world without Christian faith. The eschaton is an *historical* reality. Why, then, should it seem strange that its effects are manifest even where its sources are unacknowledged? But I would rather say, in a less defensive vein, that devotees of Christian faith do not deplore modern man's apparently independent courage and responsibility. For Christians are not bent upon converting men to Christ. That evangelistic drive is abandoned with the abandonment of direct Christology and with the dawn of the eschatological horizon. Christians are responsible for announcing the eschaton and thus for bringing the world to expression as creation, as responsible sonship. Therefore, when we hold out faith to men, we do not do so in the expectation of taking something from them, or even of giving something to them which they do not have. We do so to confirm and strengthen them in what they could indeed already in some sense have. So may their sonship be brought out of latency and fate into patency and history, and their joy become final by being made full.

TWELVE

Theology and the Worldliness of Faith
—The Prospect for a Theology as History

One of the significant points of arrival in contemporary theology is the almost general consensus that the reality of faith is historical. The logic of faith is a fully historical logic, which means that faith ought to be interpreted as history, with the kind of thinking appropriate to historical reality. At first the position may seem reductionistic. Is not reality more than history? Is there not a world of nature as well, and is there not a realm of being? The answer is that systematic theology pursued on the model of history ought not deal with nature, because nature by definition is reality insofar as it is not history, that is, insofar as it does not involve the question of meaning for man, as history does. The consequence for theology is that physicalistic concerns, hitherto included by theology in the discussion of such topics as creation, providence, miracle, and sacrament, ought to be eliminated in the interests of dominantly historical concerns. At the same time, the realm of being is relevant to theology only insofar as being "appears." But being, in its appearance, is history, at least if it "appears" in situations in which the question of meaning for man is being raised, which is the historical question.

Not even so-called "acts of God" have a claim upon theological consideration, for if they are not history they are not meaningful for man. Thus they classify as nature, and ought not be discussed by theology. The being of God-in-himself, his nature and attributes, the nature of the church, the nature of man, the preexistent nature of Christ—all these conjectural topics which have drawn theology into a realm of either physical or metaphysical speculation remote from the habitation of living men should be abandoned. Not that the concerns they express should be evaded. Every doctrine which has existed in Christian theology embraces some historical intention. The task of an historical hermeneutic, an historical mode of interpretation, is to disengage the historical intention from the non-historical expression and to conserve and elaborate the intention. In the process, nothing meaningful is lost; but a good deal of meaningless discourse in theology may be terminated.

Such a program can be called a hermeneutic. Yet, a hermeneutic involves interpretation of texts. Does not theology's text—the Bible and the history of its interpretation—include concerns which resist compression into the single category, "history"? Theology as history is based on the supposition that the revelation which the Bible and Christian literature express is thoroughly historical and that the canonical text itself embodies the struggle of the early authors to interpret the faith historically, protecting it against non-historical vulgarization. A strictly historical hermeneutic allows a text to be treated as history. This does not mean judging the text by standards of plausibility imported from outside the text. It means letting the text supply the basis for its own interpretation. When this is done, one discovers that the Old Testament, when it speaks of creation, may not really be engaging in cosmology, as more technologically oriented ages seem to have inferred. It may rather be interpreting how the historical destiny of a minor people can be a mandate with a universal validity. When the New Testament speaks of the imminent presence of the Kingdom of God, it may not be augmenting or counterbalancing a futuristic apocalyptic, as harmonistically-minded attitudes encourage one to assume. It may rather be attempting to eradicate apocalyptic. When the apostles talk about God, they may not be referring to his being, as metaphysical philosophies have conditioned us to suppose, piously drawing our attention to realms beyond our history. New Testament *theo*-logy may not be a doctrine of God at all but a doctrine of salvation, that is, a doctrine of God-in-his-word, of God-for-us. When the New Testament writers record proofs for the resurrection of Jesus, they may not be endorsing them, as epochs deficient in imagination and trust are eager to assert. Their proofs may be superseded by confessions more reminiscent of faith, in which our Lord pioneered. That is to say, the text is not to be judged in the light of some alleged doctrinal consensus in the traditional church. The text must be allowed its own initiative in revealing the character of the theological struggle implicit in its record of the formulation of the faith.

These, then, are the two most important methodological facets of theology as history. First, it is theology resolved to make no statements about reality which do not involve the question of the meaning of man's existence. Second, it is theology resolved to import no criteria into the interpretation of the Biblical faith which the Bible does not itself supply or confirm. It will read the Bible as history. Two consequences for theology flow directly from these resolutions. One is that in theology as history there will be no norms and authorities. There will be only a frame of reference, that being the Bible and its hermeneutical aid, the history of its interpretation. To call the Bible and its interpretation a frame of reference rather than an authority allows to this locus of history the opportunity of manifesting its own authority, as history anywhere must do. When the reformers employed this method, they arrived at the discovery that "word of God" was not "Bible" but "Christ." This possibility was the Bible's own warrant for criticism of the Bible. One could now read the text in the light of the intention of the text, and let that intention interpret or stand in judgment upon whatever in the Bible was not Biblical. To say there is no authority in history does not deny the quite realistic need which the church as an institution has in defending its embodiment in history. That kind of concern, however, is primarily a policy matter and only secondarily a theological matter. The question of the authority of the church becomes primarily a theological question when the authority which is responsible for making the body of Christ mobile in the world begins to manipulate the church's definition of its faith in the interest of greater mobility.

The second consequence for theology from its historical method will be that proof and explanation in theology must give way to clarification and illumination. The logic of an historical faith must be thoroughly historical, and the rationality of history inheres in its capacity to illuminate life with meaning. When this is done, the old dichotomy between the *faith-which-is-believed* and the *faith-by-which-one-believes* collapses. In the rationality of faith, "reason" and "faith" are synonyms, for one's faith becomes the source of his self-understanding and not an option for courageous acts of belief.

Why is systematic theology warranted as an independent discipline in this definition of theology as history? Why not simply Biblical exegesis, whose consequences speed immediately to preaching without the intervention of another discipline? Heinrich Ott, Barth's successor at Basel, has been tricked into oversimplifying the systematic task by the excessive simplicity of Rudolf Bultmann's comprehension of the theological situation. Bultmann has seen exegesis as embracing all the functions of theology in one. Ott breaks two functions apart—exegesis and preaching—and interposes systematic theology between them, giving systematic theology the very limited definition which it derives from its shuttle service between these two other disciplines.

My own understanding of the task of systematic theology is that it is a totalizing operation within a highly complex historical process. Historically speaking, neither systematic theology nor Biblical exegesis has been dramatically effective in the development of Christian history. Preaching, broadly conceived as the practical encounter of the world by the church's interpretation of its faith, has been the real vanguard. That is why one can say that one studies theology not to learn theology but to learn to preach. But preaching rarely springs directly from exegesis, although that is how Bultmann and his disciples have visualized its occurring. Nor does preaching emanate from systematic theology as the deductive, reflective presupposition of preaching, although Heinrich Ott is currently encouraging that assumption. Not that preaching *cannot* happen directly out of exegesis or dogmatics. But historically the preaching of the church has emanated almost by inertia from the *doctrines* of the church as they shape the mentality of the body of Christ at any given time. The doctrines of the church are the conscious convictions of the Christian people in any epoch. This doctrinal consensus conditions the church's witness to and hearing of the word in every generation. The direct effect of either exegesis or systematic theology on the history of the church's understanding of itself is relatively sluggish and possibly even imperceptible, except for a few theologically dynamic moments in history. Moreover, the current of theological understanding does not flow in a direction from contemporary exegesis or dogmatics to the mind of preachers and congregations. Rather, the current moves back and forth between these two disciplines.

The actual movement of the theological understanding of the church is a stream traceable from its background of officially fixed dogma, through its foreground of fluid doctrinal consciousness, to its engagement with the world through preaching. The picture of theology as a process of exegesis which becomes preaching with immediacy, or the picture of systematic theology mediating between exegesis and preaching is astonishingly a-historical. It has almost wholly forgotten the reality of the church as an historical force. The church as history moves toward the future out of the dogmatic inertia of the past through the doctrinal consciousness of the present.

"Dogma" is officially fixed doctrine. The fact that it is officially fixed is no reason why the term should be thought to be pejorative. Systematic theology is known as dogmatic theology for a good reason. It conserves a priority for dogma in the life of the church that is easily by-passed in other theological disciplines. The official dogma of the church is important as the major point in the entire historical complex of Christendom where the faith expresses its unity. One can see how dogma functions when he relates it to preaching, doctrine, and exegesis. *The preaching of the church* is as erratic as the freedom of the pulpit and pew at any given time permits. *The doctrine of the church* is the church's perennial adolescence, for there the church tests its freedom, giving expression to its imagination, bending to resistance, yet reaching toward new opportunities for understanding. *The exegesis of the church* is the church continually confessing its origins, alternately baffled by how the fruit of a tradition can any longer examine its root and edified by how a tradition rooted in the past can continue to create a present.

The church does not experience its unity in its preaching, in its doctrine, or even in its canonical scriptures. Little wonder, then, that the church is wistful for some formal articulation of the oneness which it knows to be implicit in its being one body, with one God and one Lord. *The dogma of the church* is the church's expression and safeguard of the oneness of which it is conscious but which it nowhere finds explicit.

What baptism is in the unexpressed unity of the church, dogma is in its expressed unity. Thus if one were to make doctrine and not dogma the deductive phase of the hermeneutical process, he would be wrong on two counts. He would be wrong to subject exegesis to the guidance of theological expression in its adolescence and irresolution, and he would be wrong to neglect the dogma of the church as the unity beneath its doctrine. The dogma should be allowed to enter into the deductive moment of the church's hermeneutic. When doctrine alone does so, it does so not so much as the statement of the church's faith, but as the revelation of the world's interrogations of the church's faith. Doctrine is the conscious remnant of the officially fixed faith which remains after trial in the actual world, and thus it is also the sign of the continued erosion of that faith.

By the deductive phase in the hermeneutical process is meant that moment in the formulation of the faith when general comprehension is allowed to illuminate particular expressions. When dogma enters into the interpretation of the Scriptures, it has the function of keeping alive the church's legitimate drive toward unity in its understanding. That factor could otherwise be dangerously lost in the exegesis of texts, considering the fragmentation and diversity of the texts. The principle of canonicity is the acknowledgment of this connection between dogma and exegesis. When the church canonized the Bible as its official scripture, its concern was not so much with conferring authority on the Bible. Roman Catholicism is wrong to conclude that the power which confers authority retains priority over the authority which it designated. The church's relation to the Bible in canonizing it is analogous to John's relation to Jesus in baptizing him. To give the church authority over the Bible is to commit, therefore, the heresy which Paul exposed in the "disciples" at Ephesus who made John the Baptist the source of their faith, forgetting Jesus. Canonicity, rather than conferring authority on the Bible, is the church's way of holding its exegesis of the Bible to a consciousness of the living history of Christianity. Varied and fragmented, like all history, the history of the church deserves to reflect in its life and experience the unity of its basic loyalty, as its dogma attempts to do.

The systematic theology of the church, then, is a totalizing function required by the complex historical situation through which the word of God is believed to realize itself in history. It is the discipline through which the actual basis of the preaching of the church (the history of the church in its movement from dogma through doctrine to preaching) is being essentially revised in the light of the frame of reference within which the church finds its historically authentic existence (exegesis) and in response to the actual situation which the church confronts (the practice of preaching, broadly viewed).

The history of the church is the self-consciousness of the church in response to its internal heritage. It is that history which mainly influences the church's preaching, and not the exegesis of the Scriptures. Gerhard Ebeling's suggestive definition of the history of the church as "the history of the exegesis of the Scriptures" seems excessively influenced by Bultmann's oversimplified understanding of how the historical revelation insinuates itself directly into the historical world through exegesis. The practice of the church is its self-interpretation to the world against the background of the church's history. In the practice of the church, in its effort to interpret itself to the world and to expand its boundaries in the world, there is a reflex upon the church from its worldly impact. The church accommodates itself to the world in its engagement with the world. This is not entirely bad. The church must be responsible for discerning the legitimate demands of the growing world, which the church stubbornly confronts in its effort at proclamation, in order to allow these demands to influence the formulation of the faith in so far as this can be done without prejudice to the intention of the faith. A properly hermeneutical theology employs a hermeneutical circle whose function is to embrace the world's own understanding of its needs as a moment of pre-understanding which interrogates the Biblical text. Systematic theology must not act as if it knows what the world needs before it asks— as if some structure of Christian teaching could dispense with actual dialogue with the world. Systematic theology must totalize the impact of the historical world into the hermeneutical circle, into the approach to the text, simply straining out the questions which have no fundamentally historical intention.

The historical source of the faith, not simply in the sense of chronological origin but of present constitution, is the Biblical text. Being an historical text, it is dealing with human questions, and thus the rapport between the demands of a growing world and the materials of the text is not difficult to establish. For instance, allowance for this reflex upon the interpretations of the Bible from the preaching contacts of the church is more evident in Rudolf Bultmann's project than in Heinrich Ott's. The reason for this is partly that Bultmann has a different understanding of the role of philosophy in theological formulation than Ott does. The task of philosophy in Ott's theology is to provide him with a way of understanding how human thought can relate to the Being of God. The task of philosophy for Bultmann's theology is to provide him with aids in formulating the historical question which permits the word of God in the Scriptures to reveal itself in its historical relevance. Bultmann's use of philosophy is miraculously ample for an exegete. Not that exegetes do not usually employ philosophy. It is only that they usually do it unconsciously. Ott's use of philosophy, however, is too limited for a systematic position, for if philosophy is to become an instrument through which an understanding of the structure of the historical demand is communicated to theology from epoch to epoch, the theologian cannot confine his dialogue to a single philosophy as Ott does in the case of Heidegger.

Systematic theology is the comprehension of the Christian faith which emerges when the demands of the church's historical practice are conjoined with the church's historical self-understanding and constructively illuminated by the exegesis of its historical source. The very fragmentation of theological functions in modern times could, of itself, make a systematic theology as an independent discipline indispensable. If exegesis is to be an historical operation, it must be allowed its autonomy. It must not allow itself to become an aspect of the historical movement of the church, which is an unwieldy, inertial movement from dogma through doctrine to preaching, a movement characterized by a very low degree of self-consciousness. Church history and historical theology elaborate the self-consciousness of the church in this movement from dogma to preaching. There is no advantage to the church in having a special, official "church" history, as Roman emperors, for instance, had special imperial historians to adorn the case for their existence. The purpose of church history is to bare the facts of the matter as they really are, as the basis on which the church can consciously and candidly assume its responsibility toward the future.

Philosophical theology interprets to the church the structures which shape the mentality of the present, as they have shaped the formulation of its faith throughout Christian history. That is why philosophical theology is necessarily more of a secular than a sacred science. It is indispensable to the faith of the church that its information concerning the historical consciousness of the world be accurate respecting the world and not simply fawning toward the faith. Some theology exploits philosophy. Karl Barth, who leaves it alone, has a preferable grasp of the relation of philosophy to theology. At least in Barth's theology, philosophy can be what it is. On any other basis, paradoxically, philosophy's usefulness to theology is obstructed.

The theological significance of a practical theology is its responsibility for registering the reaction of the world to the church's efforts at the communication of its doctrinal consciousness. Autonomy for practical theology is as indispensable as it is for exegesis, history, and philosophy, for in historical hermeneutics deductive procedures cannot stand alone. The church ought not first decide what its faith is, then retain agencies of communication to promote that faith. An historically sensitive church will allow its conception of the faith to be held in suspension to the world's response—on the mission field, in the schools, in the social structure, from the pulpit, and in the counseling office.

Systematic theology is the discipline vocationally responsible for affecting the actual center of the church's self-understanding, which is its doctrine. Dogma is the church's official but largely subconscious basis of self-understanding. Scripture is its formative source for the articulation of its self-understanding. Doctrine, however, is the faith as the church is confessing it in any given period, irrespective of its dogma or scripture, and under the influence of its practical historical situation. It is the primary task of systematic theology deliberately to influence the doctrine of the church. It does so on the basis of the theological understanding which results from its totalizing hermeneutical process. Comprehended in this process are the tradition of the church, contemporary exegetical work, and the historical conditions of human life as the church is actually confronting them. The methodological result of this comprehension is a face to face engagement between these several disciplines which otherwise occurs only incidentally and without analytical rigor. The substantive result, to which this methodology is instrumental, is the clarification of the consciousness of the church, expressed as the revision of its doctrine. The immediate outcome of such doctrinal clarification is its influence upon the practice of the church, springing as it does from the doctrine of the church as a means of bringing the interpretation of the church's dogma into honest correlation with its doctrine, and through its doctrine with both its formative historical foundation (exegesis) and its authentic contemporary practice (preaching). This thoroughly historical character of systematic theology's responsibility should make the theologian cautious of non-historical sciences. The hopeful sense of the power of the interpreted word in shaping our historical existence should make one reluctant to form alliances with methods which cultivate defensiveness and ineffability. The freedom implicit in complete openness to the historical process should tutor one in scepticism toward any supports for traditional Christianity which do not subject it caustically to renewal.

Notes

Notes to Chapter II

1 *Endgame*, Evergreen (New York: Grove Press, 1958), p. 32.
2 *Ibid.*, p. 62.
3 Evergreen (New York: Grove Press, 1958), p. 22.
4 *Proust*, Evergreen (New York: Grove Press, 1957), p. 49.
5 *Molloy*, Evergreen (New York: Grove Press, 1955), p. 182.
6 *Endgame*, p. 49.
7 *Molloy*, p. 11.
8 *Murphy*, Evergreen (New York: Grove Press, 1957), p. 72.

Notes to Chapter III

1 This distinction was established by Plato in the *Phaedo* where he showed how dialectic is different from rhetoric, a distinction he believed the Sophists overlooked, to their discredit.
2 Martin Heidegger has warned that this word smacks of metaphysics and the technologizing of language, putting it in a class with sputnik and rocket techniques. *Unterwegs zur Sprache* (Pfullingen, 1959), p. 160.
3 Alfred North Whitehead has a similar way of suspending the requirement for "immediate guarantees of correctness" called "the delayed test, that the future conforms to expectations derived from this assumption." *Process and Reality* (New York: The Macmillan Co., 1929), p. 411.

Notes to Chapter IV

1 Paul Kalweit, *Die Christliche Welt*, J. 21, p. 562; Tr. Steinmann, *Zeitschrift für Theologie und Kirche*, n.f., XIII, p. 49; W. Thimme, *Theologische Studien und Kritiken*, J. 105, pp. 25, 35–36; Karl Barth, *Die Kirchliche Dogmatik*, II, 1, p. 225; Dietrich Bonhoeffer, *Christentum und Wissenschaft*, H. 12, p. 435; Hermann Diem, *Die Christliche Welt*, J. 46, p. 546; H. Obendiek, *Scottish Journal of Theology*, Vol. 5, No. 3, p. 259.
2 Fernand Ménégoz, *Le Problème de la Prière*, p. 203; Friedrich Traub, *Theologische Studien and Kritiken*, n.f., 1917, p. 191; D. C. Macintosh, *The Problem of Religious Knowledge*, p. 350; Rudolf Paulus, *Zeitschrift für Theologie und Kirche*, n.f., 1922, p. 201.
3 Karl Beth, *Theologische Rundschau*, J. 20, p. 94; Otto Hoffman, *Theologische Studien and Kritiken*, 1922, p. 267; Julius Kaftan, *Studien zur systematische*

Theologie: T. von Haering, pp. 37, 39; Erich Przywara, *Stimmen der Zeit*, 1926, p. 353.

4 *Das Weltbild der Zukunft*, p. iv; *Leitfaden der Dogmatik*, 2nd ed., Vol. 1, p. 64; *Das Weltbild*, p. 193; *Glaube und Leben*, pp. 518-19; *ibid.*, p. 623; *Glaubensgewissheit*, 1st ed., p. 39; *Glaube und Leben*, p. 650; *Spirit and Truth*, p. 113; *Zeitschrift für Theologie und Kirche*, n.f., Vol. 11, p. 330; *Die Wandlung im naturwissenschaftlichen Weltbild*, p. 18; *Glaube und Denken*, 2nd ed., pp. 335-6.

5 *Zwischen den Zeiten*, J. 9, H. 5, pp. 451-453.

6 Karl Barth, *The Doctrine of the Word of God*, Part I (New York: Charles Scribner's Sons, 1936), p. 21. In one of his last written statements Heim conceded that pietism dominated his thinking, but defined pietism in this way: "the conviction that there is such a thing as Christianity only on the basis of a 'conversion,' which means a turning about through which I cease to lead myself and by complete surrender put my whole existence under the leadership of Jesus Christ. If a conversion is the only way a man can be certain of his eternal salvation, then a theology can only have meaning if it serves the end of leading man to this decision." *Ich gedenke der vorigen Zeiten*, 1957, pp. 315-316.

7 Kazuo Mutō, a Japanese Christian teaching philosophy at Kyoto University, has helped me understand this about Barth. See my *Japanese Contributions to Christian Theology* (Philadelphia: Westminster, 1960), p. 133.

8 *Glaube und Denken*, p. 22.

9 *Die Wandlung*, p. 13.

10 *Leben aus dem Glauben*, pp. 3, 4.

11 *Ich gedenke der voringen Zeiten*, p. 224.

12 *The Doctrine of the Word of God*, pp. 152-153.

13 In 1932 G. C. Berkouwer wrote discerningly of Heim's theology as "the theology of the non-objectifiable." See his *Geloof en Openbaring in de Nieuwere Duitsche Theologie (Faith and Revelation in the New German Theology)*, pp. 84-103 and 182-192.

14 *God Transcendent*, pp. 230-231.

15 *Glaubensgewissheit*, 2nd ed., pp. 129-130.

16 The strategy was outlined by Heim in an article called "Der gegenwärtige Stand der Debatte zwischen Theologie und Naturwissenschaft," *Theologische Studien und Kritiken*, 1908, pp. 402-429.

17 *Der christliche Gottesglaube und die Naturwissenschaft*, Erster Teilband, p. 33.

18 Emil Brunner's works also illustrate this method. He has given it the name "eristic" or "Christian Socratism," and he refers to it as "theology's other task," which was his way of saying that the writing of a *Dogmatik* does not exhaust the theologian's responsibility. *Zwischen den Zeiten*, 1929, pp. 255-276.

19 Cf. also my analysis of Heim in *The Hinge of History* (New York: Charles Scribner's Sons, 1959), esp. pp. 70, 71.

20 Kurt Leese, *Zeitschrift für Theologie und Kirche*, J. 24, p. 120.

21 "Rudolf Bultmann: Ein Versuch, ihn zu verstehen," *Theologische Studien*, H. 34, p. 43.

Notes to Chapter V

1 See Jean Daniélou, *Origen*, trans. Walter Mitchell (New York: Sheed and Ward, 1955), p. 140.

2 Reference is to his Easter Sermon in Basel in 1943, cited by H. W. Hertzberg, "Zur neueren Auslegung des Alten Testaments," in *Theologische Literaturzeitung*, No. 4 (1949), p. 221.

3 Cited by Hans-Joachim Kraus, *Geschichte der Historisch-Kritischen Enforschung des Alten Testaments von der Reformation bis zug Gegenwart* (Neukirchen, 1956), p. 440.

4 Rudolf Bultmann, *Essays*, trans., James C. G. Greig (London: SCM Press, 1955), pp. 191ff.

5 *Ibid.*, p. 241.

6 Rudolf Bultmann, "Ist Voraussetzunglose Exegese möglich?", *Theologische Zeitschrift*, J. 13, H. 6 (Nov.-Dec., 1957), p. 413. This essay is now available in English translation in the collection of essays by Bultmann called *Existence and Faith*, ed. Schubert Ogden (New York: Meridian Press, 1960).

7 Rudolf Bultmann, *Glauben und Verstehen*, Vol. I (Tübingen, 1933), p. 161.

8 *Ibid.*, p. 295.

9 "Ist Voraussetzunglose Exegese möglich?", pp. 414, 415.

10 Cf. "Prophecy and Fulfillment" in *Essays*, pp. 205–208.

11 Tübingen, 1956.

12 *Weimar Ausgabe* 20; 579, 11.

13 Hertzberg, *op. cit.*, p. 220.

14 *Die Geschichtlichkeit der Kirche* (Tübingen, 1954), p. 4.

15 *Ibid.*, p. 12.

16 *Either/Or*, Vol. I, trans. David F. Swenson and Lillian Marvin Swenson (Princeton: Princeton University Press, 1944), p. 22.

17 Cf. *Das Evangelium des Johannes*, 1953, p. 40.

18 *Essays*, p. 117.

19 *W. A.* 3; 243, 37f. cf. Gerhard Ebeling, "Die Anfänge von Luthers Hermeneutik," *Zeitschrift für Theologie und Kirche*, XLVIII (1951), p. 212.

20 *Glauben und Verstehen*, Vol. I, p. 296.

21 *Ibid.*, p. 133.

22 *Ibid.*, p. 161.

Notes to Chapter VI

1 *Die Christliche Welt*, 1921, pp. 186–190, article entitled "Ein Apfel vom Baume Kierkegaards."

2 A striking antecedent of this view can be found in the writing of the medieval mystic Hugh of St. Victor, *De sacramentis Christianae fidei*. See Henri de Lubac, *Exégèse medievale*, Part I, Vol. I (Paris, 1959), p. 45.

3 *Les Sciences de l'Homme et la Phenomenologie* (Paris, 1961), p. 13.

4 *Unterwegs zur Sprache* (Pfullingen, 1959), p. 80.

5 *Holzwege* (Frankfurt, 1950), pp. 59, 64f.

6 *The Logic of Hegel*, trans. William Wallace, 2nd ed. (London: Oxford University Press, 1892), Par. 73, p. 136.

Notes to Chapter VII

1 *Attack upon "Christendom,"* trans. Walter Lowrie (Princeton, N.J.: Princeton University Press, 1944), p. 284.

2 *The Journals of Søren Kierkegaard*, trans. Alexander Dru (New York: Oxford University Press, 1938), No. 1117.

3 *Concluding Unscientific Postscript,* trans. David F. Swenson and Walter Lowrie (Princeton, N.J.: Princeton University Press, 1941), p. 248.
4 *Ibid.,* p. 292.
5 *Ibid.,* p. 319.
6 *Ibid.,* p. 296.
7 *Ibid.,* p. 271.
8 *The Point of View,* trans. Walter Lowrie (New York: Oxford University Press, 1939), p. 37.
9 *Either/Or,* Vol. II, trans. Walter Lowrie (Princeton, N.J.: Princeton University Press, 1944), p. 180.
10 *Ibid.,* p. 202.
11 *Concluding Unscientific Postcript,* p. 250.
12 These illustrations of the comic are taken chiefly from the *Concluding Unscientific Postscript,* pp. 70, 72, 130, 155, 163, 175, 189, 198, 202, 227, 248, 268, 296, 300, 315, 318, 350, 365, 406, 510; with the exception of one from *Attack on Christendom,* p. 31, and *The Point of View,* p. 34.
13 *Concluding Unscientific Postscript,* p. 37.
14 *Ibid.,* p. 118.
15 *Either/Or,* Vol. II, p. 178.
16 *Concluding Unscientific Postscript,* p. 382.
17 *The Gospel of Suffering,* trans. David F. Swenson and Lillian Marvin Swenson (Minneapolis: Augsburg Publishing House, 1948), p. 8.
18 *The Journals,* No. 1021.
19 *Concluding Unscientific Postscript,* p. 291.
20 *Ibid.,* p. 296.
21 *The Journals,* No. 605.
22 *Philosophical Fragments,* trans. David F. Swenson (Princeton, N.J.: Princeton University Press, 1936), p. 50.
23 *The Journals,* No. 10.
24 *Edifying Discourses,* Vol. I, trans. David F. Swenson and Lillian Marvin Swenson (Minneapolis: Augsburg Publishing House, 1943), p. 21.
25 *The Point of View,* p. 83.
26 *Concluding Unscientific Postscript,* p. 290.
27 *Ibid.,* p. 330.
28 *Ibid.,* p. 480.
29 *Ibid.,* p. 188.
30 *Ibid.,* p. 512.
31 *Training in Christianity,* trans. Walter Lowrie (Princeton, N.J.: Princeton University Press, 1944), p. 123.
32 *Concluding Unscientific Postscript,* p. 206.
33 *Ibid.,* p. 518.
34 *Ibid.,* pp. 530, 531.
35 *Ibid.,* p. 513.
36 *Philosophical Fragments,* p. 49.
37 *Concluding Unscientific Postscript,* p. 531.
38 *Ibid.,* p. 441.
39 *Ibid.,* p. 365.
40 *Ibid.,* pp. 440f.
41 *Fear and Trembling,* trans. Walter Lowrie (Princeton, N.J.: Princeton University Press, 1941), p. 54.
42 *Ibid.,* p. 53.

43 *Ibid.*, p. 70.
44 *Ibid.*
45 *Edifying Discourses*, Vol. I, p. 106.
46 *Fear and Trembling*, p. 72.

Notes to Chapter VIII

1 *Characteristics*, ed. John M. Robertson (London: Grant Richards, 1900), I, 189.
2 Sermon CXV, 12, *The Works of John Wesley* (Grand Rapids, Mich.: Zondervan Publishing House, a reproduction of the works of John Wesley from the authorized edition published by the Wesleyan Conference Office in London, England, in 1872), Vol. VII, p. 277. Except when otherwise indicated, this is the collection of Wesley's works referred to throughout. To facilitate the use of other editions, references to the *Journals* will include the date, and to the *Sermons*, as in this note, the official number of the sermon and the paragraph.
3 November 13, 1763 (III, 156).
4 January 2, 1787 (IV, 357).
5 August 25, 1763 (III, 144).
6 XXV, 9 (V, 451).
7 "A Farther Appeal to Men of Reason and Religion," Part III, iii, 13, (VIII, 222f.).
8 April 21, 1775 (IV, 41).
9 May 29, 1745 (I, 496).
10 LV, 1; LXXIV, 19 (VI, 199, 397).
11 LXVIII, 9 (VI, 328).
12 March 25, 1777 (IV, 93).
13 March 16, 1764, April 19, 1764, May 14, 1765 (III, 161, 170, 211).
14 December 12, 1756 (II, 389).
15 "All the great efforts of the reformation lay in the emancipation from Church authority, in the formation of a new, deeply inward order of spiritual life of Protestant society. But the religious and philosophical thought were laden with a chaos of tradition until Leibniz and Locke." Wilhelm Dilthey, *Gesammelte Schriften* (Leipzig and Berlin, 1914), II, 224.
16 Dilthey sees a transformation of European religiosity occurring in the thought of Shaftesbury, along with that of Bruno and Spinoza. Christian dogma paid no heed to it until Schleiermacher. *Ibid.*, II, 339.
17 August 14, 1776 (IV, 83).
18 September 15, 1787 (IV, 399).
19 XXXV, 6 (V, 453f.).
20 XXXVI, ii, 1–6 (V, 462f.).
21 XXXVI, iii, 6 (V, 466).
22 CXIII, 14 (VII, 260).
23 Hans-Georg Gadamer, *Wahrheit und Methode* (Tubingen: J. C. Mohr, 1960), p. 24.
24 "An Earnest Appeal to Men of Reason and Religion," 11, 35 (VIII, VI, XIV).
25 CVI, i, 1–13 (VII, 195).
26 XII, 8 (V, 137).
27 *Explanatory Notes upon the New Testament* (London: The Epworth Press, 1952), p. 847. Hereinafter simply *Notes*. On Hebrews 12:2. I do not claim that Wesley consistently applies this "phenomenological method." For instance, he has endorsed the Thomas legend in which Jesus allegedly invites Thomas to

"handle me, and see." "Take away the certainty of sense, and there is no discerning a body from a spirit." It should be noticed, however, that this particular argument is used in attack upon the medieval view of transubstantiation: "Grant substantiation, and we take away the certainty of sense." "A Roman Catechism," Question 64 (X, 119).

The association of Wesley with phenomenology is not excessively odd if one sees how he anticipates, if only accidentally and ever so slightly, its understanding of appearance in his remarkable interpretation of δόκειν, the verb customarily translated by the ambiguous "to think" but with the connotation of "to seem." Appearances by which we think are customarily treated as "mere" appearances, hence they have only the status of "seeming." In this view, δόκειν could be said to weaken a word to which it refers. That is how Immanuel Kant treated phenomena in his philosophy, contemporary with Wesley. Wesley, however, gives to δόκειν more the connotation later given to appearances by Edmund Husserl. δόκειν "strengthens the sense of the word to which it is annexed," Wesley said. See LXXXII, 2; XC, i, 4; *Notes*, p. 615 on I Corinthians 10:12. (VI, 476; VII, 41).

28 "An Earnest Appeal to Men of Reason and Religion," 60 (VIII, 23).
29 October 9, 1777 (IV, 110f.).
30 December 13, 1739 (I, 254f.).
31 LIV, 17 (VI, 196).
32 VIII, ii, 3 (V, 90).
33 "Minutes of Some Late Conversations," II, Question 8 (VIII, 276).
34 *Notes*, p. 690, Galatians 3:25.
35 October 9, 1777 (IV, 110f.).
36 CVI, 123 and i, 1–13 (VII, 195), CX, 10–14 (VII, 236); cf. *Notes*, p. 519f., Romans 1:17.
37 XXXVI, ii, 3 (V, 463).
38 *Notes*, p. 847, Hebrews 12:2.
39 XXXVI, ii, 2 (V, 462).
40 "Principles of a Methodist Farther Explained," ii, 3 (VII, 430).
41 February 22, 1741 (I, 299f.).
42 V, iv, 3; XLIII, iii, 1; December 13, 1739 (V, 61; cf. VI, 48; I, 251).
43 May 14, 1738 (X, 96, cited by Wesley from a letter of a friend received by his brother Charles).
44 *Notes*, p. 862f., James 2:22.
45 May 1, 1774 (IV, 13).
46 LXI, 19 (VI, 259).
47 April 9, 1777 (IV, 95).
48 XLII, iii, 7–10 (VI, 50f.), LXI, 10 (VI, 256), LXII, iii, 6 (VI, 277), CXXXIX, iii (VII, 497).
49 "A Roman Catechism," Question 80 (X, 125).
50 November 22, 1760 (II, 27).
51 December 20, 1760 (III, 31), LXXXIX, 8 (VII, 29), XCI, iii, 11 (VII, 56), XCV, 4 (VII, 88), November 17, 1760 (III, 25), "A Roman Catechism," Question 15 (X, 95), "Popery Calmly Considered," ii, 3 (X, 143).
52 May 17, 1777 (IV, 96).
53 May 24, 1738 (I, 98ff.).
54 XIX, i, 8 (V, 226).
55 "An Extract from 'A Short View of the Difference Between the Moravian Brethren, (so called) and the Rev. Mister John and Charles Wesley'" (IX, 201f.).

56 *Notes*, p. 520, Romans 1:17.

57 *Ibid.*, p. 593, I Corinthians 3:8.

58 *The Letters of the Rev. John Wesley, A.M.*, ed. John Telford (London: The Epworth Press, 1931) III, 80.

59 XXV, Discourse V, ii, 2 (V, 313).

60 XXXV, iii, 3 (V, 455).

61 CXX, 18 (VII, 317).

62 LXXXIII, 10 (VI, 488).

63 XI, i, 1–5 (V, 66ff.).

64 XXXIV, i, 3 and 4 (V, 436).

65 VI, i, 8 (V, 69).

66 XX, ii, 20 (V, 244).

67 XXXIV, iv, 4 (V, 444).

68 LXV, Introduction (VI,296); cf. "A Second Dialogue between an Antinomian and his Friend" (X, 279).

69 XXIX, Discourse IX, 21 (V, 388).

70 XXV, Discourse V, i, 2 (V, 311f.).

71 *Notes*, p. 602, I Corinthians 6:13.

72 XXXIV, iv, 1–3 (V, 442f.). Another possible reference is in the *Notes* on I Timothy 1:8, the standard text for the distinction of the uses. "*The* whole Mosaic *law is good* . . . and of admirable use both to convince unbelievers, and to guide believers in all holiness." The relatively standard *triplex* or *duplex usus legus* was considerably loosened up for Wesley by a treatise on the use of the law by the seventeenth-century theologian Isaac Ambrose, included in Volume VIII of the *Christian Library,* in which a *septemplex usus* is proposed, pp. 132ff.

73 "An Earnest Appeal to Men of Reason and Religion," 19 (VIII, 8).

74 XXV, Discourse V, i, 3 (V, 312).

75 November 17, 1750 (II, 211).

76 *Letters,* III, 79.

77 XXXIV, ii, 6 (V, 439).

78 L, iii, 6 (VI, 135).

79 XXXV, i, 1 (V, 449).

80 *Ibid.,* iii, 4 (V, 455).

81 XXV, ii, 2 (V, 313).

82 *Ibid.,* ii, 3 (V, 314).

83 *Letters* III, 80. cf. *Notes,* p. 48 on Matthew 8:32. Jesus, ordering the evil spirit to leave the demoniacs and enter the swine, only apparently commanded them when he said, "Go!" On this one interpretive word, Wesley comments, "A word of permission only, not command."

84 XXXIV, 3 (V, 435).

85 LXXVI, ii, 2 (VI, 415).

86 *Notes,* p. 35, Matthew 5:48.

87 "A Dialogue Between an Antinomian and His Friend" (X, 270). What Christ does to convert the law from command to promise has not been touched upon here. Lurking behind the whole discussion is Wesley's very traditional asser- tion of one of the "fundamentals," Christ's reconciliation of God to sinners. Because of the reconciliation, the power of the Holy Spirit is available to justified sinners, restoring man's capacity to fulfill God's laws, man no longer being broken by the effort to keep them. In this way Wesley has overlaid the ministry of Jesus with the post-resurrection theology of the apostles. John Locke, in his *Reasonableness of Christianity,* edited by I. T. Ramsey (Stanford:

Stanford University Press, 1958) does include Christ's "promise of assistance" in his discussion of the advantage Christians have over Jews and Gentiles in the keeping of the law, but he specifies several understandable forms which Christ's assistance gives: (1) in his preaching he has revealed God in a way not limited to nature or even to the hiddenness of the old covenant, (2) his clear commands give aid to the otherwise unassisted reason, (3) by inaugurating a spiritual worship he put an end to cumbersome ceremonies. Wesley relies on supernaturalism; Locke, only politely nodding to it, misses the theological depth of Christ's preaching of the law.

88   *Letters* III, 89.
89   *Notes*, p. 735, Philippians 3:15. Cf. "Some Remarks on Mr. Hill's 'Review of All the Doctrines Taught by Mr. John Wesley'," xxiv (X, 395f.).
90   *Notes*, p. 863, James 2:22.
91   *Letters* III, 81.
92   LXXVI, iii, 1 (VI, 421).
93   *Ibid.*, i, 4 (VI, 413).
94   *Ibid.*, i, 6 (VI, 413f.).
95   *Ibid.*, iii, 12 (VI, 424).
96   *Ibid.*
97   December 19, 1762 (III, 124).
98   P. 9.
99   Wilhelm Dilthey, *Gesammelte Schriften*, II, 135.
100 *Gnomon of the New Testament*, ed. Andrew R. Fausset (Edinburgh: T & T Clark, 1859), I, 65.
101 *Op. cit.*, V, 185. The texts referred to in this connection are John 5:47, Romans 15:4, but especially Isaiah 55:2.
102 February 14, 1736 (I, 25).
103 September 10, 1739 (I, 224).
104 XVI, ii, 3 (V, 188).
105 November 5, 1746 (II, 34).
106 April 15 and May 4, 1788 (IV, 413, 416).
107 *Ibid.*, June 8, 1788 (IV, 423).
108 April 14, 1788 (IV, 413). (Italics mine.)
109 XXIV, Discourse IV, iii, 7 (V, 307).
110 June 7, 1746 (II, 15); "An Earnest Appeal to Men of Reason and Religion," 17 (VIII, 7).
111 XLVI, iii, 5 (VI, 87).
112 May 1, 1779 (IV, 151).
113 April 1, 1748 (II, 90).
114 March 28, 1739 (I, 176).
115 March 13, 1738 (I, 103).
116 July 3, 1774 (IV, 22).
117 November 4, 1770 (III, 420).
118 May 15, 1774; April 8, 1787 (IV, 13, 367).
119 May 13, 1788 (IV, 418).
120 October 12, 1780 (IV, 192).
121 September 19, 1788 (IV, 437), May 30, 1756 (II, 363); Yet cf. October 18, 1757 (II, 429).
122 XCI, Introduction (VII, 45f.).
123 XXI, Discourse I, ii, 3 (V, 258f.).
124 April 11, 1748 (II, 92).

125 "Minutes of Some Late Conversations," I, Question 5 (VIII, 276).

126 "An Earnest Appeal to Men of Reason and Religion," 28 (VII, 12).

127 Hans-Georg Gadamer, *Wahrheit und Methode*, p. 25. Cf. also Carl August Auberlen, *Die Theosophie F. C. Oetingers* (Basel, 1869), pp. 69ff. Wesley refers to his reading of Oetinger's *de sensu Communi et Ratione* as a disappointment. "When I had with huge labor read fifty or sixty pages, finding the sense did by no means make amends for the time and pains bestowed in searching it out, I took my leave of him forever." January 27, 1759 (II, 467). While I am not claiming direct influence upon Wesley for Oetinger's view, it is not inconceivable even from this reference.

128 XVIII, 3 (V, 214).

129 VI, iii, 3; XIV, iii, 3 (V, 75, 169). Instances where "deep conviction of our demerit *after* we are accepted is certainly necessary in order to our seeing the true value of the atoning blood."

130 XXXV, i, 3 (V, 449).

131 XXXV, i, 8 (V, 450).

132 XXI, Discourse I, i, 4 (V, 253). In Volume V of his *Christian Library* Wesley includes Robert Bolton's "Instructions for Confronting Afflicted Consciences," in which he says, "Were it not absurd in surgery, to pour a most sovereign balsam upon a sound part? It is far more senseless to proffer the blood of Christ, and promises of life to an unwounded conscience." The procedure recommended: "First, to wound by the law, and to heal by the Gospel." Is this what Jesus did? "Christ Jesus tells us, that he was anointed by the Lord 'to preach good tidings'. But to whom? To the *poor;* to the brokenhearted." Pp. 17f.

133 XXXV, i, 11 (V, 452).

134 June 2, 1742 (I, 375, the words of Mrs. Holmes' sister, reported approvingly by Wesley). There is a notable exception in Wesley to the preaching of the law as preparation for the Gospel, and that is the circumstance in which consolation seems to be called for. July 4, 1788 (IV, 429). In the same "Instructions for Comforting Afflicted Consciences," Bolton says of this "high and heavenly art," "were it well known in practise, what a world of tortured and troubled minds would it prevent." P. 17.

135 "A Farther Appeal to Men of Reason and Religion," I, vii, 5 (VIII, 123).

136 CV, i, 710 (VII, 188f.). Wesley's only objection to this analysis was that these powers are no longer completely intact in man, considering sin.

137 CV, i, 1 (VII, 186).

138 *Notes*, pp. 181f., Mark 12:33.

139 *Notes*, pp. 912f., I John 3:20–21.

140 CV, 12 (VII, 190).

141 *Notes*, p. 913, I John 3:21.

142 "A Short Method of Converting All the Roman Catholics in the Kingdom of Ireland," 8 (X, 131).

143 *Notes*, p. 56, Matthew 10:32.

144 P. 949. A treatise on "The Apostles Creed" by the seventeenth-century archbishop of Glasgow, Robert Leighton, included in Volume XX of Wesley's *Christian Library*, develops the position that "the mystery of faith" and "a pure conscience" are "inseparable." "They are preserved and lost together." *Fides quae creditur* and *fides qua creditur* are united in the soul by conscience. Pp. 237ff.

145 March 30, 1764 (III, 165).

146 "A Dialogue Between an Antinomian and his Friend" (X, 267).

147 March 12, 1767 (III, 274).

148 XLIII, iii, 7 (VI, 50).

149 LXXXIX, 5 and 6 (VII, 28).

150 September 15, 1762 (III, 113).

151 "Remarks on Mr. Locke's *Essay on Human Understanding*" (XIII, 456). While this comment on Locke was written in 1781, the work from which it is derived was referred to by Wesley as early as 1745 and had been in print since 1690.

152 XIV, 20 (V, 165).

153 *Notes*, pp. 529f., Romans 3:20.

154 *Letters* III, 80f.

155 "Minutes of Some Late Conversations," II, August 2, Question 18; After 10 p.m., Question 8 (VIII, 284 and 286).

156 *Notes*, p. 86.

157 CXXXII, 8 (VII, 426).

158 XXXVIII, i, 13 and iii, 3 (V, 483 and 487).

159 LXXII, ii, 7 (VI, 387).

160 "A Farther Appeal to Men of Reason and Religion," Part II, iii, 5 (VIII, 185).

161 *Notes*, p. 588, I Corinthians 1:23.

162 LXVI, ii, 4 (VL, 308).

163 LV, 14 (VI, 204).

164 Part III, iii, 9 (VIII, 220). This is not unlike the position of John Locke on miracle, to the effect that in Christianity the power of the outward miracle has been lodged with the state.

165 *Ibid.*, 29 (VIII, 234f.).

166 *Ibid.*, (VIII, 235).

167 *Ibid.*, Part I, i, 3 (VIII, 47).

168 *Ibid.*, Part II, iii, 17 (VIII, 195).

169 "An Earnest Appeal to Men of Reason and Religion," 42 (VIII, 16).

170 September 3, 1741 (I, 327).

171 IV, iii, 1 (V, 45).

172 LXI, 27 (VI, 261).

173 LXVI, ii, 4 (VI, 308), although Wesley's omission from his *Notes* of the heavy apocalypticism of Bengel's *Gnomon* is noteworthy.

174 February 3, 1753 (II, 279).

175 September 3, 1774 (IV, 28). Wesley has even been accused of basing his view upon texts in the New Testament which were redactions of early Catholicism.

176 October 30, 1763 (III, 155).

177 June 15, 1783 (IV, 249f.).

178 L, ii, 2 (VI, 131).

179 January 25, 1785 (IV, 296).

180 July 29, 1765 (III, 231).

181 January 14, 1772 (III, 451).

182 June 12, 1774 (IV, 18).

183 May 6, 1776 (IV, 73).

184 September 12, 1776 (IV, 87).

185 XC, 2 (VII, 38).

186 XCIV, iii, 7 (VII, 82).

187 December 23, 1755 (II, 352).

188 XXII, Discourse II, ii, 6 (V, 269).
189 "An Earnest Appeal to Men of Reason and Religion," 43 (VIII, 17).
190 July 2, 1777 (IV, 104).
191 May 17, 1785 (XV, 307).
192 May 12, 1765 (III, 211).
193 July 3, 1788 (IV, 429). In the very first volume of his *Christian Library*, Wesley included John Arndt's "True Christianity." In it man is characterized not as a wanderer upon the earth but as a tenant, whose situation is no more permanent but considerably more responsible than that of a wanderer. P. 189.
194 May 15, 1738 (I, 103).
195 December 11, 1739; December 28, 1740 (I, 253, 292).
196 November 5, 1741 (I, 346).
197 "An Earnest Appeal to Men of Reason and Religion," 48 (VIII, 19).
198 LXXXVII, iii, 6 (VI, 433).
199 *Ibid.*, iii, 5 (VI, 432). "Happy" was Wesley's translation of μακάριοι in the Beatitudes.
200 January 15, 1777 (IV, 92).
201 CIX, 13 (VII, 229).
202 "A Farther Appeal to Men of Reason and Religion," Part I, iii, 1 (VIII, 58).
203 July 21, 1777 (IV, 106).
204 April 19, 1775 (IV, 42).
205 "An Earnest Appeal to Men of Reason and Religion," 48 (VIII, 19).
206 LXXVIII, i, 14 (VI, 440).
207 XCV, 8 (VII, 89).
208 LI, ii, 5 (VI, 146).
209 LXXXVII, ii, 11 (VII, 11).
210 "Minutes of Some Late Conversations," II, After 10, Questions 5-6 (VIII, 285f.).
211 *Notes*, p. 606.
212 March 9-12, 1747 (II, 48).
213 IV, i, 5ff., VI, ii, 1ff. (V, 40ff., 71f.).
214 II, iii, 9; XIX, i, 8 (V, 24, 226).
215 January 18, 1736 (I, 20).
216 "An Earnest Appeal to Men of Reason and Religion," 26 and 45 (VIII, 11, 18).
217 December 14, 1768 (III, 349).
218 November 13, 1776 (IV, 89).
219 February 8, 1753 (II, 279); May 19, 1764 (III, 177); II, i, 1 (V, 17).
220 September 4, 1788 (IV, 436).
221 March 1, 1776 (IV, 69).
222 L, i, 7 (VI, 130. As is generally known, two other injunctions were coupled to this one: "save all you can" and "give all you can.")
223 XC, 2; CV, i, 8 and 9 (VII, 385 and 189).
224 CXIV, 20 (VII, 271).
225 Sermon XXII (V, 262-277).
226 Sermon IV (V, 37-52).
227 CVIII, ii, 2 (VII, 218).
228 January 9, 1786 (IV, 325).

Notes to Chapter IX

1 Philadelphia: Westminster Press, 1960

Notes to Chapter X

1 *The Uses of the Past*, Mentor Book (New York: New American Library, 1952), p. 47. Yvor Winters in his *In Defense of Reason* (Denver: University of Denver Press, 1947), p. 400, cites this passage from *The Education of Henry Adams* and adds his comment:

> Adams must inevitably have begun by asking Sir Isaac for an intelligible reason why the apple fell to the ground. He did not know enough to be satisfied with the fact. The Law of Gravitation was so-and-so, but what was Gravitation? And he would have been thrown quite off his base if Sir Isaac had answered that he did not know.

To this Winters says, "This neurotic and childish impatience, amounting almost to insolence, is the final fruit of the Christian doctrine in New England; the patience and humility of an Aristotle or a Newton are incomprehensible."

2 Archibald MacLeish, *J. B.* (Boston: Houghton Mifflin Company, 1958), scene 11.

3 See the account of Islam by Edmund Perry, *The Gospel in Dispute* (New York: Doubleday & Co., 1958), Chapter VI.

4 Harvest Book (New York: Harcourt, Brace & World, n.d.), p. 72.

5 *Ibid.*, p. 172.

6 Quoted by Alan Watts in his article "Beat Zen, Square Zen, and Zen," *Chicago Review*, Summer 1958, p. 8. Reprinted by permission of Allen Ginsburg.

7 *Ibid.*

8 See *Azia ni okeru Kirisutokyo* (Christianity in Asia), ed. H. R. Fox and Kano Yamamoto (Tokyo, 1955), pp. 117ff. James Bisset Pratt in *The Pilgrimage of Buddhism* may have had in mind the *iki-yabo* contradiction when he likened the conversion of a Buddhist to Christianity to making Thomas Aquinas into a Methodist. See Heidegger's vote for the *iki* mentality in his dialogue with a Buddhist recorded in *Unterwegs zur Sprache* (Pfullingen, 1959), pp. 85ff.

9 See his short story "Teddy," in J. D. Salinger, *Nine Stories* (Boston: Little, Brown & Co., 1953).

Notes to Chapter XI

1 Rudolf Bultmann, *Das Evangelium des Johannes*, 16th ed. (Göttingen, 1959), p. 476.

2 "Minutes of Some Late Conversations," I, Question 5. *The Works of John Wesley*, Vol. VIII (Grand Rapids, Mich.: Zondervan Publishing House, authorized edition of 1872), p. 276.

3 Sermon XVI, i, 12.

4 New York: Pocket Books, Inc., 1965, p. 118.

5 Bultmann, *Das Evangelium des Johannes*, p. 106.

6 Wolfhart Pannenberg, *Grundzüge der Christologie* (Gütersloh, 1964), p. 189; Blumenberg's phrase, used approvingly by Pannenberg.

7 Gerhard Ebeling, "Der Grund christlicher Theologie," *Zeitschrift für Theologie und Kirche*, J. 58, H. 2 (August, 1961), p. 232.

8 *The Autobiography of Michel de Montaigne*, ed. Marvin Lowenthal, Vintage Book (New York: Random House, 1956), p. 206.

9 *The Disappearance of God* (Cambridge, Mass.: Harvard University Press, 1963), p. 73.

Index